# HIDDEN
## UNDER THE CORPORATE LADDER

*Based on a true story*

**J.K. LaMAY**

Hidden Under the Corporate Ladder

Copyright© 2005 by J.K. LaMay

Printed and bound in the United States of America. All rights reserved. No part of this book may be reproduced in any form or by any electronic or mechanical means including information storage and retrieval systems without permission in writing from the copyright holder, except by a reviewer, who may quote brief passages in review.

ISBN: 978-0-9754803-6-6
ISBN: 0-9754803-6-7

Published by

2100 Kramer Lane, Suite 300
Austin, Texas 78758

Tel: 512.478.2028
Fax: 512.478.2117

E-mail: info@turnkeypress.com
Web: www.turnkeypress.com

*Dedication*

*Dedicated to The Spirit That Drove Me. I hope you find peace with what I've done.*

## CHAPTER ONE

*Pittsburgh PA*
*November 27, 1984*
*5:15 a.m.*

The telephone's shrill ring awakened John MacAlfie from a sound sleep. Quickly, he snatched it to his ear. "Hello… Hello!" No one answered. Fumbling in the dark, he returned the phone to the cradle, rolled over, and sighed in disbelief. By now, both he and his girlfriend Gwen were wide awake.

"Who was that?" Gwen murmured in a voice still thick with sleep.

"Probably just a wrong number—they hung up." John replied as he held her next to him while listening to the rain peck against the bedroom window. Gwen snuggled against him, dreading the thought of going outside.

"Why don't we stay in bed all day?" she asked. "If this rain turns to ice, traffic's gonna be a nightmare."

"There's nothing I'd like better, but you can't miss any more work without getting fired. And that's not something we can afford right now." He sighed again and pulled her closer. "Besides, I've got important business in court today."

"What's going on?" she asked.

He kissed the top of her head. "Top secret. I'll tell you all about it later." At that he climbed out of bed and stumbled to the bathroom, turned on the radio, and stepped into the shower.

Realizing skipping work wasn't an option, Gwen reluctantly followed John into the bathroom. Standing in front of the gold trimmed mirror, she splashed cold water on her face and rubbed briskly with a towel. She'd just stepped back into the bedroom and peeled off her robe when the phone rang again. She glanced at the clock on the radio. It was now almost 5:30. Still in the shower, singing along with the radio, John hadn't heard the phone. Gwen reluctantly picked up on the second ring.

No one answered at first, but the eerie silence kept her hanging on until she heard a man's hoarse voice echo from what sounded like the inside of a phone booth with rain pounding against it. He stated, "There's a cab on its way. You got ten minutes to get out. The choice, right now, is yours."

He hung up without waiting for a response, and Gwen dropped the receiver onto the bed. Her heart pounded in her chest as tears welled up in her eyes. She stood trembling, looking through the bathroom doorway, watching John through the fog collected on the glass door of the shower. Soaping his head vigorously, he sang off-key to a Van Halen tune.

She looked back at the clock, and with her voice quivering, she asked God to help him. Without further hesitation, she threw on the clothes she'd laid out the night before, grabbed her purse, and paused to steal one more glance before she whispered, "I love you, John." Seconds later, she slipped out the door and ran for the elevator.

John turned off the shower and called, "Honey, can you dry my back?" There was no reply. He wiped a clearing off the shower door so he could see through. Again he called out, "Gwen, honey. Where'd you go?" He finished drying himself off, got dressed, and ambled into the kitchen, expecting to see Gwen at the table. But she wasn't there. Instead, he noticed her purse and keys were gone from the table beside the door, and the safety latch dangled loose.

"What the hell?" Mumbling to himself, he ran back into the bedroom, put on his shoes, and grabbed his jacket. He bolted down the hallway to the elevator and punched the down button. No response came from the cranky old elevator above the print shop where they lived. After waiting a long thirty seconds, he ran into the stairwell and flew down two flights of stairs. He burst out the front door just in time to see Gwen getting into a cab.

"Honey, wait!" By the time he cleared the front steps and reached the curb, the cab was pulling away. "Gwen!" He shouted.

She sat motionless in the back seat, looking straight ahead. Then, as the car moved onward she turned and quickly wiped a clearing on the back window of the cab. At that moment, John saw nothing but fear in her eyes that froze him in his tracks. Then his fear escalated when she screamed, "RUNNNNNN!" as the cab sped out of sight.

Immediately he reached inside his jacket for his gun, but it wasn't there. The realization of vulnerability set in as John raced back into the building and attacked the elevator button in an effort to make it work faster, all the while trying to figure out what had just happened with Gwen. Her craziness was a total surprise. As the elevator door opened, he leaped inside and hit the close button with his fist. The old steel cage creaked upward to the second floor. He leaned forward, head bowed, bracing both hands against the wall.

"How could I have been so stupid?" he asked, pounding his fist against the door. As a federal undercover officer, he knew better than to go anywhere without his gun, but in his haste to catch Gwen he'd left the apartment without it. When the door slid open, John stepped into the hallway and sighed a deep breath of relief as it closed behind him. Jogging down the dark, narrow hallway toward his apartment, he noticed the apartment door was standing wide open.

Just then a tall lanky man wearing a long black raincoat stepped from inside. He was wielding a 9mm pistol with a silencer attached. He raised the gun, pointing the muzzle at John's face. John stopped in midstride. Fear had taken his breath as he stared down the cold steel barrel, eye-to-eye with the very drug lord he was scheduled to testify about before the grand jury that same day.

Evidently the deal he'd made with the Feds to protect Gwen had gotten to her, he decided. Even so, her behavior didn't make sense. How did she know about this? John and his partner had secretly worked on this case for quite some time, and their testimonies would convict several men linked to a major drug ring between the US and Colombia.

John inhaled a deep breath, knowing this was the end. "How'd you know it was me?"

"Your partner. I bought him off." The kingpin chuckled, an ugly sound. "Then I gave your old lady ten minutes to get out."

In violent anger, John lunged toward the smug bastard, but before he completed the first step, a bullet ripped through his skull. He stared into his executioner's face for a single moment, raised one hand as though to ward off another blow, and fell backwards in the hallway.

The kingpin stomped toward John as he pumped three more shots directly into his head. Straddling John's limp body, he fired two more shots, precisely placing a bullet through each eye socket to ensure that his face was the last thing John would see before approaching God.

Enthralled by the execution, the murderer panted until he reached a climactic stage and then leaned forward and vomited on his victim. Wiping his mouth with his sleeve, he slipped into the stairwell and disappeared.

## CHAPTER TWO

*March 1995—Dallas Texas*
*6:30 a.m.*

Thinking Jackie was still asleep, George leaned over the bed, breathing in the scent of her perfume. She lay sprawled on her stomach with her blonde hair spread across the pillow. He kissed the nape of her neck.

"Don't try and sneak off. I felt that." She rolled over, grabbed his hand, and pulled him onto the bed.

"I didn't want to wake you," he said, smoothing her hair. "But I needed a kiss."

"And I need to tell you something." Jackie replied as she stuffed the pillow behind her neck and sat up so she could look George in the eye. "I'm sick of Missouri winters, and my big project is finally over. How about I just stay in Dallas and find a job here?"

"You're serious?"

She nodded, watching his face.

"This is great news. I've missed you, and I know the kids have too. We can tell them over dinner tonight."

"No, not yet. Wait till I make a few calls and find some work here. Let's just keep it to ourselves for now, because I'd hate to disappoint them."

"That's fine, honey. You just make those calls." George kissed her on the forehead and she pulled him into her arms.

"Let's celebrate!"

\*\*\*

Later that morning Jackie called Jim Smith, president of the Manufactured Housing Association, knowing he'd have the scoop on everything in the industry. He invited her to stop by the office that afternoon.

Located alongside a busy highway, the factory had doubled in size since her last visit. She parked her Nissan sports car in the visitor's lot and entered through the main door. A surprising amount of activity was going on in and around the factory, and the employee's parking lot was crammed with dusty pickup trucks. Seems there'd really been an explosion to the industry and economy since she had been away.

Inside the building, she had to sign in at a security desk and leave a copy of her driver's license with the receptionist. The small office in front was for retail sales, and Jackie was escorted into the main office waiting area where she settled in a chair while the receptionist announced her arrival. Looking around the stylish room, Jackie realized things had changed since she'd moved to Missouri a year ago. She hadn't really kept up with the hometown economy, and now it was exciting to see all the activity going on.

Just then Jim stepped through the door and shouted, "Jackie, how in the world are you? Come in, come in, come in! My office is just down the hall." Jim was approximately five eleven and stocky, with his shirtsleeves rolled up to his elbows, and no tie. His thick dark hair looked a bit shaggy, and she noticed with a smile that he still crammed half a dozen pens and pencils into his shirt pocket.

Walking beside him down a carpeted hallway lined with fine art, Jackie exclaimed, "Wow—I'm impressed."

To Jim's questioning look she replied, "Just look at this place. Business must be good."

"Hey don't give me a hard time. I worked my butt off while you were vacationing up north." He glanced at his watch. "In fact I've got to hit the streets in about an hour and drum up some new business."

"What new business? Don't buyers still come to you, or have you started selling these wobbly boxes door to door?"

Jim chucked, "You've been away too long. Things have completely changed. We learned from the great depression of the 80s that we have to be self reliant and not allow the finance companies to have complete control over our destiny ever again." He ushered her into a corner office with windows overlooking the factory floor. Jackie stepped to the window and looked around. Below, a rail assembly line moved the homes along from stage to stage as the workers put them together. A catwalk along the top allowed the roofers to work. Each corner of the building held an office where supervisors monitored the crews from overhead.

Strolling back to Jim's desk, Jackie sat in a padded chair and hung her purse across the back. "Really? And how do you also control the economy that goes along with this?"

"The economy's holding—we now buy in volume, and we've formed an organization for the entire industry, so we have purchase power. Everything we use is purchased in bulk, by the trainload or shipload—whatever we need. We save a ton of money that way. And… we control who joins our organization and who gets to share in the savings."

"And that's legal?" Jackie demanded.

"Sure it is. The little guy in business for himself joins our group and gets to benefit from each purchase just like he was one of us big guys buying volume. They're elated to share in the savings. Believe me, it's not only legal, it's a blessing to the little guys in business."

"So what do you big fish get from this?" Jackie asked. She looked around the office, taking in the framed photographs of Jim posing with the governor, several congressmen, and a state senator.

"More volume at a cheaper cost, and bigger savings for everyone. It all adds up." He leaned back in his chair. "So how did things go with that housing development you were working on? I heard you ran into some problems."

"My, but you do keep up with everyone, don't you?"

"Hey, everyone knows everyone in this business."

"No, Jim, everyone knows everyone's business in this industry. Anyway, I solved that little glitch and finished the project. Now I'm ready to move on to another development—and I just might explore my options here in Dallas."

"How long were you up there in Missouri?" Jim asked casually.

Knowing his mind was working behind that relaxed looking facade, Jackie answered, "One very long, cold year. My part of the project is finished, and they're ready to move families into the homes."

Jim scratched his head. "Wasn't that a two-year project?

"It was scheduled for two years, but I worked sixteen-hour days to get things finished up."

"Damn, woman, don't you have a life? I guess the investors were pleased with that. I'm surprised they're willing to let you go."

Jackie knew this was the crucial moment in their conversation. "Trying to have a life! I've met a wonderful guy who owns his own company here in Dallas. He has custody of his two kids, so he doesn't want to move or change anything in their lives. Besides, I'm ready for a warmer climate."

"So tell me, what happened between you and Kevin?" Jim asked.

Jackie's stomach tightened. "What do you mean between me and Kevin? We weren't dating!"

Jim waved his hands in the air. "Hey, That's not what I meant. I heard Kevin was kinda pissed off because you didn't stay and run the business for him."

She took a deep breath, and then let go with both barrels. "Would you work for free for a year? That's what I did to get Kevin's business going, under the promise that IF I got it up and running we would sit down and negotiate our partnership. The problem was—Kevin never thought I could pull it off. His girlfriend dropped in every day asking how things were going so she could make future plans for herself. He showed up every Friday to sign checks for his bills, and other than that I never saw him."

Jackie paused as Jim's secretary popped in and handed him a folder. "After I sold the first house, I cut myself a $3,000 check, which was only about twenty-five percent of the profit on that sale. You'd have thought I was robbing him. He screamed "I can't afford to pay you three grand on every house sold from this lot. I'll pay you a flat $500 per house."

"I hope you told him he was nuts," Jim said. "You should've been an equal partner in that operation from get-go. At least that's what Pierre told me when he approved that half-a-million-dollar line of credit to get that business off the ground. But, like they say, hindsight is 20/20. By the way, Jackie, did you know Pierre works for us now? Eventually, he'll be my second in command. We want to build our empire with people who are familiar faces in the industry at high levels. That gets attention. Plus, Pierre knows who our competition is and how they operate."

"So you lured Pierre away from his company. I've heard that called corporate sabotage."

Jim chuckled. "I call it knowing your competition." He folded his hands behind his head and leaned back in the chair. "Have you ever thought about working in Louisiana?"

"No! I don't like the humidity," she snapped.

"Just thought I'd ask. I know a guy in New Orleans who could sure use someone with your experience to be a road warrior for his product."

Jackie shook her head no. "I really need to get off the road, Jim. I've logged too many miles over the last couple of years. I want a schedule that lets me keep all my clothes in the same closet. The way things are now, half the time I'm looking for something that's in another house in a different state." She sighed. "I'm just ready to get my career life organized and stabilized, and I'd like it to happen in Dallas."

"In that case, you need to meet Richard Spaniel. He's area manager, in charge of all the retail lots in the Texas, Oklahoma, New Mexico region."

"Do they build developments like I'm used to?" Jackie asked.

"No, they're not that far along—they're into just the home-building part right now." He added, "I think you really should think about going retail now. They have 401k and insurance, plus room for advancement. With your experience and expertise, you'd be a real asset to Richard. Want me to set up an interview?" He held his hand over the phone.

Jackie's pulse quickened. This was why she'd come to see Jim, but things were moving even faster than she'd expected. "Sure I'm interested. I'd like nothing more than to get in with a new company and be able to grow and prosper along with them."

"You just wait outside for a minute, and I'll set this up. Richard's office is just down the hall."

Jackie found the ladies room and spent a few minutes freshening her makeup. She brushed a few blonde hairs off her black double-breasted business suit and refolded her white turtleneck collar. Her hair looked fine, but she nervously redid it anyway. Back in the waiting room, the receptionist brought her a cup of water and she flipped through a company magazine without really seeing the articles. She mentally prepared herself for the interview, ticking off her accomplishments inside her head.

Jim reappeared a few minutes later, smiling. "Richard's excited about meeting you, so I'll just show you to his office."

Jackie offered Jim her hand. "It still pays to have friends. Thanks, Jim. I really appreciate this."

"Hey, you'd do the same for me." He said as he cupped her hand inside his. They entered Richard's office together, but Jim excused himself after the introduction. On his way out, Jim shook Jackie's hand and whispered, "I know you'll be a real asset to this company. I'll be watching your stats." As he stepped out the door he turned and leaned inward as he remarked. "Oh, by the way, Jackie. We don't do business with Kevin anymore. He was just too big a problem after you left him." Then Jim turned his thumb in a downward motion before hastily continuing down the hallway toward his office.

## CHAPTER THREE

When they entered the office, Richard was leaning over his desk, fumbling through a stack of papers. Jackie couldn't help but notice he had a slight paunch above his baggy dress pants. Wearing a crisp, monogrammed white shirt with a flashy print tie, Richard would've been right at home in a used car lot or discount furniture store.

"Have a seat, Jackie. I'll be with you in a second. If I don't find this invoice, my secretary's gonna have a stroke."

Standing in front of Richard's massive desk, which occupied most of the room, Jackie heard the muffled sounds of power saws, hammers, and loud music from the factory floor as the workers completed their part on the assembly line of homes. The office décor mostly focused on Richard's accomplishments—pictures of him handing out awards to salespeople or receiving awards himself. A few photos of his children graced the desktop. Looking around the room, Jackie noticed a familiar face in one of the group photographs. Taking a step closer, she recognized someone she'd worked with in another state, but she couldn't place the other people in the snapshot.

Just then Richard returned and approached her with his hand out, apologizing for the inconvenience. "Got to keep the bills paid, ya know."

"Oh, that's no problem. Customers always come first," she said, accepting the handshake.

"You can say that again! Have a seat." He motioned her into a plush chair in front of his desk." He settled into his leather chair and adjusted his oversized cuff links. The ring on his right hand reflected the light, a cluster of diamonds in the center of a company logo. He peered at her face. "Have we met before? Where do I know you from?"

"That picture." Jackie stated.

Richard turned and squinted at the picture on the wall. "I know you aren't in it."

"No, but I think I know a couple of those people."

"Really? That was taken last year on our cruise to Switzerland. He got up, removed the picture from the wall, and began naming the faces. Jackie walked around the desk and stood behind him until he pointed to the familiar faces. They said the names in unison: "DeDe and Dawn."

"So you do know them," Richard said.

"I worked on a project for them a long time ago. I doubt they'd even remember me. Isn't he from Pittsburgh?" She asked.

"I think he is," Richard replied.

"Well, I've heard good things about you from Jim and Pierre, so what can you tell me about yourself?" Richard tilted back in his chair.

Jackie described her most recent project and then gave him the highlights of her career, including the ill-fated venture with Kevin. Richard asked a few general questions, and soon they were engaged in conversation like two old school chums. After an hour of conversation, Richard checked his watch and chuckled as he smiled and remarked, "You're so charming, I nearly forgot my lunch date. Why don't I send you over to meet with Stan Decker, our VP. You'll either work directly with me or with Stan—I'm not sure yet. But we'll find a place for you."

Still talking, they made their way down the hallway to the reception area. They parted outside as Richard moved toward his silver Mercedes and Jackie unlocked her sports car. She grinned all the way to Stan's office. Everything was happening fast, and this was exactly what she wanted.

Half an hour later, she was escorted into Stan Decker's office. He introduced himself and prepared to sit down when Jackie said, "Stan, before we go on, there's something I'd like to take care of up front."

He froze, staring at her. "Okay."

She removed her wallet from her purse and held a fifty-dollar bill out to Stan. "I know this seems awkward, but I feel I have to take care of something with one of your employees before we even try to move on."

Stan looked surprised, but he listened intently while Jackie explained that she'd seen Dickie Vaughn standing in front of the building as she drove in. "We worked together several years ago, and one day my ex husband showed up at the office, created a huge scene, and got me fired."

"And?" Stan interjected.

"I owe Dickie fifty dollars for a briefcase I bought from him, and I never had a chance to pay him." Jackie felt her face turning red. "I don't want any hard feelings from anyone if I work here."

Stan shook his head, accepted the money, and said. "I'll be right back."

Jackie stared at the floor for ten minutes, awaiting her fate. As the minutes ticked away she grew more anxious and wary that things would not end well for her in this interview. Finally, Stan hurried back through the door and passed her the money.

"Dickie doesn't even remember, so I guess the money's yours," he shrugged. "This is an unusual way to start an interview."

"I'm sorry," Jackie said.

"For what? I know this had to be embarrassing for you, and I admire your integrity." He picked up an ink pen and rolled it through his fingers. "Let's talk about how we can get you on board with the company."

After forty-five minutes, Stan checked his watch and said, "I'd love to have you work for me here, but Richard has one other interview for you before we make the final decision." He passed her a piece of paper with an address and map showing yet another location. "Fair enough?" he asked.

"Fair enough," she replied, saying a quick thank you to the powers above that she hadn't botched the interview when she mentioned Dickie.

Once on the road, she glanced down at the map Stan had drawn for her and realized the next interview was less than five minutes from George's house, where she'd be living. Things were looking up! Navigating traffic on the highway, she considered how perfect this would be—instead of six hundred miles, she'd be within five miles of home. *No more late-night runs to the airport on Sunday. No more tearful goodbyes or long telephone conversations at bedtime*, she thought as she dialed up an oldies station on the radio and sang along with the music while letting the wind blow through her hair.

At the next location, she was met by a man who introduced himself as Dexter Kuykendahl. He motioned for her to enter his office.

Dexter stared intently into her eyes and then said, "Can I ask you a personal question?"

*Damn*, Jackie thought. *Stan must've tipped him off about the Dickie thing.* Smiling demurely, she said, "Of course."

"Are your eyes really that green? Are those contacts? You have the prettiest eyes I've ever seen!"

Not quite sure how to respond, she kept it simple. "Yes, they are green, and I'm not wearing contact lenses, but thank you for the compliment."

Dexter continued, "You remind me of Morgan Fairfax. Hey, I've had wet dreams about Morgan Fairfax before."

The conversation had taken an ugly turn before it even started, and Jackie knew she'd better take control of the situation. "Can we please just get on with the interview?"

Dexter said. "Sure, why don't you tell me about yourself and your experience in the business. I know you went over this with Richard and Stan, but I'm probably the one you'll be working for."

"Well," Jackie replied. "What else would you like to know about me besides my personal genetics?"

Dexter chuckled and thumbed through some papers on his desk as she openly discussed her experience.

They were well into discussing her background when a woman popped open the door directly behind Jackie and demanded Dexter's attention.

"Can it wait? I'm kinda in the middle of something right now," he explained.

Jackie's mouth dropped open. The woman babbled on and on about supplies and ignored the fact that Dexter was in the middle of an interview. Moments later, Jackie understood when Dexter explained.

"Jackie, this is my wife. She works here she takes care of the decorating." Turning back to the woman, who was still talking, he asked, "Honey can we talk about this when I get home?"

"No," she demanded. "We'll talk about it now!" Mrs. Kuykendahl tossed a fabric swatch onto the desk. "They've brought the wrong color carpet—again!"

Jackie stood, saying, "You know I think we were through anyway, so you just go ahead."

As she left the office, Dexter shouted above his wife's shrill voice, "Thanks for coming by. We'll be in touch."

Jackie drove home shaking her head. Dexter was not her first choice for a boss, and Mrs. Kuykendahl would be a handful.

# CHAPTER FOUR

By this time the day was pretty much gone, but she needed to pick things up at the grocery store for dinner. When she came through the back door carrying grocery bags, she noticed the answering machine on the kitchen counter was blinking. The message was from Richard Spaniel, asking her to please call him immediately.

"No way." Jackie shook her head as she hit the erase button. She needed to discuss the day's events with George and get his male perspective before she decided if she'd even talk to Richard again. While she was putting away the groceries, the phone rang again. She trotted into George's office and checked the caller ID.

It was Richard Spaniel, calling from his home this time. She decided not to answer, and he hung up after three rings.

Back in the kitchen, she greeted Jason, George's oldest son, who announced he had a baseball game and wouldn't be home for dinner as he grabbed a handful of granola bars and an apple before he darted out the door.

Jackie was well on her way to creating the perfect lasagna when George arrived home with Brandon, the ten-year old, in tow. Brandon burst through the front door, charged into his room, and emerged with his baseball bat and glove so he could practice in the back yard.

George shouted, "Stay in the yard Brandon!" As he made his way into the kitchen, sniffing his favorite seasoning—garlic.

"Honey, that smells great! Lasagna?"

Jackie winked and shook her head up and down before she kissed his cheek, looking like Betty Crocker wearing her red-checkered Kiss the Cook apron. "Hope you like it. Does Brandon eat lasagna?"

George opened the oven door for her. "I hope not. Then I can have it all!" As Jackie slid the lasagna pan into the oven, he asked, "I thought we were taking the kids out for dinner tonight?" He put his arms around her so she couldn't escape and stared into her eyes. "We were gonna talk about you staying in Texas. Ah Jackie, this is big stuff—don't rain on my parade. I don't want you to leave again."

"And that's why I don't want to say anything to the kids yet. We need to be sure before we make any announcements."

"So what's not right with it?"

Jackie stood motionless, thinking before she replied. "Let me tell you about my day, and then you help me decide." She described her visit with Jim and then said, "After that, things went downhill a little bit. In Richard's office I noticed a picture of some people I'd worked for several years ago. They screwed over their employees and pretty much everyone they did business with before they skipped out to Switzerland. That was seven years ago."

She pulled loose from George's embrace but took his hand. "They clipped me for over five grand on just one house, George. I almost went under because of it. Seeing them back in the business again makes me sick. I don't know if I can walk past them when we have meetings and hold my thoughts to myself. I'm wondering if I should've said something to Richard right then. I mean, they took off with the money from six houses that had been sold off the lot and didn't pay the builders or commissions. They took the money and zoomed off to Switzerland, telling us they were going to Florida because his mother was sick. His own brother who worked for him was left holding the bag. They didn't even pack up their house—they just left everything."

"Maybe you should call them now that you know where they are."

"Why?" Jackie asked. "You think they're gonna have some feelings of remorse and wanna pay me the money after all this time? I don't think so. They know they owe me and a lot of other people, too. Besides I tracked down his mother's phone number and called her, which is how I found out they were lying about the whole thing."

"Well, would they have anything to do with you in this company?" George asked.

"No." She responded.

"Do they make any management decisions with the company that would involve you?"

"No."

"Would they be responsible for or have any say so over your position or your paycheck?"

"No," Jackie replied again.

"So what are you worried about?" he asked.

She thought for a moment and then said, "You're right. I shouldn't worry about them. They should worry about me! Once they see me and know I'm working for the same company, operating under the same guidelines, they'll probably avoid me like the plague. Besides they won't want me to tell what they did with their last business, so they probably won't even claim to know me." She gave a sigh of relief. "You're right, George, I'm probably making something outta nothing. Let's set the table for dinner."

Half an hour later, Jackie pulled the lasagna out of the oven as George called Brandon in for dinner. Jackie excused herself for a moment, and Brandon, who was ravenous, took a huge bite of the lasagna. He grabbed his mouth, spitting the food back into his hand.

"What are you doing?" George shouted. Brandon looked around to see if Jackie was nearby and then whispered, "Dad! The noodles aren't cooked!"

Looking both ways, George gritted his teeth and replied, "Eat it anyway!"

Moments later, Jackie returned to the table, where both Brandon and George sat, each sporting a peculiar smile.

"Thanks for waiting. Let's eat, guys."

"After you," George responded. He and Brandon watched Jackie take a bite of the uncooked noodles. As she bit down and the lasagna crunched between her teeth, she froze. They could see her thinking back, trying to remember if she'd left out a step when she was preparing the lasagna.

She, too, spit the uncooked food into her napkin. "Why didn't someone stop me?" They all laughed hysterically. Jackie said, "I can't believe I was so worried over this work stuff that I couldn't even remember to cook the noodles. I guess we'll eat out tonight after all."

They all three picked up their plates and scraped the remains into the sink. With a flourish, George turned on the disposal and they both followed his salute as the lasagna crunched between the blades on its departure down the drain.

Brandon whispered, "Dad, you do the cooking from now on, okay?"

Jackie and George laughed hysterically, and George replied, "Okay, son."

They turned around to see Jason watching them with a puzzled look on his face while they rinsed away the remnants of the lasagna.

"What's for dinner?" he asked.

Still laughing, Jackie said, "You pick it. We're going out."

"How about Italian?" he suggested.

Again they burst into hysterical laughter. Throwing his arm around Jason's shoulders, George said, "I'd sure like some lasagna. Let's go!"

## CHAPTER FIVE

The phone started ringing about 9:00 the next morning, but Jackie refused to answer before she'd had her morning cup of coffee. She suspected it was Richard Spaniel. However when the answering machine picked up, she heard the familiar twang of Larry Russell, an investor from Oklahoma. Jackie grabbed the phone just as Larry began leaving a message.

"Hey, Larry, I'm here! Sorry I didn't pick up. I thought it was someone I don't want to talk to."

"Oh yea? Trouble in Paradise?" he asked.

"Oh, nothing I can't handle. What's up?"

"I just took a call about a new startup in Oklahoma, and I'm checking to see if you're ready to tackle another development."

Jackie grabbed her coffee cup and carried the phone into the living room, where she settled on the sofa. "Maybe. "Where's it located?"

"Somewhere between Oklahoma City and Tulsa," Larry replied.

"Hmmm. Sounds interesting. Why don't you get all the info together and call me? I'll catch a flight up there and we can look it over together."

"I knew I could count on you," Larry said. She could almost hear the wheels turning in his head.

"Hey don't count your chickens yet. I'm working on some other things that'll keep me closer to Dallas."

"Do I hear wedding bells?" Larry asked.

"Maybe. I haven't made my mind up yet. I'm thinking out my options, and Oklahoma ain't that far from Texas."

"Ya'll could still see one another on weekends," Larry added. "I'll send a report within the next few days, Jackie, if you promise to consider the offer."

"Okay, okay," she agreed. "I'll call you back after I've looked it over."

She headed back to the kitchen for the last cup of coffee in the pot, thinking hard about the offer. The phone rang again, vibrating across the counter. This time she answered on the first ring, thinking Larry was calling back.

It was Richard Spaniel. "Well, what'd you think about our product?" He asked.

"We didn't get that far," Jackie replied. She hesitated, not wanting to go into details about Dexter's witchy wife. Before she could think what to say, Richard added, "Look, I've got something going on at that location I can't quite put my finger on, so I'd appreciate your input."

"Well, Richard, since you put it that way, I'll tell you." She then explained how Mrs. Kuykendahl sabotaged the interview by bursting into the office with carpet swatches.

"Damn, what a bad impression. Thanks for being up front with me. Hang on a sec." She heard him speak to someone, and then he was back on the line. "I can't apologize enough, Jackie. But you can see that the office really needs someone with your expertise to get it up to par."

Jackie drummed her fingers on the counter. "I just made a commitment to look over a development in Oklahoma, so I'll be out of town the rest of the week."

"I'd sure like to talk with you again before you make a commitment anywhere. Will you do that for me?" Richard requested.

Jackie thought fast. She didn't want to burn any bridges, and the Oklahoma deal might not work out. What could it hurt to hear Richard out? "Okay, I can do that," She said. "I promise to call you in a few days—before I make a commitment elsewhere." She hung up, sighing with a relief.

## CHAPTER SIX

Several days passed and Jackie didn't hear from Richard again. She was thankful because this gave her time to check up on his company and think about other options. Unfortunately, the Oklahoma job was moved to the back burner due to zoning problems, so Richard's company began to look like her best option for staying in Dallas. She waited another twenty-four hours, playing hard to get.

The next morning, Richard called again. She carried the phone into the office, put her feet on the desk, and stared out the window at the garden.

Richard's hearty voice boomed in her ear. "I was hoping you'd stop by my office again, so we can have a serious talk. You remembered your promise, right? I'm free later this morning. How 'bout it, Jackie?"

At that, they arranged a meeting, and Richard closed the conversation with, "I promise you won't be sorry."

Jackie decided that since all she got to wear on her last job was jeans, this time she would dress for success. She chose a tailored navy blue dress with a skirt that accented her trim legs. When she arrived at the factory, she was glad she'd worn upscale office attire because a managers' meeting was in progress, with stuffed coats and pin stripes everywhere. She was accustomed to being the only woman on a job site, so the men's stares didn't bother her as she made her way to Richard's office.

As they continued the interview, Richard discussed what the company had to offer should she decide to accept the position. He stressed that she was exactly the type of material they were looking for to build their empire. Her knowledge and expertise would help her move toward obtaining her own lot in due time.

This was exactly what Jackie hoped to hear—she'd like nothing better than to have her own housing lot close to home, while producing a six-figure income. It was her dream come true! Naturally, the dream came with a price.

Richard said, "Before I put you on your own lot, I need you to straighten out the Midway Park location. That lot should be a number one producer, and we can't seem to get more than three or four homes delivered a month. It just hasn't taken off like I think it should, and I need someone with your expertise to straighten it out."

Seeing her frown, he tilted his chair back and eyed her over the rim of his glasses. "Then, in less than a year tops, I'll have you on your own lot. In the meantime I'll have you over here periodically doing some training to prepare you for management. Our way. You should do very well with your experience on that location—probably sixty to sixty-five K until we get you onto your own lot. How does that sound?"

"Sounds good," she replied as she nodded. It wasn't perfect, but so far the company looked good, and they'd promised her a retail lot within twelve months. That would give her time to make sure things were going to work out with George, too.

"Great!" Richard shouted. "I promise you won't be disappointed!!!" He picked up one of his cards, scribbled something on the front, and passed it to Jackie. "Here, this is my home phone number and my wife's name. I want you to keep it with you and report back to me—I don't care what time it is. If I'm not there, my wife, Sue, will take a message."

"Report about what?" Jackie asked.

"Whatever you need, or anything I can do to assist. I'm calling that manager, Dexter, right now and let him know I've hired you. Can you go by there today and pick up your employment package?"

"Sure," Jackie said. "Might as well get started." She and Richard shook hands to seal their agreement and she left the office feeling she'd made the right decision. She held her head high, looking forward to a promising future.

## CHAPTER SEVEN

Jackie stopped at home long enough to call George before she headed to the Midway Park office. He'd been worried she might accept a job out of town, and she wanted him to hear the good news right away.

"Guess what!" she blurted. "I just accepted the position with Midway Housing right here in Dallas, and I'll be working from the Midway Park office five miles from our house."

George let out a whoop. "That's terrific! Let's do dinner and celebrate, just the two of us. Where would you like to go?"

"I can't even think about food right now—I'm too excited. I've still got to pick up my employment package and go over inventory at the Midway office. Why don't you just surprise me?"

George said, "That I can do! You just have yourself ready tonight by 7:30 and we'll do it up right."

At the Midway Park location, Jackie was greeted by a tall man with bulging biceps who introduced himself as Tom Kerakasco and then quickly added, "But my friends call me Tommy."

"Nice to meet you, Tom. My name is Jackie Weatherby. My friends call me Jackie."

"Oh a wise guy," he replied. "I like that!"

Dexter kept her waiting outside his office while he took a phone call, and she chatted with Tom, who leaned against the wall beside her chair. His dark hair was trimmed short and stood stiff with hair mousse. Although his shirt was a bit too tight, it emphasized the fact that he obviously worked out a lot.

"So where are you from, Tom?" she asked.

"I just moved here from Minnesota."

"Minnesota? I would have bet that was a New York or Jersey accent. What brings you to Texas? Did you get tired of those awful winters up there?"

Tom shook his head no and uttered, "Ugly divorce." Before she could respond, he asked, "So, are you married?"

A little surprised by the question, Jackie said, "No, but I'm attached."

Tom proceeded to ask a string of personal questions about her family and George. "So what does your ole man do?" Jackie quickly replied, "My father is retired." Tom laughed, "No, no not your father—your attachment. What does he do?"

"Oh, George. He owns a flooring company." Now really embarrassed, she answered his next questions in as few words as possible, wishing Dexter would hurry with his phone call. Between her conversation with Tom, Jackie heard bits and pieces of Dexter's conversation from the other side of the door. Apparently it was a loan officer from one of the mortgage companies they did business with, and from the gist of the conversation, there was no hope for Dexter to get his the loan approved.

This was none of her business, so she simply sat there waiting her turn, trying to ignore Tom's looming presence. Finally, Dexter ended his conversation and escorted her into his office.

He apologized for his wife's actions at the last interview, and she brushed it off as no problem. Then he called Tommy into the room, saying, "I wanna visit with the two of you together, so have a seat."

Tom settled in the chair next to her, giving her a big smile as Dexter began speaking.

"Tom here is my assistant—the sales manager, right now. However, my plans are to have two leaders to whom the sales personnel will report."

That seemed logical, Jackie thought, and she wondered how the teams would be divided. Since there were twelve salesmen, she figured each manager would supervise six employees.

She tuned back in to Dexter, who was saying he'd implement the changes in two weeks. He added, "I'm about to take care of something I've been needing to do for a while. Now that you're on board, Jackie, I'm going to relieve someone of their job so you'll have an office."

"What!" Jackie sat up, thinking she'd heard wrong.

"I didn't mean it that way," Dexter said. "But this lady hasn't sold anything in two months, so it's really time for her to go back into real estate sales. I just don't think she's cut out for our office." He grinned. "Besides, I don't like her—she has a mustache bigger than mine!"

Jackie stared, not sure he was joking.

Dexter headed for the door, calling back over his shoulder, "Tommy will show you the inventory while I relieve Ms. Raleigh of her job."

Tom led Jackie out the back door toward a model home, beginning with the most expensive model on the lot. She was truly impressed with the home, but still she had to ask: "Do you always start off with the most expensive home when you're showing your customers?"

"Sure, why not?" Tom replied.

"Will you try something new with your next customer?" Tom nodded, and she continued. "I want you to do a step up. Start off with the least expensive home, one you know they won't like. Then step up to something similar to what they want, and lastly go to one that's the perfect match. That way they have to open up to you between houses, describing what their idea of the perfect home is. Then you've hooked 'em and you just reel 'em in."

"Hey, that makes sense. I'm gonna try that."

She followed Tom from house to house, looking over the different floor plans and decor packages as they talked about the business, the product, the company, and the people who worked in the Midway

Park office. This also gave them time to become better acquainted and learn each other's work styles.

Looking at his watch, Tom said, "I really need to get back to the office. I've got some calls I need to make." As they started back, he added, "I really appreciate the sales tip, and I'm gonna try it next time."

Jackie stayed in the sales area so she could walk through the homes again and make a map of the lot, knowing she'd need this jump-start before she started meeting customers on Monday morning. She needed to know every detail of each home—the last thing she wanted was to fumble in front of a customer.

When she walked back into the office, brushing dust off her skirt, Dexter called her back into his office and shut the door. When she was seated, he looked at her with a huge grin on his face. "Tom tells me you passed the test."

"What test?"

"Just a little thing we put every sales candidate through while Tom walks them through the homes. He always starts with the most expensive one first. You're the only person who's ever questioned him on that, and you even told him how to change his methods."

Jackie laughed. "So that's why he gave me that dumb look when I stopped him. I almost felt sorry for him." She shook her head. "He pulled that one off perfectly—I thought I was really teaching him something. Don't I feel stupid!"

"Hey, you should feel pretty smart. You're the only one who's ever passed the test!"

After a few minutes of conversation, they agreed that Jackie would start work Monday morning, and Dexter promised to introduce her to the staff at that time.

"See you then!" She said, gathering her notes.

## CHAPTER EIGHT

Jackie stood in the shower with her eyes closed, deep in thought, allowing the hot water to cascade down her body, taking away the stress of the day with it. When she turned off the faucet and opened the curtain, there stood George, holding a towel, a dozen red roses, and wearing a smile that covered his entire face.

"George! You are so sweet!" Still dripping wet, she flung herself against him, pushing him against the sink as she deeply kissed him for his thoughtfulness.

"Whoa! I'm gonna bring home roses every day," he proclaimed.

They were abruptly interrupted as Brandon shouted, "Dad! Mom's on the phone," as he pounded his little fist nonstop against the bathroom door.

"Hang up!" George shouted. He looked down at himself. His pants were wet where Jackie's wet body had been pressed against him, not to mention bulging in anticipation.

"I swear, that woman has radar," he snapped as he wrapped the towel around his waist, stepping out in front of Brandon and leaving Jackie behind laughing at his misfortune.

"Dad, why are you wearing a towel over your clothes?" Brandon asked.

George snatched the phone from his hand and sent him off to play in his room. Minutes later, Jackie emerged from the bathroom wearing George's robe and carrying her roses. As she sashayed past to find a vase, she made kissing noises. George waved her off, trying to block the phone with his hand and whispered, "I'm gonna get you for that!"

Just out of his reach, Jackie stopped and let the robe fall open. "You gotta catch me first," she whispered back. Securing the robe with the belt, she darted into he kitchen while George finished the dreaded weekly call from his ex.

Jackie was placing the roses in the center of the dining room table when the doorbell rang. Apparently, no one else was available to answer, so she went to the door wearing only George's robe. Luckily, it was Mandy, the babysitter, who'd stay with Brandon while she and George went out for the evening.

Jackie looked like a million dollars in the red dress she'd been saving for a special night on the town, and George insisted on taking pictures of everyone together before they left the house. He drove them to an upscale restaurant in Las Colinas—one that required reservations.

"This is great. I didn't think you even knew about places that required reservations," Jackie said as the doorman opened the door.

"I'm hoping this is a special day for us," George whispered in her ear as they followed the maître d' to their table beside an indoor waterfall.

Jackie thought the night was absolutely perfect, but after they finished the main course, things got even better. George reached into his pocket, pulling out a ring that was absolutely the biggest thing she'd ever seen. There was a huge, sparkling diamond in the center, at least a full carat, and smaller ones all around. Her mouth fell open as George said, "I'm not going to ask you, because I know what the answer would be right now, but can I just give this to you and say, 'Whenever you're ready I hope it's me you choose?'"

Jackie reached for his hand, linked her fingers with his, and kissed it. He then took her left hand and removed the ring she was wearing from her ring finger. He replaced the ring with his. They'd talked about marriage—well, George had talked about marriage—but Jackie just didn't feel ready. Accustomed to her independence, she wanted to accomplish some things on her own before she settled down. Fortunately, George had always seemed to understand her need for independence. Until now, anyway.

"I just want you to know I'm serious about this relationship," he explained.

"I can see that," Jackie said, twisting her hand to watch the diamonds sparkle in the candlelight. Much to her embarrassment, a tear trickled down her cheek. "George you've taken my breath away! I am profoundly impressed with your thoughtfulness, not to mention your consideration for me, and I do want you to know I love you. But I—"

George interrupted, "I know."

Jackie tried again after clearing her throat. "We'll have to start with some ground rules. We must allow each other space and room to grow."

"I hope I don't grow any more—I'm already six-six and two hundred forty pounds."

She laughed. "You know what I mean, wise guy."

"Yeah, I do, but I don't want to lose you, Jackie. I thought this separation for the past year was so you could accomplish something for yourself."

"And I did. I just want to be self-reliant."

"I thought you were self-reliant," George said. "I don't provide anything for you—you won't let me."

Jackie couldn't deny his words were true, but she'd been married to her career for a long time. Could she make George happy, or would she end up ruining his life?

He watched her, smiling tenderly. As usual, he was reading her thoughts. "Can we at least live in the same house and meet in the middle?"

She sipped her wine, stalling while she considered her next words. "George, we can dwell under the same roof, we can share our lives, and I do want to marry you—just not right now. I want to make sure we can blend our families together, as well as our lives. And then there's our careers." She reached for his hand again. "There has to be a separation between four entities: your business and you; my business and me.

"I agree." He nodded.

"I don't want to work for your company or know the details about your company. I don't need to take on that responsibility. Nor do I want your employees thinking that just because we're attached I'm going to be in there running your business. And then I don't want to bore you with the details of my business dealings. I simply want us to have something different to discuss together over the dinner table. Something that you did that day and something I did that day, not directly involving one another. I think couples who work together set themselves up for failure, and I don't want that for us. Different careers would give us the separation we need to maintain our individuality. Is that okay?"

"No problem. I already have a secretary and a bookkeeper. I don't need you in my business, but I want you in my life."

"Then it's settled—separate careers." Jackie held her glass aloft and they drank a toast.

# CHAPTER NINE

Monday was the start of Jackie's new career with a new company, and she felt ready to take on the world when she arrived at the office, carrying her new briefcase. Tammy Aikman, the office manager, introduced herself, and she and Jackie realized they'd worked together previously at another company. Tammy handed Jackie a pile of corporate forms to fill out, along with the official job application, and escorted her into an empty office.

While Jackie was working on the forms, Dexter popped his head in the door and said, "When you're finished, stop by my office. I'll call everyone together for a meeting and introduce you."

"Sounds great," Jackie replied. She completed the paperwork in an hour and headed down the hallway to Dexter's office. Passing through the lobby, she walked in on a group of salesmen who were being entertained by a bulky guy with a military haircut. He was demonstrating how he'd bent his wife over the back of a chair and humped her the night before. Jackie felt her face burn with embarrassment as she walked through the room, but the guys seemed oblivious to her discomfort. The big guy continued his performance, fueled by their laughter.

She quickly stepped into Dexter's office and closed the door behind her to separate herself from the hoopla and regain her composure. She couldn't tell whether or not Dexter had heard the performance—he was just hanging up the phone when she came in and announced the paperwork was completed.

"I'm ready to move into my office and start greeting customers," she added with a big smile.

"That's fine," Dexter said. "But first we'll have a little meeting so I can introduce you to the guys."

The men were still assembled in the lobby as Dexter and Jackie stepped through the door. Tom brought a chair for Jackie from his office and she took a seat beside him.

Dexter cleared his throat and the men quieted, staring unabashedly at Jackie. "Good morning, group. I've called this meeting to introduce a lady who'll be a genuine asset to us. She has several years' experience in the business, and she'll be helping Tom and me put your loans together, or anything else you need help with. I ask that you each spend some time with her and use her to help you close some deals. Any questions?"

No one uttered a word. Dexter went around the group and introduced each man to Jackie. None of them made eye contact or spoke. The troublemaker who'd provided the merriment earlier was named Shane Sturmer, she noted. His sidekick was Royce Hader, a surly looking man with nicotine stained fingers.

"Any comments?" Dexter asked.

Just then Royce Hader rose and walked down the hallway toward his office. Moments later, Shane also got up.

Dexter asked, "Where you goin buddy?"

"My office," Shane snapped.

Then Royce stomped back through the lobby, carrying his keys, banged through the front door, and headed toward his truck.

Dexter stood as though to follow Royce, then changed his mind. "I'd like everyone to go to their offices until I get this cleared up." Just then, Tammy paged him for an urgent phone call, and he disappeared into his own office. The other men drifted away, leaving Jackie alone in the lobby.

Royce stormed back into the building and into his office, where he raised the window and began throwing things into the bed of his truck, which he'd parked alongside the building. "Ain't no bitch gonna tell me how to run my motherfucking business!" he shouted.

Jackie watched in shock as Tom emerged from his office, slammed the door behind him, and rushed into Dexter's office, announcing, "Royce is outta control, and you need to intervene, NOW!"

But before Dexter could get off the phone, Royce was packed and had climbed through the window. He threw the truck into gear and peeled rubber all the way across the parking lot.

By this time, all the sales personnel had regrouped in the lobby. Shane spouted off, "Royce don't need any motherfucking help from anybody to get his loans through."

Realizing she wasn't going to get any support from Dexter, Jackie decided to defend herself. She turned to Shane and asked, "If Royce was such an expert in the housing and mortgage industry, why did he have to maintain a paper route at night to supplement his income?"

Everyone laughed, and she added, "I'm here to help you guys, not hinder anyone's ability to make a living."

Shane shouted, "I don't give a F U C K why you're here, lady. I'm still working my own deals!"

"You know what, Shane?" Jackie replied. "You can get pissed off and cuss all you want, but not at me, and not within my hearing distance. You got that?"

"I'll say what the fuck I want, when the fuck I want, to who the fuck I want—and there ain't a fucking thing you or anybody else can do about it." Shane snarled. "And if you don't like it you can take your motherfucking cocksucking ass and go somewhere else to work. You got that?"

Forcing herself to stay calm, Jackie smiled up at Shane. "You think so Shane? I'll tell what—I'm going to make one phone call and give one person an opportunity to help you see the light if I hear one more motherfucking, cocksucking, son of a bitch come from your mouth. Believe me, there are things I can and will do to stop this from happening. I don't care if I have to go outside of this company, You

Are Not Going To Talk To Me Like That Ever Again. Got It?" Jackie spun on her heel to leave, when she heard Sam Massick, the business manager begin speaking.

"Shane, she's right. You need to control you mouth. You need to watch what you say and when you say it. Everyone around here, me included, has a problem with foul language, and we all need to be more considerate—especially with our customers. These people come in here to make a big purchase, and they can hear you guys through the walls. This language thing may be the reason some of them never come back."

Shane turned without a word and walked into his office, slamming the door. Everyone assumed he'd be the next to leave, but in a few minutes he came out with his briefcase in hand and announced, "I'm going to lunch."

# CHAPTER TEN

Jackie took refuge in an open office, wondering how much worse things could possibly get. She was tempted to follow Shane out the front door and never return, but then he'd win. She was much too stubborn to let a redneck pig like Shane scare her off.

Sam followed her into the office and offered his hand. "We haven't formally met, so I'd like to introduce myself and apologize for that outburst."

In his mid fifties, standing over six feet tall with broad shoulders, a bald head, and a deep booming voice, Sam always wore khaki pants and a plaid shirt. Relieved to have at least one ally, Jackie took his hand. "Thanks, I'm grateful for what you just did. Does this kind of thing happen a lot?"

Sam settled into the chair opposite her desk. "When they don't get their way or feel threatened, they tend to throw tantrums, but this is the worst I've seen."

"Well, maybe that's why this location hasn't shown a profit. Lack of discipline can bring down an operation," Jackie said.

"You're probably right." Sam said, "But getting someone to listen is also a problem."

"Well maybe that's why they put me here." She watched his face. Sam raised his eyebrows. "Oh yeah?"

"Richard asked me to look things over and give him a report. He said there's a problem with this location that he just can't put his finger on."

Sam laughed. "Oh, boy. This should be interesting. Keep me posted would ya?" He closed the door, returned to his seat, and continued in a softer tone, "I've been in this office for over a year and I can't tell you how many times I've tried to clue Richard in. He either won't listen or denies everything I tell him. I hope you have better luck."

"That's interesting," Jackie said. Before she could ask further questions, Dexter summoned them to the lobby again. This time he announced, "I want to meet with each one of you alone in my office, starting with Todd. Everyone else stay in your offices with the doors closed until I call you."

Still unsure which office would be hers, Jackie returned to the empty office and stared at the walls. Sam slipped back in a few minutes later, and they spent nearly an hour discussing the business, discovering they had several mutual acquaintances. As they talked, some of the morning's tension subsided, and Jackie realized she felt more comfortable with Sam than anyone she'd met there so far. He seemed to have a genuine interest in the business and they both shared the same views. At least there was one person in the office she could relate to.

After each individual one-on-one conference and Royce's departure, the office seemed to mellow out for a few days. However, on Thursday, Jackie was escorting an elderly couple into the office when they walked past Shane and Roberto. The term "motherfucker" reared its ugly head, right in front of Jackie's customers!

"You two shut up and take this conversation elsewhere," she hissed. By the end of her first week at the Midway location, she'd heard the "boys" talk about how their buddy did business down the street and had listened to all the profanity she could stand. She decided to call Richard from home that evening where she could speak to him in private. The office obviously suffered from a major breakdown in responsibility and personnel management, and she felt there had to be a change.

At nine o'clock that evening she went into the office at home, where George and the boys couldn't hear her, and dialed Richard's number. He seemed delighted to hear her voice. "How are things going? I've been wondering about you."

"I'm having serious doubts about working at Midway, and I'd like to be considered for another location if I'm going to stay employed by your company."

"Why? What's wrong?"

Jackie outlined the week's events, including Royce's departure through the window, Shane's tantrum, and the constant profanity, adding that Dexter and Tom had counseled the salesmen, but it did no good.

"I'm sorry to hear that," Richard said. "But I'm sure we can handle this. Is there anything else I need to know about?"

"Unfortunately, that's the least of your problems." Jackie continued explaining to Richard. "Shane, Roberto, and Royce are taking the applications from customers and then delivering them on their two-hour lunch breaks to their buddy Drew, who runs a lot down the street. They do this because they don't know how to write up the deals, and won't let Sam help them. When Drew closes and funds the deals, he pays them a commission."

She heard Richard take a deep breath. "How do you know this?"

"One of the customers stood me up for a second appointment. When I called him at home, he said Drew followed them home from our lot and offered them a better deal."

"This explains a lot," Richard's voice trembled with rage. "Jackie, I thank you. I knew I could count on you. I'll take care of this immediately, and you have a good evening. You'll be seeing me sometime next week in the office."

The next morning when she reported to work, Jackie found Hillary, Dexter's wife, in her office, moving furniture and pulling up the rugs.

"What's going on?" Jackie asked.

"I bought this rug for my husband, and I hope you don't think you're gonna keep it," Hillary snarled.

"I don't want the rug," Jackie said, stepping out of Hillary's way. "Just put things back when you're finished." Looking for an excuse to leave the office, she stepped out onto the lot to examine a new house that had just arrived. All houses were inspected upon arrival and checked for parts that were shipped on board for other houses. Jackie had performed this task a thousand times on other jobs, and since no one else seemed interested or available, she decided to go ahead and inspect it herself.

She knew from experience where the weak spots were in the factory, and she always checked them out before letting the driver unhook a house from the truck. Her policy was to write down every problem, and then have the driver observe the damage and sign off on it with her. Just as she was finishing the inspection, Hillary stuck her head in the door and asked, "What are you doing out here?"

"I'm just checking out the new house. Why?"

"That's my job. My husband wants me to inspect all the houses." Hillary reached for the clipboard Jackie carried.

Jackie shrugged and handed it to her. "I just thought I'd help out, that's all." She walked back inside the building, pondering why Hillary was acting like a thirteen-year-old junior high school hormonal bitch defending her boyfriend from the new girl in school. Still hoping to avoid a confrontation, Jackie retreated to her office to check on what kind of a mess Hillary had left. Her office was a total wreck. Hillary had removed pictures from the walls, scattered paperwork across the desktop, and placed Jackie's photos and other items in piles on top of the desk. Even the chairs were overturned.

This time Jackie was pissed. She marched into Dexter's office and firmly closed the door, forcing herself not to slam it. Turning around, she stumbled on one of the rugs, which Hillary had evidently dumped in Dexter's office for safekeeping.

Looking sheepish, Dexter held up both hands. "I'm sorry about the rug deal."

"This has nothing to do with the damn rug," Jackie said. "I don't care about the rug. My boyfriend owns a rug company and I can have a dozen of 'em any time I want."

"Look, I know you've had a bad week," Dexter responded, but next time you have a problem with someone here, I wish you'd come to me first instead of going to my boss."

Jackie realized that Richard had made a phone call. "I'd like to honor that request, but Richard asked me to call him, and he even gave me his home phone number. He wanted to know exactly what was going on here. Since he hired me with those instructions, I didn't have much choice."

Dexter looked sullen, but he didn't answer, so Jackie continued.

"I'm here in your office today to ask that you resolve the problem your wife has with me so I can move forward with my job here without being harassed. The chain of command around here is more like a family tree, with your sister-in-law as warranty manager and your stepson running the lot maintenance. And then, every time I try to do something, there's Hillary in my face telling me how her "Husband" wants it done. It's obvious she dislikes me, and I really don't give a damn about that—but, she does need to respect me and my office."

"As I understand it, Hillary decided to move one of the rugs to a different location," Dexter said. "I'm not sure why you gals are fighting over a rug."

Jackie clenched her hands to keep from socking him in the jaw. "I suggest you take a look at my office. She completely trashed the room, after I spent days cleaning and putting it together. It looks like a tornado went through."

Dexter heaved a sigh. "I'll take care of it. I promise you it won't happen again."

"Thank you," Jackie said. As she started out the door, Hillary stalked in, giving her a stare that could melt paint off the walls. Jackie sidestepped around Hillary without so much as a look in her direction.

Dexter and Hillary shouted at one another for a few minutes, and then Hillary exited the office, slammed the door, and went to her office. She grabbed her purse and left the building.

Jackie began putting her office in order, and Dexter stopped by with an offer to help. "What are you doing in this office anyway? Why don't you move up front and we'll turn this one into the sample room?" He suggested.

The front office had a large window, which Jackie coveted, so she readily agreed and began packing her things. She'd just filled a box with files when Tom stopped by.

"Hey, I know you're upset about all the profanity around here. So we've adopted an outline for everyone to use." He handed her a piece of paper and walked away with a huge smile.

"Thanks, Tom," she called. With both hands full, she didn't have time to examine the form, but tucked it inside one of the folders. She smiled to herself, thinking that maybe the guys were starting to come around. This was a positive development.

With Hillary off the lot, Dexter decided to call everyone together for a sales meeting to go over pending sales and discuss areas that needed improvement. Expecting a long session, Jackie carried a tablet of paper, plus an extra pen to take notes. She kept notes so well that she could go back to any day during the past three years and report even the weather and temperature. Noting these things in her journal had saved her butt many times when she talked with upset customers because she could state legitimate reasons for delays and problems. This helped customers to know what exactly was happening with their home and helped Jackie keep up with each of her customers' needs at a glance. She considered the journal her secret to success.

Dexter opened the meeting by announcing, "By now all of you have met Jackie, and I want to thank her for riding out the storm last week. She's here to stay, boys, so get used to it." He explained that more changes would be made, and Jackie felt hopeful. Perhaps the worst was over, and she could get serious about building her customer database.

Dexter asked each salesperson to introduce himself and describe what deals they were working. Todd Hunter, a goofy looking kid with short shaggy hair, told everyone that he was still trying to figure things out and needed help, or he'd have to find another job. "I've been here three months without a sale," he added.

"I'll help you work on that," Jackie said. "Stop by my office right after the meeting, and we'll get started."

Next to speak was Stuart Carlson, a handsome, quiet young man who'd remained in his office during all the shouting and tantrums. Stuart was working a few deals and expected to reach a higher level within the company. Jackie figured he was the only one in the group who showed any sign of professionalism.

Half way through the second hour of the meeting, Richard Spaniel strolled in the door, escorting another man no one seemed to know. Dexter froze in midsentence. Without introducing the man with him, Richard said, "Where can we meet?"

"My office," Dexter squeaked. The group scattered, consumed with curiosity. After ten minutes, Sam was summoned to Dexter's office. Jackie tried to listen, but the phones kept ringing and vendors were coming and going, making it hard for her to hear the conversation.

Trying to keep busy, she decided to look over the memorandum Tom had handed her. The paper was laid out as an interoffice memo, addressed to All Associates from Executive Management Regarding Elegant Language. It stated:

It has come to the attention of Eraphmus that some associates have been using foul language during moments of extreme stress. Due to complaints from some other associates, we are instituting a new policy of elegant language. The following list is management's suggested phrases:

| OLD PHRASE | NEW PHRASE |
|---|---|
| No fucking way. | I'm not certain that's possible. |
| You've got to be shitting me! | Really? |
| Ask me if I give a fuck. | Of course I'm concerned. |
| Tell someone who gives a fuck. | Perhaps you should check with… |
| It's not my fucking problem. | I wasn't involved with that. |
| What the fuck? | Interesting behavior. |
| Fuck it. It won't work! | I'm not sure I can implement this. |
| Why the fuck didn't you tell me sooner? | I'll try to schedule that. |
| When do you expect me to do this shit? | Perhaps I can work late. |
| Who the fuck cares? | Are you sure it's a problem? |
| He's got his head up his ass. | He's not familiar with the system. |
| Eat shit. | You don't say. |
| Eat shit and die. | Excuse me. |
| East shit and die, Motherfucker. | Excuse me, Sir. |
| What the hell do they want from my life? | Weren't they happy? |
| Kiss my ass. | So you'd like me to help with this? |
| Fuck it, I'm on salary. | I'm a bit overloaded at the moment. |
| Shove it up your ass. | I don't think you understand. |
| Who the hell made you God? | Do you want me to take care of this? |
| Blow me! | I see. |
| Blow Yourself. | Do You See |
| Another fucking meeting! | Yes, we should discuss this. |
| He's a fucking retard. | He's confused. |
| Fuck you! | Certainly. |
| I'll do it, Asshole. | Just hold on. It will be my pleasure. |
| What the fuck do you want? | What can I do to help? |
| I don't give a shit. | I don't think it will be a problem. |
| This job sucks. | I love a challenge. |

Jackie dropped the paper on her desk. Never in her professional career had she seen anything so blatantly disrespectful. She shook her head in complete disbelief.

Just then she heard Dexter's door open and watched Sam head back to his office. She gave him a few minutes and then placed the memo inside her jacket and headed down the hall. She stopped short in the doorway when she saw he was packing his things.

"You can't be leaving!"

He grinned. "It's okay. They're just moving me down the hall to another office and replacing me with that new guy Richard brought in. You know him, don't you?"

"I don't think so," Jackie said.

"That's Jose Hernandez from World Atlas Bank."

"Then I know him by telephone. We've never met in person, but we certainly have done our share of business together."

"Well, he's gonna be your new business manager, and I'll go back to sales, which is a big relief. Let Hernandez have the headaches associated with this title."

Jackie was helping Sam carry his things to another office when they saw Richard go into Shane's office and close the door. Richard began explaining the chain of command in a voice that rumbled through the building. He then asked Shane to open his briefcase and allow him to look inside. Shane refused. Richard fired him on the spot and immediately escorted him out the front door.

Richard then met with Dexter briefly behind closed doors and departed without speaking to anyone else.

Jackie spent the afternoon moving into her new office, thinking this was like a game of corporate musical chairs.

# CHAPTER ELEVEN

It looked like spring cleaning, and everyone welcomed the changes. Almost everyone. Those who didn't were left with no choice, because the boss's boss had spoken. The next employee to leave was Roberto Rodriguez. He was a link to the old crew, and Richard feared with Roberto around there was still an opportunity for business to go out the door.

Jackie felt that things were really beginning to take shape, and every passing day brought more improvement. By the third week, she'd begun to feel comfortable in her new workplace and decided she'd made the right decision. There were deals on the board for the first time in a long while. Customers often returned for second visits, and business was looked good for everyone. With Jackie's help, Todd even had a couple of deals pending.

She liked Todd, but something in the way he looked at her made her feel funny, as though he were touching her with his eyes. For that reason, she kept her distance from him whenever possible. Todd confided that he was living with Tom, but wanted to become successful so he could move on with his life and get his own place. The two guys had met because Tom's wife and Todd's girlfriend were in school together, training to become surgical assistants.

After Richard reconstructed the sales staff and initiated a step-by-step sales procedure, the system was in place for everyone to succeed. If they simply followed the steps, the profits would come. Both Richard and Jackie expected the lot to move up in the rankings and become a top producing location. With the new business growth and customer interest, they needed to increase the sales staff by replacing the men who'd left. Dexter announced in one of the meetings that if anyone knew of a salesperson looking for a job, they should send them in for an interview.

"I think I know someone," Jackie said. She'd just remembered a salesman she recently met in a dress shop. She'd stopped in to browse and ended up leaving with over $400 worth of new dresses and accessories—thanks to the gentle spirit and helpfulness of the salesman. "This guy was such a good salesman, he could sell a Bible to an Atheist." She told the group.

Tom laughed. "We don't need no Bible salesman around here."

"That's not what I said, Tom. This man was a true professional, an excellent dresser, and genuinely caring toward his customers. I think he'd be an asset to our group."

Dexter replied, "Okay, have him stop by and fill out an application. I'll see."

Since Jackie was scheduled off the next couple of days, she stopped by the dress shop on her way home to look for the salesman. He was busy with a customer when she stepped in the door, but still acknowledged her and offered a soft drink. Jackie turned down the drink, but took a seat and watched him work his magic on someone else. He was GOOD. Everyone who entered his store left with a purchase, even if it was only a five-dollar scarf. Each customer filled out a customer card, giving him their name, address, phone number, and date of birth. She figured his closing ratio had to be at least ninety-five percent.

After he "allowed" the customer to leave, he approached Jackie with his hand extended in greeting asking, "What can I do for you today, Ms. Jackie?"

"You remembered my name! I'm impressed." Jackie stated. "But I'm actually here on business." Jackie looked at his nametag. Victor. "I'm wondering if you've ever considered selling something besides dresses."

Victor rolled his eyes, but he listened as Jackie explained about her company and how she thought he'd be a natural at selling big-ticket items like mobile homes.

He chuckled and then said, "I majored in business finance, so I've certainly thought about selling something bigger than myself." He pointed to his large frame, "But I've just never had a change to pursue it."

"Then you're interested?"

"I'm willing to check it out," Victor replied.

She handed Victor her business card. "I'm off for the next two days, but stop by the lot and ask for Dexter. I think you'll be surprised and pleased with the potential, and I know you'll be good at it."

When she returned to the office on Friday, Jackie found a thank you card on her desk from Victor. Anxious to hear how the interview went, she set the card aside for the moment but made a mental note to discuss it with Dexter.

At a group meeting later that morning, when everyone had discussed their pending deals and Dexter was wrapping things up, Jackie asked, "So how did the interview with Victor Champion turn out?"

Dexter hesitated, rolled the paper he was holding in his hand, and glanced at Tom. Jackie got the impression something was wrong, but she didn't say anything. Instead, she kept looking at Dexter, waiting for an answer.

"Well, there is going to be a new addition to our sales staff."

Jackie smiled, thinking—*Yes!*

"But it isn't Victor," Dexter added.

"Then it must be someone transferring from another location with much more experience if he beat out Victor," Jackie said.

Dexter cleared his throat. "Actually, my wife wants to try her hand at selling." He couldn't even look Jackie in the eye.

Jackie felt her smile evaporate. She could hardly believe what she'd just heard, forcing herself to remain calm as she stated. "I'd love to have Hillary on my team."

"I decided to put her on Tom's team." Dexter quickly responded.

"No doubt," Jackie said. "That's a good choice." Then she left the meeting and went to her office to ponder for a while.

Within a few minutes, Tom came her office and closed the door behind him asking, "Can we talk?"

She waved him into a seat. "Right now, I can't even think. What kind of hare-brained idea is this?"

"Well we both know it won't work. Hillary is not the person we need on the sales floor interfacing with customers. She can't control her temper or her jealousy."

"It's a horrible idea," Jackie agreed. "Like turning the Wicked Witch of the West loose on the sales floor."

Tom grinned. "So who is this guy you sent over her yesterday?"

Jackie outlined how she'd met Victor Champion and described his qualifications.

"So he isn't a personal friend of yours?" Tom asked.

"Just an acquaintance," Jackie replied. "Is there a problem?"

Tom hesitated for a second and then replied, "Well, he's black. That's the problem." When Jackie didn't respond, Tom sat with his chin leaning down on his fingers, chewing on the side of his mouth. Finally he said, "We don't hire no triggers 'round here."

Jackie stared into Tom's face as she leaned forward, spitting each word at him, "Trigger is a dead horse that belonged to Roy Rogers. Do you wanna explain your Minnesota slang? Cause I'm not following you."

Tom made a gesture with his hands. "Come on, Jackie. Do I gotta spell it out for you? This company don't hire no niggies."

"Niggies?" She shouted. "Niggies! What the fuck are you saying! Don't you ever say that word to me again!" She slammed her fist on the top of the desk. Just then her phone rang and she snatched up the receiver, but instead of answering the call she beat the phone base until the receiver broke in half. "You're telling me Dexter hired that empty-brained, hot-headed, jealous, vindictive hormonal idiot over an intelligent, educated man just because he's black?"

Tom held up both hands. "Let me—"

"No! Let me—there's something I need to tell you." She shook the broken receiver at Tom. "And you can share this with everyone here. I don't like your ethnic jokes. I hate prejudice, and I won't tolerate it from anyone, my supervisor included. Right now I don't have the right to hire or fire anyone, but, I do have the right to tell you never—ever—use that word around me again. Now, leave my office! Please. I need time to think."

"Jackie, listen," Tom said.

Instead she stood and left the office, closing the door behind her, leaving Tom alone while she went onto the lot to cool down. After pacing for a few minutes, she climbed into her car and drove away to remove herself completely from the situation before it got any worse. Besides, she needed to use a telephone, and hers was broken.

Jackie took the time to stop by to see Victor instead of calling him. He seemed somewhat evasive when she first walked in, but after they talked for a few minutes, he said, "I don't want to offend you Jackie or hurt your feelings, but I don't care for those people up there and I don't think it would work out."

"I really owe you an apology," she said.

"No, Jackie," he answered. "No need to apologize for trying to help me. That's what you did, and I want you to know it means a lot to me. I wouldn't take the job even if they offered it to me. But, I'd like for us to remain friends."

Jackie smiled and said, "You know, Victor, you're right about the job. I picture you working for some Wall Street company someday. Either way, I'd be honored to count you among my friends."

When she came back to the office, no one said anything to her about what had happened, and there was a brand new phone on her desk.

## CHAPTER TWELVE

By July, the teams were truly making headway with the Midway location and it was time again for the quarterly sale. Jackie was going full speed ahead, and the month was looking profitable for everyone. Every deal she'd worked for the past three months was coming together. The show was scheduled to take place on the last weekend of the month, with loan officers coming in to make on-the-spot decisions for customers.

A total of twenty-three mobile homes sold at this show, and eight of those were Jackie's.

She was ranked third of over four hundred sales people throughout the country, and she'd been with the company only four months. Her stats proved she had the knowledge and determination to be a great asset to the company.

At the end of July when the company statistics were totaled, Midway was on top and ranked number one among all locations throughout the country. As the result of all her efforts and in addition to $19,000 in commission (after taxes), Jackie earned a plaque for salesperson of the month, plus a trip to Cabos in September. Altogether, nearly a hundred other company employees were also going, and Dexter and Tom told Jackie it was their way of saying thanks for a job well done. Jackie accepted the award, along with the trip, and started making plans for Cabos.

## CHAPTER THIRTEEN

Hillary was another story. Several times a week she'd get angry with Dexter about something that happened at home and then want to duke it out at the office. Once she was yelling at Dexter, in front of everyone as Jackie walked in the front door and through the lobby, so Jackie said in a loud voice, "Not in front of the kids!" Meaning the employees, but Hillary just kept shouting.

Then to avoid listening to Dexter's side, she stormed out of the office and stayed gone for two to three hours. Nobody minded when Hillary left—it was a welcome relief. Then Hillary began showing up later and later for work, until one Saturday when Tom tried to reprimand her for delaying an early morning progress meeting, and Dexter did a 360 on Tom, pulled rank, and took up for Hillary, telling Tom it was none of his business. That was a shock for everyone.

When Dexter finished, Hillary yelled, "Dexter's motherfucking son stole my car last night and wrecked it or I would have been on time today. So you can yell at him not me. This one is on him." Then she turned to Jackie and snarled, "And if you've got anything to say about that, well I wouldn't, because I'm not in the mood to put up with your shit today. But if you feel you must, go ahead, and I'll slap the shit out of you!"

Jackie stood to address Hillary, and everyone knew that shit was about to hit the fan. Just then both Dexter and Tom screamed,

"Hillary!" and dashed toward her as if to stop her from assaulting Jackie.

Jackie said, "Please gentlemen, allow me to address this issue with Hillary by myself." She stepped right up to Hillary's reach and said, "You might get away with slapping at home, but now you're in a place of business and if you want to work around me then you'll need to conduct yourself in a professional ladylike manner. Now, if you weren't such a pathetic, mentally inadequate, pretentious, obnoxious, jealous idiot, I might take personal offense at your threats. So, if you feel that you can handle the consequences of slapping me, then go right ahead. But I need to warn you—I don't fight fair. I don't care what I have to do to defend myself."

Jackie raised her voice slightly to make certain so everyone in the room could hear. "Effective immediately, Hillary, I'm not going to excuse any more of your threats as just a bad choice of words." She stood her ground, staring at Hillary eye to eye as Dexter grabbed his wife by the arm and escorted her outside, where they both got in his truck and drove away.

Tom then conducted the morning meeting and told everyone he'd talk with Richard himself if the disruptions continued. Everyone agreed they were sick of Dexter and Hillary's arguments. One of the men said he felt sorry for Jackie, because Hillary seemed to have some kind of vendetta against her.

Tom remarked, "Jackie can handle Hillary. She's got the biggest set of balls around here." Everyone laughed except Jackie. She found the whole thing nauseating and retreated to her office for a shot of Pepto Bismol.

After the meeting, Tom stopped by Jackie's office, closed the door, and asked her in a quiet voice, "Can I talk with you for a minute?"

Tom sat down as he began by asking, "So, are you all right?"

"Yeah, I guess so," Jackie said. "I'm not quite sure what to make of that woman. She has some serious jealously over Dexter and it's aimed right at me for some reason. I just know I'm sick of it, and I'm not quite sure what to do."

"I think what you did was perfect." Tom adjusted his tie. "She now knows she can't bluff you because she's married to the boss. You sent a clear message by not backing down from her. That took balls, and I'm proud of you for doing it." Then Tom held up his right hand in gesture for Jackie to give a high five.

About three hours later Dexter returned to the office without Hillary. He'd apparently dropped her off at their house, leaving her without her wrecked car, which was still at the office. Dexter immediately took Tom into his office and closed the door to talk in private. After twenty minutes or so, Dexter called Jackie via the intercom and asked her to join them. Not sure what to expect, she knocked on the door.

Before she even got inside, Dexter was apologizing again for his wife's behavior. She said, "Dexter maybe it wouldn't be so bad if she could leave her "wife" title at home and take on a salesperson's title when she gets to the office, but I can't tolerate any more of her physical threats."

"I'm not asking you to," Dexter said. "I talked with Richard, myself. He needs a secretary, and Hillary needs to be somewhere else, so he said she could work for him. But, it'll be about two weeks before he has an office for her."

"That's good news." Jackie relaxed a bit.

"As of Monday, she'll be working a different schedule from yours, and she is to report to Tom exclusively and not to direct any questions or comments to you at all until she transfers over there. Is that okay with you?"

"Absolutely," Jackie said. "But does Hillary understand she is not to make any more threats toward me?"

Dexter nodded. "I believe she now understands."

"Good," Jackie replied. "I don't like working in such a stressful situation. I go home every day with a sick headache because of it."

"Well, in a couple of weeks things should straighten out," Dexter reassured her. "Just hang in there, Jackie. We really need you around here. You're the best producer I have, and I don't need for you to go anywhere else."

# CHAPTER FOURTEEN

Since Saturday was the busiest day for the business, everyone stayed at the office all day, and lunch was brought in. Occasionally someone's wife or maybe a friend would drop by, and on this particular Saturday, Tom's wife stopped by with their daughter Frankie Paige, along with a friend named Crystal and Crystal's son, Hanley. Both of the children were about the same age, Jackie assumed. Tom introduced his wife to Jackie as Lucrezia Ravetti.

Jackie, Tom talks about you all the time, so I just had to come meet you," Lucrezia said. Their daughter immediately reached out for Jackie to take her. "That's strange," Lucrezia said. "She never goes to a stranger."

Jackie smiled at the little girl. "This happens to me all the time. I can be in a department store minding my own business, and a child will come up to me like they know me and the parents are just amazed." By this time Jackie was holding Frankie Paige, talking to her and showing her things around the office. Frankie stared into Jackie's face as though fascinated.

"How old is she?" Jackie asked.

"She's almost eleven months old, and Hanley's two weeks older. They're almost like brother and sister, since they've been together all their lives."

"So are you two sisters?" Jackie asked, referring to Lucrezia and Crystal.

"Just good friends," Lucrezia said. "Crystal lived with us after she had Hanley until recently. But they still see each other on a regular basis, and they stay with the same babysitter during the day.

By this time Todd had made his way over and reached to take Frankie Paige from Jackie, but Frankie turned around in Jackie's arms, ignoring him. So Todd took Hanley from Crystal and walked away with him.

Jackie asked, "Is Todd your boyfriend?"

Crystal laughed. "He wishes. No, he's not, and he's not Hanley's father. He just plays with him a lot when we go over to Lucrezia and Tom's house to visit."

Jackie knew right away that Todd really liked Crystal and wanted people to think that there was something between them. After all, Crystal was attractive and available, with an incredible body. Most of the men in the office considered her a perfect catch.

Half an hour later, the two girls left, saying they'd bring the babies by periodically to visit Jackie. Both babies waved goodbye as the mothers carried them out the door.

After they left, each of the guys had his own comments to make about Crystal, but Tom took the opportunity to brag about having Crystal living with them and how he got to watch her breast-feed Hanley. Although it wasn't uncommon for him to discuss Crystal around the office with the guys, it seemed this time he wanted to really make an impression. He described how Crystal would pop out one of those big bazookas, as he called them, and just breast feed lucky Handley right in front of him!

Jackie found his comments revolting, so she retreated back into her office to get away. Leave it to Tom to make something as personal and beautiful as breast feeding sound dirty. He'd even compared Crystal to a Jersey cow and made hand motions as if milking a cow. He added, "I've tried to drink right from the spout before, but lucky Hanley won't share."

In the meantime, Jackie had taken a call back from a customer of Todd's, and she needed to discuss the possibilities of making some changes on their plans so she consulted with Todd in his office. Still reeling from Crystal's visit, Todd was hardly able to concentrate on what Jackie was explaining to him. Placing the folders on the desk, she questioned Todd.

"So you really like Crystal, huh?"

"Oh yeah!"

"Well, I thought you were engaged."

"I am, but if I ever thought there was a possibility with Crystal, I wouldn't be."

"Is that fair to your fiancée?" Jackie asked.

Todd shrugged and said, "Who cares?"

Feeling shocked, Jackie couldn't help but ask, "Then why are you engaged to Angie?"

"Well, her daddy has a lot of money, and he kinda supported us for quite a while and still does sometimes."

Staring speechless at Todd, Jackie couldn't even think what to say next. She just stood and walked out of his office.

Todd called after her, "What's you're problem? It's the truth, and you asked for it."

Jackie just kept walking, shaking her head. Even if it was true there was no need for Todd to discuss it with her, and this proved exactly how shallow Todd really was. Plus he was a disgusting womanizer.

## CHAPTER FIFTEEN

Later that same day Tom received a phone call from Alvin Waters, a manager at another lot, asking for suggestions on solving a problem. Several customers had refused to sign contracts because of problems with their linoleum. Remembering that Jackie's "significant other" owned a flooring company, Tom asked Jackie if George would be interested in helping.

"I'm sure he'd be glad to help out, but I don't know anything about his business and don't want to," Jackie said. "You can call George and work things out with him."

Within fifteen minutes, Tom was in Jackie's office explaining he'd made a deal with George, who was scheduled to check into the problem on Saturday. Tom was excited he'd found a solution and called Alvin back immediately. "If George does good work, we'll use him again," Alvin said.

After Tom finished talking with Alvin, he tried to draw Jackie into a discussion of her relationship with George, but she cut him off, saying, "I'd prefer not to discuss my personal life with you. George and I have an understanding about business. It's not a big deal."

"Would you be opposed to having George work with us?" Tom asked.

"Of course not," Jackie said. "I'm just not wanting to get involved in his business, and I don't want another spouse involved in mine. The last time my ex husband got pissed off, he caused a scene at work, and I lost my job over it."

"We'll have Connie take care of the scheduling from here with George's secretary—that way you're completely out of it," Tom promised.

George did the initial job himself instead of sending one of his guys because he wanted to make sure it got done right the first time. The customers were very pleased with the new linoleum and wrote a thank-you letter commending George for his work. They then closed their loan, which meant Alvin was also pleased with George.

With all the new homes suddenly being sold from the Midway location, the company really needed a contractor, so Tom and Dexter discussed the options with George. He told them he'd love to have the contract, but he didn't want it to interfere with Jackie's job in any way.

That night after dinner, George and Jackie talked through the possibilities. Jackie agreed, on the condition that George would work through Tom and Dexter. After all the conflicts between Dexter and Hillary, she certainly didn't want the other employees to worry about interoffice problems between her and George. Plus, she didn't want to be caught in the middle in case an unhappy customer complained about the flooring. George agreed and told Jackie that he had covered this with Tom and Dexter and told them it had to be this way or he would not accept to take the contract.

After a long discussion, they agreed that George could handle the contract without interfering with Jackie's relationship with the company, and it sounded like a win/win situation for everyone.

George called Dexter the next day and accepted the contract as their executive floor installer. There were so many jobs, George had to hire an additional crew just to handle the Midway contract, and before long he became so busy he didn't have time for any of the other business coming into his store. He called his brother and developed a partnership to run the store business so he could keep up with everything. George kept his crew working twelve-hour days just to keep up with the Midway Park business. Within a few weeks, Alvin wanted George to work for him too, but Tom and Dexter didn't want George to work for other lots. Alvin was persistent—he called Dexter every day until finally Dexter asked George if he could expand and install for Alvin, too.

By recruiting enough installers for a new crew, George was able to take on the extra work. Since this was an exclusive contract, George cut his profits to get the best workers for the job. Pretty soon other managers were calling, wanting to use George also. He became so busy with the Midway contract installations he could hardly keep up.

Soon they were talking to George about handling a four-hundred-house development opening in Austin. They suggested George restructure his company to sell off the outside business, allowing him to concentrate solely on their contract needs. George's crew was scheduled out so far into the future he couldn't see daylight, so he agreed to sell his interest in the store and focus on the housing industry. George's brother was obliged to take over the business, which had been up and running over twenty-five years and was well established. Thus, George was working exclusively for Midway.

## CHAPTER SIXTEEN

Tom and Dexter had recently hired a salesman named Chris, but felt they needed at least two more people for the staff. Tom needed to conduct a job interview off site, but his wife had dropped their daughter off at the office on her way to class. Since it was closing time, Tom asked Jackie if she'd mind taking Frankie Paige home with her for an hour or so while he completed the interview.

"I don't have a car today." Jackie said. "George dropped me off."

Tom replied, "That's okay. Just take my truck. It has her car seat in it, and I'll have someone bring me by your house later."

Thinking nothing else of it, Jackie agreed, and carried Frankie to Tom's truck, where she strapped her in and headed home.

It was after 10:00 p.m., and Frankie Paige was asleep on the couch, wrapped in a blanket, before Jackie even got a phone call from Tom. He was so plastered she couldn't understand him. He finally gave the phone to his wife so she could get directions to the house to pick up Frankie. They weren't far away, but Tom couldn't remember the address or directions, and they'd been driving around for some time looking for Jackie's house.

Lucrezia was furious with Tom. He stayed in the car and she came to the door by herself. Jackie was waiting, with Frankie Paige in her arms. Lucrezia thanked Jackie profusely for taking care of the baby.

She added, "I didn't know Tom had an interview or I wouldn't have dropped her off at the office."

"No harm done," Jackie said. "We had fun with her and she fell asleep about eight o'clock. Why don't you come in for a minute?"

"You have such a nice home." Lucrezia stood in the living room, looking around. "I'm so glad my daughter was with you and not Hillary," Lucrezia said. "One time I left her with Hillary for a couple of hours, and when I came back, Frankie Paige was still sitting in the garage, strapped in her car seat."

"Oh, my God!" Jackie replied.

"Can I ask you one more favor? Would you keep Tom's truck overnight and drive it to the office tomorrow? I don't want him driving tonight."

Jackie looked at George, who nodded. "That's a good plan. I'll bring the truck back tomorrow."

The next morning when Jackie arrived at work driving Tom's truck, people obviously wondered what was going on. She didn't feel any need to explain as she made her way into the office and dropped the keys on Tom's desk. He said thanks, and slipped them inside his pocket without any further comment.

One member of the sales staff was missing from work, but no one noticed it until about ten o'clock, at which time Tom entered Jackie's office and said, "Club Boy didn't show for work today." That was Tom's nickname for Chris, because he had a bad arm.

"Have you called him?" Jackie asked.

Tom hesitated and then said, "No, but we were out late last night."

"It was only ten when you left my house," Jackie reminded him. "And you were with your wife."

Tom grinned sheepishly. "Well Lucrezia was pissed at me for misplacing Frankie, so I called Club Boy, and we went out and got plastered. I think something happened, but I can't remember 'cause we were drinking pretty heavy and smoking."

"Like what?" Jackie asked as she stood to leave the room.

"I can't say for sure, but I think we wrecked his new Mercedes."

"What? You wrecked his car?"

"Shhhh," Tom waved her back into her seat. "Don't say anything. Just call his house for me and see if he's there. See if he's okay."

Jackie stared at Tom in disbelief. "You mean to tell me you left him out there somewhere in a wrecked car? What were you thinking? How bad was the car?"

"I think it flipped," Tom replied.

"What if he's hurt? He could be dead! Did you ever think about that?"

"Hell yes, I thought about it. Why do you think I left? I panicked! I was already in enough trouble with my wife without that. I walked several blocks and called a cab."

"Did you call 911 for Chris?" Jackie asked.

"No, because I figured someone would find him pretty soon and call in."

Tom handed Jackie the phone number and she immediately started dialing. Chris answered, "Helllooo," in a deep, scratchy voice.

She said, "Chris—this is Jackie. Tom asked me to call you. Are you okay?"

"I don't know yet," Chris mumbled. "I still can't feel anything from the head down, but I'm fucked with my insurance company. We totaled my new car."

"How?" Jackie asked.

"I think we were driving on the wrong side of the road. All I remember is Tom yelling 'Look out,' and swerving to miss a dog. I swerved too hard and flipped the car. I think Tom was thrown out, but we couldn't find him. The paramedic said it was a good thing I had the sun roof open or it would have crushed me."

"I can't believe this!" Jackie exclaimed. "You had that car less than twenty-four hours. I'll bet the insurance company is fit to be tied."

"Oh yeah, that's an understatement," Chris said. "And, I don't think they're going to replace the car either."

She hung up the phone, speechless for almost a full minute, and then looked at Tom. "Does Lucrezia know about this?"

"No, and I don't want her to." Tom propped his feet in a chair.

Later that day they learned that Chris was on probation for DUI, and when his probation officer received the police report they threw him back in jail. Because Tom had left the scene of the accident neither the police nor paramedics believed there was anybody else in the car with Chris when the accident occurred.

## CHAPTER SEVENTEEN

Jackie knew Tom was afraid Lucrezia would find out about the wreck, and he asked her not to tell anyone else at the office. He could also lose his job if anyone in upper management got wind of the wreck. Jackie agreed to keep her mouth shut, on condition that Tom get help for his drinking problem.

"I'm going to quit altogether after this," he promised.

For the next several weeks, Lucrezia stopped by the office almost daily, and Jackie assumed she was checking up on Tom. Sometimes she came alone, but usually she brought along her friend Crystal and the children. Since Frankie Paige saw Jackie almost daily at the office, they developed a close relationship and Jackie began feeling almost like her grandmother. The two children copied one another, so little Hanley would race Frankie to Jackie's office, where she always had suckers to hand out and toys to keep them occupied.

The two children looked like twins and were constantly together. Hanley quickly warmed up to Jackie and would reach out for her to take him. He was a snuggler, and when Jackie held him, he would wallow back and forth, rubbing on Jackie until he was firmly planted, as if to melt into her, while placing his face against her neck and resting his head onto her shoulder. He was such a sweet baby and so easy to love! He rarely fussed and he always smiled. His presence was almost angelic. Jackie would hold Hanley and rock him, and it was hard to say which of them enjoyed it the most.

However, It wasn't long before Jackie discovered the true reason for Lucrezia's daily visits. She asked Jackie if she'd lost a pair of sunglasses, to which Jackie replied, "Yes, I lost a pair a week." She often left her glasses lying around in one of the houses on the lot until a customer would pick them up and carry them off. Jackie finally decided she couldn't afford to furnish all the customers with nice sunglasses, so she started buying Dollar Store sunglasses.

"What kind did you find?" Jackie asked.

"Ray Bans," Lucrezia said.

Jackie laughed. "Ray Bans aren't in my budget, but I think Hillary wears them. You might check with her." Jackie found out later that Lucrezia had discovered a pair of women's sunglasses on the bar in their house and was trying to find out which female employee owned them.

Lucrezia stated, "I don't think these belong to Hillary." She knew Tom couldn't stand Hillary and wouldn't have her in their home, much less have an affair with her. Lucrezia didn't actually come out and say she thought Tom was having an affair, but a few days later Tom confided to Jackie that Lucrezia had blown up at him and accused him of having an affair with Connie, the warranty manager at the office, when she found the glasses.

"Aha," Jackie exclaimed. "That's why she asked me if I'd lost a pair of sunglasses. Well, who do they belong to?"

Tom shrugged. "I really don't know. I apparently had them when I got home the other night after Chris and I went out."

"That's another good reason to quit drinking."

Tom and Lucrezia continued to have problems from Tom's drinking and bar hopping with the guys, and eventually they separated. One afternoon on Jackie's day off she received a phone call from Tom. Calling from his house, Tom begged her to pick him up, because Lucrezia was beating him after she came home to find another woman there with him.

Jackie was shocked. Why would he call her for help? Besides, he and Lucrezia were supposed to be separated. She told Tom she had no intention of helping him and hung up the phone, completely bewildered.

A few days later Lucrezia showed up at the office and walked into Jackie's office where she closed the door and sat down. Jackie sat speechless not sure what to expect from this. Lucrezia said, "I'm sorry about the other day." Jackie didn't respond.

Then Lucrezia said, "You know, when Tom called you and we were having a fight."

Jackie held up one hand as if to signal her to stop. "Lucrezia, I've worked with men all my adult life, and I was raised with three boys. I kinda know how stupid they can be. But, I don't want to know about their personal lives, marriage problems included. I have plenty of my own problems to deal with without getting involved in yours and Tom's." She passed Lucrezia a tissue because she had started to cry.

"I don't want to hurt your feelings, but I will lose respect for someone when they aren't respectful of me or my time. I'm not a counselor or a social worker, and I'm not the reason for your marital problems."

"Oh, I'm not saying you are," Lucrezia said, "and I want to apologize for bringing you into our problem the other day. I hope you won't think badly of us because of it."

"It's too late. I already do. But I won't continue to think badly of you two if you'll just keep it out of the office and to yourselves. Agreed?"

"Agreed." Lucrezia held out her hand to shake hands with Jackie.

Jackie half-heartedly returned the handshake, but as Lucrezia departed the office, one word came to mind: F L A K E.

## CHAPTER EIGHTEEN

The date of the Cabos trip quickly approached, and Jackie looked forward to time away from the office, plus the opportunity to meet people from other offices who'd also booked the trip. However, she had one concern. She discovered her trip had originally belonged to Tom's wife, but since they separated it had become available and was awarded to her. Tom and Jackie were the only two employees from Dallas making the trip. Since they were scheduled to meet others at the airport in Phoenix and continue as a group to the final destination in Cabos San Lucas, Jackie was concerned how people would view their arriving and traveling together. But she could only wait and address problems as they arose.

Once on the plane, Jackie felt very uncomfortable because Tom openly talked about his personal life and problems that Jackie thought he shouldn't be discussing. From his conversation, it was obvious that Tom and Lucrezia were still having marital problems. Jackie got the impression some of his comments were made out of frustration and felt compelled to let him vent some of those frustrations. However, Jackie was not prepared to handle what Tom confessed to her next.

"Yeah, Lucrezia was the 'Shot Girl' in the club where we met. Ya know what that is Jackie?"

Jackie shook her head back and forth, as she turned her face looking out the window of the plane, ignoring him as he continued on with his descriptive story:

"It means she went from table to table selling single drinks called shots." He explained before adding. "She took an instant liking to me!"

Although, Jackie thought it was probably the other way around. Tom chuckled as he went on telling his outlandish story.

"She was everything I had dreamed of in a woman. Long brown hair, brown eyes, long legs and tits!" He explained as he held his cupped hands out in front of himself as if to represent her large physique.

Jackie interrupted him as she sternly jeered, "T-o-m-m-m . . . T.M.I!" Tom starred back for a minute then asked, "What's T.M.I?"

"Too Much In-for-ma-tion," she enunciated.

"Oh," he replied as he sat in silence starring down into his drink glass. Jackie pretended she was reading a magazine, hoping that he would just shut up and leave her alone. Tom finished his drink and leaned forward pulling up his pant's leg revealing a flask containing liquor attached to his leg. Jackie could not believe what she was looking at.

Tom sheepishly confessed, "I always get cut off by the stewardesses, so I have to bring my own stash."

"Tom, your drinking alcohol is comparable to throwing gasoline on a fire. You really need to slow down, it's still early, and we aren't even half way there yet," Jackie remarked as she held up her arm tapping on the face of her watch. She was obviously embarrassed, and she tried to reason with him to stop drinking at lease until they got to their destination, so she didn't have to be tortured any longer by his conversation. However, her pleas went unheard as Tom only got louder and more voluble, confiding to everyone that was within hearing distance that he knew that he had to do to "have" Lucrezia the first time that he laid eyes on her.

"Yea, she looked just like one of those characters from a soap opera, you know that old soap, Ryan's Hope? I fantasized about that girl on there for years. Then I saw Lucrezia, Italian descent. Wow, I just sat back and watched her that first night in the bar, working her magic on those unsuspecting smucks. I knew the first time I laid eyes on her, she wasn't no Jer-sey trash. I could tell that they were all thinking the same thing, and I knew that I had found my challenge of the day, and I knew in my heart it was me that she was going home with."

"What ever," Jackie replied.

"What? You don't believe me?" Tom asked. "She came to me." Tom explained but before he could finish -

"It was her job!" Jackie snapped.

"Oh yea, then why did she accept my offer?"

"Om, let me guess, because you paid her? Why are we having this conversation, Tom?" Jackie asked before she excused herself to go to the rest room.

Stepping over Tom's extended legs and into the aisle, she came eye to eye with a priest sitting two rows back. She was so embarrassed she felt sick to her stomach. Hoping to find a vacant seat elsewhere, Jackie made her way to the restroom at the back of the plane. However, the plane was full, and Jackie had no choice but to return to the seat next to Tom, whether she liked it or not.

Jackie settled herself back in and motioned for Tom to lean toward her.

She whispered, "There's a priest sitting across the aisle."

Tom immediately attempted to look around at which Jackie grabbed onto him, demanding between her gritted teeth, "Don't stare!"

"How do you know it's a real priest?" Tom asked.

"Because he's wearing the collar," Jackie whispered.

"That collar don't mean he's a real priest," Tom declared. "I'll introduce you to my friend, Doug Greenback, sometime, and he can tell you first hand about priest's in hiding in the church."

"Priest's in hiding? Tom, you really need to stop. That's disrespectful."

"I'm just telling you the truth. Doug got into some trouble, and instead of sending him to the big house, he was put inside a monastery. He tells me the church if full of 'em. It's like this big secret inside the Catholic church. They harbor some of the biggest bad boys in the world under their frocks and collars. In exchange the underworld contributes millions of dollars to them, and everybody benefits and nobody says a word.

"That's why you never hear of the church going outside the Vatican to handle priests molesting little alter boys. If you think those bastards are really priests, you're believing a made up fairy tale.

"But if it makes you feel better, we'll talk about something else." Tom paused only to draw a breath as Jackie silently questioned herself why she ever accepted this trip.

"I think Lucrezia picked me because she knew I would be a good daddy for her little girl after I asked her, 'What za nice girl like you doin in a joint like this?' She saw my concern." Tom confessed while shaking his head yes.

"Really?" Jackie questioned. "I thought you were Frankie's daddy."

"Nope." Tom replied, shaking his head back and forth. "Her daddy doesn't even know she exists, and Lucrezia wants it to stay that way.

"He's some high paid engineer living around Ft Worth that Lucrezia went out with once. She said he's a genuine prick, so when she found out she was pregnant, she never even called him. She figured why bother? He's a prick, and I don't need him.

"Anyways, I asked Lucrezia what time she got off work, and she said 2:00. So I asked her if she wanted to get something to eat before she went home. She then told me she had a baby at home and had to be there no later than 3:00 for feeding because her roommate has a baby, too, and they are on the same schedule."

Hearing this, Jackie assumed that he must be talking about Crystal and Handley. She listened intently as Tom continued with more personal confessions of his and Lucrezia's relationship, yet she wasn't quite sure why Tom was telling all this to her.

Tom pondered quietly momentarily then burst out, "Oh, I've gotta tell you about her boss at the bar - what a prick!

"He didn't like Lucrezia talkin' with me that first night, but she told him she could talk to who ever she wanted to.

"Then he tried to have a personal conversation with Lucrezia, but she snubbed him, closed out her tab and left the bar. I knew right then I needed to make my move, so I left the bar and caught up with her in the parking lot. We talked for a few minutes, then decided to go down the street to Denny's to get something to eat, so we could talk inside in a warm spot."

"She just didn't seem like the kind of girl that would work in a place like that, and I told her that."

"What did she say to that?" Jackie asked.

"Oh, she agreed, but she said she made up to $500.00 each night, and that was the only way she could live the life she was used to without any help from her family or the baby's father. Then she told me who her father was, and I 'bout shit on myself."

"Oh really?" Jackie exclaimed. "Who is he?"

"He's the CEO of one of the largest companies in the entire state. They handle a lot of government contracts. Yea, she felt really uncomfortable talking about it, so she turned the questions to me."

"I told her I'm from the Bronx, but she didn't believe me and said she thought I was using a phony accent."

"Me too," Jackie replied.

"Then I explained to her about my bad divorce and how I used to own a concrete company with my old partner until I came home early one day unexpectedly and found them together. Then I explained to her that my uncle and me were in business together now, and he had sent me here to check out the area for possibly opening up a jewelry store. I told her I wasn't sure that I was gonna stay here in this area or not."

'Well, I guess that didn't work out either," Jackie commented.

"What?" Tom asked.

"The jewelry store!"

"Oh, yea, but if you ever want a piece of jewelry, let me know. I can get it for you and save you some money," Tom offered.

"I'll keep that in mind," Jackie remarked with a chuckle in her voice.

Tom just picked up his story from where he left off. "Then, before we knew it, an hour had gone by, and Lucrezia had to go home. I wrote my phone number down on the back of the ticket the waitress gave me and slid it across the table to her.

"I sat there with a sinking feeling inside my stomach as she got up and walked out the door. I didn't even know where she lived. I just sat there in my own little world after watching her drive off into the night. The waitress stopped by and offered up her condolences with another cup of coffee as she rubbed on my shoulder. I don't like nobody touching me, especially some ugly broad I'm paying to wait on me. So I told her, 'I'll take your coffee but your opinions you can keep those to yourself.' Then I shrugged her hand off my shoulder and told her to hold my table till I got back from the john. I couldn't believe it when I got outta the john she was still sitting there, in the booth where Lucrezia had been sittin.

"I raised my voice and shouted 'Hey!' at her and was about to tell her off when I noticed that it wasn't the waitress sitting there in the booth but Lucrezia waiting for me to get back!

"She asked me, 'So, you wanna see the baby?'

"She wasn't gonna have to ask me twice. I took a twenty outta my pocket and threw it on the table, and we were out the door and on our way to the parking lot.

"When we got to her apartment, she took me down the hallway and into the baby's room. I couldn't believe how tiny that baby was when I first saw her. Lucrezia whispered for me to sit down on the side of the bed, while she picked up the baby and laid her in her lap to change her diaper. Then she asked me to get her a wet wash cloth. I thought she was gonna use it to wipe the baby's bottom, but when I got back to the room, she was sitting there without her shirt. Her huge breasts were completely exposed, and she used that wet rag to wash herself before she breast fed the baby right there in front of me."

"Haven't you ever seen that before?" Jackie questioned.

"Yea, but this was different. This was real, and she made me a part of it.

"At that very moment, I made up my mind she and that baby was gonna be mine, and she wasn't gonna work another night in that seedy, run down bar."

Jackie sat mesmerized, listening to Tom's story. She felt sorry for him now that she knew his side of the situation.

"Do you think Lucrezia used you?" she asked.

"Yea, and now that I'm emotionally attached, she wants to move on," he confessed.

"I slept on her couch that night, and the next morning, I woke up feeling like a new man who had just got a new lease on life. The next day, I went straight to that bar she was working in and told her boss, Randy, that she wasn't gonna be working there anymore, and he could find him someone else to work. I even offered to work there in her place helping him, not as a shot girl or nothin like that, but as an extra set of eyes to watch for employees stealing liquor and stuff like that. He didn't like my idea. It was just as good. I didn't like him neither."

Finally, after a long, agonizing two hours, the pilot came over the speaker announcing their arrival into Phoenix.

"Thank God!" Jackie exclaimed.

After meeting the other group of company travelers inside the terminal, they settled in for an unexpected delay caused by a severe weather situation that prevented them from landing in Cabos. Everyone scattered, going his or her own way. Tom headed straight to the bar, and Jackie went to the nearest ticket counter. So far the trip had been miserable, and she knew she'd never survive a week with Tom. Since she and George had just purchased a new home together, there were lots of things she needed to do around the house anyway.

She waited patiently in line at the ticket counter, but just before she got to the counter someone tapped her on the shoulder and asked if she'd please go to the bar because they needed someone to help with Tom. Unsure just what that meant, Jackie rushed into the bar thinking there'd been an accident.

Tom was completely plastered, shouting at the bartender and demanding another drink. The bar manager ordered Jackie to remove her husband immediately. Totally embarrassed, she said. "This is not my husband!"

"I wouldn't claim his ass either," the manager said, "but I need someone to get him out of here. He's disturbing my customers and insulting my waitresses."

Meanwhile, Tom put his head on the bar and appeared to be asleep or passed out. Jackie shook him she called his name in a demanding voice. "Tom, you need to get up. We have to go, the plane is here."

He raised his head, looked at Jackie in silence for a moment and then stated, "Jackie, I need to talk to you about something."

"It can wait," she said. "They want you outta here."

"No, it can't wait. I hafta ask you now: How serious are you about George? I really like you a lot and I need to know if there is any chance that we might—"

"Don't say it. Don't even think it. There Is Absolutely No Chance For Anything Between Us—You Got That!" Jackie left the bar and walked toward the ticket counter, more determined than ever to exchange her ticket.

Tom shouted as she walked across the terminal, "Well then, will you at least call me Tommy?"

Before she reached the counter, there was an announcement over the intercom for everyone from their group to assemble at the ticket counter for instructions. They were instructed to exchange their tickets and fly back to home base because the weather had turned really nasty, and a tropical storm on the opposite end prohibited them from landing safely.

Jackie was first in line and the first on the plane headed back to Dallas. Finally, twelve hours after her original departure, she arrived back in Dallas. She felt relieved and comforted when she saw George waiting there for her.

"Where's Tom?" George asked after they'd hugged.

"Who cares!" she snapped. "Probably passed out somewhere." As they walked toward the baggage return, Jackie noticed Lucrezia sitting in the terminal, awaiting Tom's arrival. She waved to her and steered George in another direction. "Strange couple," she muttered.

## CHAPTER NINETEEN

Jackie awakened early the next morning and drove to the new house, where she'd planned to check on some things the contractors were supposed to do. Everything seemed fine, so she made plans to begin moving things in later that day.

Jackie and George felt incredibly lucky to get the house. Dexter's aunt and uncle had wanted to purchase a new mobile home for their lake property for early retirement but needed to sell their condo in order to make the deal work. Since Dexter knew Jackie and George were looking to buy another home, he recommended they look at the condo. It truly did fit their needs, so they worked things out so the original owners would carry the note on the property for two years.

Because of Uncle Frank's retirement, he couldn't make any legal changes with the property for this two-year length of time. Therefore, George and Jackie would get their own outside financing after that time, and until then Frank and Lita would carry the financing themselves.

Excited about having their own place together, Jackie and George both immediately began investing money in the home: new paint inside and out, carpet and linoleum, a full security system, new outdoor lighting, and a privacy fence. Not to mention the larger washer and dryer they purchased. The initial investment was just over ten grand before they even moved in, plus the ten grand down payment. However, they both felt it was a good investment, and they enjoyed the new surroundings as their first home together became a reality.

After using a few days of her vacation to move into the new home, Jackie decided going back to work was the only way she'd get some rest. On the first day back in the office she didn't even realize Hillary wasn't there until around 6:30 p.m. when she appeared driving a new Lexus. She bragged to several people about making Dexter buy her a Lexus after his "degenerate son" wrecked her car. Jackie ignored both her comments and her car. She closed her office door to get away from Hillary's loud voice and continued making her phone calls for the day.

Everyone, including Dexter, seemed to really tense up when Hillary was around, partly because her comments and actions were so unpredictable. No one—child or adult—was safe from Hillary's wrath. Through the closed door, Jackie heard her shrill voice bragging about being corporate and working for the big bosses, therefore she had to keep up appearances. She added, "Ya'll need to keep yourselves in line now, 'cause Dexter has a direct line to the Big Boss!"

Jackie reached under her desk and pulled the trashcan out, so when she threw up she only had to turn her head and lean over. Knowing Hillary's comments had offended everyone, Dexter left his office and escorted her outside, where they discussed where they'd meet for dinner before departing in separate automobiles.

After they drove off the lot, Tom tapped on Jackie's door and asked, "Do you mind if I come in?"

He settled in a chair beside her desk. "Do you believe that Hillary? Who the hell does she think she is? If it weren't for Dexter she wouldn't have a job, that ungrateful cunt! Did you hear her threaten everyone?"

Jackie just chuckled, "What do you expect? It's Hillary's perception of authority. I feel sorry for Dexter—he puts up with her at work and at home."

Tom shook his head in disbelief. "I don't know how he does it. I wouldn't put up with half the crap she pulls." He sighed. "Jackie, about the other day in the airport…"

Jackie felt her face turning red, not sure what to expect. She said nothing and stared down at the desktop, waiting for the other shoe to drop.

"I owe you an apology. I'm known for saying and doing stupid stuff when I drink. I only hope I didn't offend you too badly and we can keep a good working relationship. I'm truly sorry for whatever I did or said to offend you."

Silence hung in the air for what seemed an eternity. Finally, Tom asked, "Jackie, what did I say to you?"

"Don't you remember?"

Tom looked puzzled and then replied, "No, really I don't have a clue."

"Good," Jackie replied. "We'll just leave it at that and forget about it."

"If you say so," Tom answered.

"Oh, by the way," Jackie said, "Someone named Levi Chance called for you earlier when you were with those customers. He said to tell you he called and he'll catch you later. Is he a customer?"

"Nah. Just someone I've known for a long time," Tom replied.

# CHAPTER TWENTY

Over the next couple of months everyone seemed to relax around the office—especially without Hillary's demands and threats. However she still made it into the office on a regular basis to check in and flaunt her "corporate position." One evening while Jackie and Dexter were working together on a month-end deadline, trying to get one more problem deal closed, Dexter made the comment to Jackie that his neck was really tense and asked if she'd rub it.

Jackie stepped back and shouted at him, "Hell no! Are you crazy! You aren't going home with my fingerprints anywhere on your body!"

Dexter quickly replied, "What do you mean? She can't do anything to me because she needs my income to maintain that corporate image she's trying to uphold."

"It's not you I'm worried about," Jackie said. "Think about it, Dexter. She already threatened to slap me, and I hadn't said a word."

Just as she finished her sentence the door flung open, and in stepped Hillary.

"See," Jackie said, giving Dexter a smile.

"See what?" Hillary demanded, hands on her ample hips.

Jackie stared into Dexter's face with a smile and answered, "See if you can get your wife to pull those strings at corporate so we can close this deal next week and still fund it in this month's business."

"Absolutely not!" Hillary replied.

"Okay with me," Jackie said. "It's your only deal. Anyway my six closings for the month are long since done." She sat back in her chair, basking in her glory and smiling at Hillary as if to say *take that*. She waited for the next outburst.

Not about to admit defeat to Jackie, Hillary looked over the paperwork as though she knew what she was doing and then replied, "I'll talk with Richard tomorrow."

Dexter snatched the file from Hillary and stated, "I'll take care of it myself. I don't need you to take anything to Richard!" Dexter was truly afraid Hillary would take the deal to Richard and ask him to make a determination, making Dexter look incompetent to his boss.

Jackie knew this was something he needed to discuss in private with his wife, the Corporate Connection, so she excused herself and closed the door on her way out. And the fight was on once again between Dexter and Hillary. Jackie thought to herself, this time Dexter deserved whatever Hillary dished out to him. Asking her to rub his neck, indeed!

The next day Dexter and Jackie both had an appointment in Arkansas to look over a mobile home trade-in, so they were together out of the office for the majority of the day. Because all trade-ins required an appraisal, Jackie needed to go along because she was the appraiser on staff. It was always clumsy traveling with a fellow employee, but under the Dexter-Jackie combination there was bound to be chaos somewhere after Hillary got involved.

However, it wasn't until a couple of months later that Tom approached Jackie as she stood at the counter in the sales lobby working on a file, yet within hearing distance of Dexter, chuckling as he stated, "So Jackie. Did you know Hillary thinks that you and Dexter are having an affair?"

Deep in her project, Jackie wasn't certain she'd heard him correctly but looked up and said. "Excuse me, Tom, would you repeat what you just said?"

He grinned. "Yeah, Hillary accused Dexter of fucking you when you two went to Arkansas that time." Jackie was appalled and distraught by his comment. Unable to speak, she turned, looking directly into Dexter's office where he sat with a shocked look on his face, yet smiling back at her.

Just then Tom added, "Yeah, can you imagine that? It would look like a Chihuahua fucking a German shepherd."

Jackie screamed, "YOU THINK THAT'S FUNNY OR WHAT? I don't appreciate that comment, and you and Hillary both owe me an apology!"

Tom then followed Jackie as she walked toward her office and slammed the door. Unsure what had just taken place or what she should do about it, she wanted to be alone and think things through before she did or said anything else. Just as she sat down at her desk, the door burst open and there stood Tom laughing hysterically, humping the door facing, then throwing his head back, howling like a dog baying at the moon!

Jackie screamed, "Get your ass out of my office—Now!" She was horrified by the whole incident and trembling with rage, while desperately resisting the urge to cry. Jackie picked up her purse and stalked out of the office to gain her composure, leaving the men to wonder if she'd ever be back.

After taking the rest of the day off, Jackie sat alone in her living room to think the situation over. She decided that she had to go back. There was a written company policy that Jackie had signed off on stating if she should quit, she'd forfeit any commission she had coming. With over $17,000 owed her for the current month alone, she was not about to walk away. Not to mention what would happen if George got involved in this act of stupidity. She had to consider his job, too.

Just then the phone rang and she picked it up without even looking to see who was calling. It was Dexter, and she didn't even get to finish saying hello before he started apologizing.

"Jackie I don't know what got into Tom, but he's lying to you. It didn't happen."

"I don't know who to believe anymore, Dexter," she said. "I just know I can't work around this. I don't like to be humiliated."

"I know." Dexter's voice took on a soothing tone. "Please come back to work tomorrow, I'll make sure nothing else happens, and Tom will apologize. Please, Jackie what do ya say? I know that you're a bigger person than he is and you can't let this bother you so much that you quit over some stupid remark."

"Dexter, I'm giving you fair warning. I'll go to Richard if this happens again."

I telling you, Jackie, it won't! You have my word. Pleeease, just accept my apologies and give it another try."

She hesitated for a moment and then replied, "I'll think it over and let you know tomorrow at 9:00 a.m." Her first thought was to first discuss this with George as she hung up the phone and turned on the television to clear her mind of the day.

It wasn't very long before George came through the door and asked, "Are you feeling better honey? I stopped by the office and Tom said he was worried because you went home not feeling well."

"I'm fine," Jackie replied with a chuckle, as she thought *that liar.* "Nothing to worry about. How did your day go?"

George sank into a chair. "Really busy. I had to shut the crew down because I ran out of supplies. Between the Midway Park lot and Alvin's lot, I've not been this busy since I had all three stores running at the same time—and that's been a long time." He sighed. "But I love it. I haven't had this much satisfaction out of a job in a long time."

"I'm happy for you," Jackie said. At that moment, she knew she wouldn't mention her day to George, and the decision for her to stay had just been made without any discussion between them at all.

Jackie went in to work the next morning and walked past Dexter's office as he looked up from his paperwork. He followed her into her office and closed the door behind them before he said, "Jackie, I hope that you are here to stay. I've talked with Tom and instructed him to not say anything to you at all."

She didn't want to be patronized, nor did she want everyone walking around on eggshells because of this. She blasted back at Dexter, "Hey, do you think I enjoy going through this crap every day? Well if you do, you're just as sick in the head as Tom is. I'm damn tired of his shit and I'm tired of covering his ass every time he does something stupid in the name of drinking. He sat here the other day and confessed to me every woman he's slept with in this company. He even had the nerve to call me for help once when his wife walked in and caught him with one of them in their home. Why does he do this stuff?" she shouted.

Dexter shook his head. "I can only guess that it's because he really likes you—as a friend, I mean."

"Well let me make it clear for the record: I don't give a shit who he likes or has slept with in this company, and I don't want to know anything about who he's screwing. Nor do I want ANY gossip started about me. Can't You Understand That?"

"Yes I do, Dexter replied. I'll make sure that he keeps his big mouth shut from now on."

As Dexter started to leave the office, Jackie called his name. He paused and again closed the door, turning toward her in silence. "Did Hillary really say that about us?"

He looked down as he thought for a second, and then nodded his head yes before stepping through the door, closing it behind him and leaving Jackie alone in her office.

Over the next several months, keeping Tom quiet was not a promise Dexter was able or willing to keep. The entire group of guys gradually became more lax in their actions, which resulted in a large number of people quitting on a regular basis. They might hire three or four people every month, and at least half of them would quit. Some just stopped showing up for work, while others voiced their dislike of the bad language or the disrespectful way in which they were treated by either Tom or Dexter.

Even Sam quit in search of a better situation. It wasn't easy for Jackie with Sam gone. She'd known she could rely on him to say something to the guys when they let their language or stupidity get out of hand. They did respect him for his age—or perhaps it was his size and deep, loud voice they respected. Either way, when he spoke, the windows rattled and they had no choice but to listen.

Jackie knew she'd also miss Sam because he was the only person she truly felt comfortable around at work. But she'd made a commitment to Richard Spaniel to get the Midway location straightened out, and she knew she'd have to interface with Tom on a daily basis in order to accomplish her goals. Dexter had indeed instructed Tom to keep his mouth shut around Jackie, and he did so for two weeks, until he just couldn't stand it any longer. He bounced into Jackie's office one evening and sat down, looking across the desk at her. She looked up, without any expression or comment, staring at Tom in silence until he said with a stupid grin on his face. "Hey Jack, how ya doin?"

"What do you want?" she asked.

"I just want to be friends with you, Jackie, that's all. Can't you forgive me?"

"No!" She looked back at the contract on her desk.

"I was only telling you the truth—can't you understand? I thought you needed to know, that's all."

"No, that's not all, Tom. You had entirely no business ever telling me what you told me. You got that! You embarrassed and humiliated me, and you made fun of me. I don't appreciate your sick humor. I don't forgive you. You were totally disrespectful to me and I don't see how anyone in their right mind can't see that."

Tom interrupted her. "You're right, I'm stupid! What can I say?"

"Nothing!" Jackie shouted back over the ringing phone sitting between them, "Not a God damn thing!" The phone continued ringing, and she finally answered after the fifth ring. It was Levi Chance on the other end, "Hey Jackie this is Levi Chance. Is my um—my friend Tom around?"

"Yes, as a matter of fact he's sitting right here." She handed the phone to Tom. The two men conversed like old pals before Jackie finally left the office, not wanting to become part of his personal conversation.

## CHAPTER TWENTY-ONE

After leaving the office, Jackie strolled down to the lobby, where she greeted a customer who'd just come in the door. He told her he was looking for a mobile home and wanted to see what she had to offer. She responded to him like as she had with a hundred customers before, introducing herself and then escorting him down the hall to her office. As she entered her office with the man, Tom placed his call on hold, left the room, and closed the door so they could have privacy.

The customer, whose name was Neal Garretson, explained what he was looking for in a home, but before they could go out to the lot Jackie asked him to fill out an application so she could do a credit check and further qualify him financially. As she asked him questions, Jackie couldn't help but notice the large scar on Neal's left cheek, which somehow added to his rather rugged California look with his tanned skin and long, wavy sun-bleached hair that he constantly brushed away from his face. After he completed the application, Jackie excused herself to pull a credit history. Just as he said, his credit was flawless, and with the income he verified by check stub, he could qualify for pretty much whatever home he wanted to purchase. Together, they walked outside to look at the homes.

Neal seemed especially taken with one of the homes Jackie showed him and wanted to price that model with some upgrades. Excited about the possible sale, Jackie led him back inside to write up the deal. After taking notes on the changes he wanted, she told Neal she'd get back to him with a firm price within the next two days. Jackie was surprised at this easy sale on the man's first visit, but she wasn't quite prepared for what happened next.

When she prepared to shake hands with him, Neal pulled Jackie forward and pressed her against him with one arm around her shoulder and the other down her back. He quickly kissed her on the lips. Jackie was so shocked she couldn't believe it. She immediately pushed him away.

"I'm sorry," he stammered. "I'm just so excited and you're such a comfort to work with. I got carried away."

She opened her office door and motioned him out, saying, "I think you know your way to the front door."

As Neal left, Jackie marched straight into Dexter's office and told him what had just happened. He replied, "You're kidding right?" Then he took the man's credit application from her and looked it over.

"No, I'm not making this up," she answered. "If I call you to come to my office the next time he's here, don't hesitate."

Just then, Todd tapped on the door and opened it just wide enough to put his face inside and say, "Jackie, you have a call. I think it's the guy who was just here."

"I'll take it here." Sure enough, it was Neal.

He said, "Jackie, I want you to know I'm serious about buying that house, but I forgot to talk to you about a place to put it. Can you help me with that?"

"I probably can," Jackie replied.

"Will you come with me to look at some land tomorrow?"

"We have a land locator on staff who handles that for us. I can put you in contact with him."

"That's not necessary," Neal said. "I just thought we might get you out of the office and maybe have a little afternoon delight—I mean lunch together."

"Neal, I don't date customers, and besides that, I'm attached. So, if you're looking for a girlfriend, I'm not it."

"Oh no," he replied. "I just thought if we were out looking for land together we'd eventually have to get something to eat. That's all. I didn't mean anything else. I'm sorry if you thought that."

"No problem," Jackie said. "I'll check on that price thing tomorrow at the factory and get back with you as soon as I know something. Okay?"

She hung up the phone and sat there, expecting some kind of backup from Dexter. But instead he said, "If you can't take this motherfucker down, let me know, and I'll give the deal to someone who can! From the looks of his credit he can buy any fucking thing he wants, and we need this deal, so don't let this guy get away without closing him on a house. Take the emotion out of it—you got that?"

Jackie was so shocked she didn't trust herself to answer. Instead, she grabbed the folder back from Dexter and left his office.

Just as she returned to her own office, she received a page over the intercom for a telephone call, line three. With Neal still on her mind she answered rather hastily, thinking it was probably him calling again. But instead, it was Richard Spaniel.

"Jackie, everything all right? You're kinda out of breath."

"Oh, it's nothing I can't handle," she replied. What can I do for you, Richard?"

"Well, it's been a while since we last talked, and I wanted to know if we could get together some time this week and go over some things."

She and Richard agreed to meet on Friday at her office for lunch with the corporate HR manager and to make plans for moving Jackie to her new location.

As she hung up the phone, Jackie felt so restored she couldn't stop smiling as she thought, *Finally, I'm gonna bust out of this den of iniquity and get my own lot!!!* Nothing could stop her now. She was rekindled and filled with energy at the thought of the meeting with Richard. The next few days seemed to creep along. The Friday meeting just couldn't come soon enough.

On Friday morning, she dressed for the occasion and was ready to make a good impression on the corporate human resources executive Richard was bringing with him. She was shocked to see who came in with Richard: It was John Turner, the president of the company.

John shouted, "Jackie, is it really you? How are you? It's been years!" He took both her hands, kissing her on the cheek. "So, are you ready to have lunch with us?"

Jackie glanced across the room and saw Dexter sitting in his office with his mouth hanging open because John Turner was everyone's boss, and Dexter had no idea she knew him. Nor could anyone believe the company president kissed her right in front of everyone! They were all in shock. Richard included. He asked, "Jackie, is there anyone you don't know in this business?"

Over a nice meal at a local steak house, the three discussed numerous things about the business, including John's father. Jackie had worked for the senior Mr. Turner several years earlier in another state. John told Jackie his dad was still very much involved in the company and would probably die at his desk. The business had become a family enterprise since his mother became an office manager, plus his sister and her husband had also joined the company and were running a retail lot. They discussed the few people who were still in the business and then John took a sip of his water and said, "I'm certainly glad you're working for our company, and we have every intention of moving you to your own lot in time. However, a few things need to happen before that takes place. One of the main things is that we need you to train and work with Tom Kerakasco very closely for several months to make sure the transaction goes as smoothly as possible for the two of you."

She looked at him, frowning. "I don't understand what you mean—the two of us."

"Our intention is to move both you and Tom; not necessarily at the same time or to the same place, but we need you to fill his position after we move him so you can then transition smoothly to your own lot."

"That makes sense. But, who's doing the training?"

"Well," John replied, "I'd intended for you to meet her today, but unfortunately she couldn't make the trip to join us. Our HR trainer is Emma Woods, and you may know her. She was with the company several years back and recently came back to work as a trainer. Her husband's a regional VP in one of our area districts." John held his coffee cup out and paused while the waitress filled it. "Anyway, I'll get her in touch with you soon so she can fill you in and get you started on the training 101 session. If all goes well, we plan to have you moved in about three to six months. But in the meantime, Richard tells me you've taken a major interest in this location, and with your help it turned into a money maker, like we always knew it should be."

He paused again, adding a packet of sugar to his coffee. "I want to thank you personally and ask you to hang in there for whatever time it takes us to get things moved around and people placed in order to move you up where we feel you belong so that you can start making that big six-figure money."

"Alright!" Jackie exclaimed. "That sounds good to me."

Richard added, "Emma should be back in town early next week, and we'll get things going then."

"Sounds great," Jackie said. Her smile lit up the room.

After much conversation and reminiscing over lunch, a couple of hours had passed. Because Richard and John still needed to visit one other lot in the area before John's flight departed, they left the restaurant and headed back to drop Jackie at her office. Jackie couldn't contain an ear-to-ear smile as they walked back into the office together. Both John and Richard said their good byes to Jackie before stepping into Dexter's office and closing the door behind them for a quick private conversation with Dexter.

Tammy, the office manager, stopped by about an hour later and asked, "Do you know a customer named Neal Garretson?"

Jackie sighed. "Unfortunately, I do. What's going on?"

Tammy said, "I think you need to be very cautious around him. Don't stay alone in the building or leave by yourself. I think he might try to follow you home."

Jackie froze. "What are you saying?"

"The guy called here asking for the office manager, and when I took the call he said that it was imperative that he get in touch with you right away and insisted I give him your address and home phone number."

"You didn't—uh…"

"Of course not," Tammy said. "When I told him that was against company policy, he got pissed and told me he was buying a house from you and needed to talk with you right away. He said you'd be very upset if I didn't give him the information."

"Yep, I can believe that." Jackie explained to Tammy what happened on Neal's first visit. "I'd appreciate you telling Dexter about this, because I tried to tell him, and I think he didn't believe me."

Tammy smiled. "I'll tell Dexter he needs to keep a handle on this idiot or get rid of him, because you shouldn't take chances with this guy. He gave me the creeps just talking to him on the phone." Tammy started to leave the office and then turned back and added, "Jackie, I mean it. Watch your back—this man could be dangerous."

Not even five minutes later, a messenger arrived with a huge bouquet of roses. One of the guys called out, "Jackie, come to the lobby, quick!"

At sight of the flowers she stopped in her tracks. "Wow! These are gorgeous." Thinking they came from George, she searched for a tag, but there was no card inside the envelope. Thinking the florist made a mistake, she called the number listed on the envelope. They told her that the man who ordered had paid cash for the flowers and specifically requested that no card be sent. The woman on the phone hadn't seen the man, and no one seemed able to describe what he looked like.

Jackie left the flowers in the front office for everyone to enjoy, since she wasn't sure who sent them or why. She didn't mention them at home, waiting to see if George would ask about the surprise bouquet. He didn't. After a few days, she was pretty sure who sent the flowers, and why.

She'd thought Neal was a little warped from the first time she met him, but she doubted he'd do anything to harm her. He always tried to spend a long time with her each time he came to the office. If she was with another customer he'd sit and wait for whatever time it took, until finally Jackie insisted he start setting an appointment before stopping in. She could hardly wait for his closing date to arrive and the home to be delivered so she could finally be rid of this character. However, a couple of days after the home was delivered and set up, Neal stopped by the office right before closing and asked Jackie if she'd walk through the model home with him so he could show her something that was missing from his house.

"Sure," she replied, "but first I need to take care of something." Still feeling uncomfortable about being alone with Neal, she stopped in Dexter's office and asked him to come out to the home in a few minutes and tell her she had an urgent phone call. Dexter laughed, but agreed. Otherwise, she wouldn't have gone outside with Neal. When she returned to the lobby, the guy was not there. Jackie stepped back to her office, expecting to see Neal waiting there for her. However, he was nowhere to be found. Assuming he'd already walked out to the home, she headed that way, hoping to find him and get this final meeting over with. Once inside the model home, she called out his name. When he didn't answer, she noticed the bedroom door was shut. She stepped inside, still calling his name. She was completely unprepared for what happened next.

The bedroom door slammed shut behind her. She turned, grabbing for the door and preparing to scream—too late. Neal grabbed her by the back of her neck with such force that her skin stretched tight against her windpipe choking her. He pressed his other hand pressed tightly over her mouth. As they struggled and fell across the bed, Jackie's heart pounded in her chest. She feared she'd pass out from lack of oxygen, or even worse be choked to death before anyone found her. She continued struggling, beating her hands against Neal's chest.

"Open your eyes and look at me!" Neal demanded. "You've been ignoring me and teasing me long enough! You didn't even thank me for the flowers I sent you!"

By now Jackie was becoming disoriented and weak from lack of oxygen, and it became more difficult to struggle as she lay underneath him. His full body weight pressing down on her, pinning her to the bed. When she opened her eyes they stared at each other, their faces only inches apart. Unable to help herself, she began to cry in fear. But as tears streamed over her cheeks and across his hand, a thought came to her mind. Surely he wouldn't harm an unborn child, but she had to somehow get this untrue message to him.

One of her hands was caught between them, the other pulling on his hand pressed against her mouth. She began frantically moving the hand between them as if patting herself on the stomach repeatedly until he looked down at her stomach and back into her eyes, hesitating before he asked, "You're pregnant?"

With what seemed to be the last ounce of strength left in her body, Jackie motioned her head yes. He took his hand off her mouth and leaped to his feet as she rolled off the bed where she lay gasping for air. He shouted at her; "You don't understand! I just wanted to take you to dinner. I never meant to hurt you. I'm sorry!"

Finally, there was a knock at the front door and Jackie thought, *Thank God, it's Dexter!* But Neal also heard the knock and quickly left the bedroom. He rushed to the front door so he could lock it and met Dexter, keeping him from entering the house.

In a surprised voice Neal said, "Oh, I was expecting Jackie. Have you seen her?"

Dexter replied, "I thought she was in here with you. She has an urgent phone call."

"Last I saw her she was with some people going in that house up front." Neal pointed toward a house on the other side of the lot, as he stepped out of the house closing and locking the door, leaving Jackie lying on the bedroom floor struggling to regain her strength.

Dexter said, "I'll just have to page her"

As they both turned and walked toward the office, she heard Neal shout, "Hey, Dexter. Would you please have Jackie call me when she gets time? I have some things I need to talk to her about."

Jackie lay on the cold floor of the house for a long time before she gathered enough strength to move herself to go back into the office. However, once she started moving she was really scared Neal would return and in his crazy way might decide to finish her off. It was now dark outside, and there were no lights connected to the house, making it even harder to get her bearings. After quite a while she heard Dexter paging her over the intercom. She finally figured out which direction she needed to go as she struggled to crawl toward the front door. But just as she reached to open it, she saw a man's shadow that scared her so badly she began screaming. This time it wasn't Neal—it was the serviceman doing his rounds to lock up for the night.

He shouted, "Jackie! It's only me! Leon. What's wrong with you?" Flashing his light toward her he saw something smeared on her face and red marks on her neck, and he knew something was wrong. Fearing her attacker still lurked inside the house, he grabbed Jackie, pulled her out the door, and helped her into the office.

Jackie was a mess. Her lipstick was spread all over her face, and she had streaks of mascara around her eyes and down her cheeks, making it apparent that she'd been struggling with someone. She fought to hold back tears, resisting her personal thoughts and feelings.

It was apparent to everyone what had happened, but Jackie withdrew to her office, avoiding any conversation as she adjusted her clothes and ran her fingers through her hair. She stated in a matter-of-fact tone. "I'm going home now. I don't feel well."

She grabbed her keys off the counter, leaving behind everything else that she normally took home with her, including her purse. Everyone just looked at her in silence, but no one offered to help.

Jackie drove herself straight home, where she removed all her clothes, tossing them into a trash bag before stepping into the shower to wash away the part of him she could still feel. She could even smell him as she closed her eyes to shampoo her hair. Just then the warning Tammy gave her came to mind and she began to tremble with the thought of what he might do if he'd followed her home. She'd never experienced anything like this before, but somehow she felt like she was at fault for the whole thing. After all, hadn't Neal said she teased him? She punished herself with the thought that she was at fault as she continued to scrub until her skin was raw and in places bleeding.

In her reasoning, Jackie was then afraid the incident would cause problems in her relationship with George. Not wanting to risk loosing him, Jackie felt she needed to put the attack somewhere far away. She slipped further into denial, convincing herself that only she actually knew what Neal had done and she was certain he'd never admit anything. Besides, it was her word against his and no one even ever saw them together. She decided to keep the assault to herself, letting all thoughts of it swirl down the drain to never return.

# CHAPTER TWENTY-TWO

Since George was working out of town on a job for Alvin, Jackie decided to stay home by herself for a couple of days and recuperate. After much thought, she'd decided it was probably best to tell George what happened, but she would wait until he was back in town rather than tell him over the phone. On her second day off, she was awakened with a phone call from Tom. As she answered the phone, Jackie could hear people talking on the other end—obviously Tom was calling from the office, and other people were in the room with him.

"Jackie?" Tom said. "How ya doing? How ya feelin? When are ya coming back to work?"

She paused, taking a deep breath and trying to gather her thoughts before she answered, "Tom, I'm not sure I can."

"Why not?" he demanded. "Let me tell you, Jackie. First of all, if I'd been around, that creep would not be alive today. Leon told us what happened and how he found you. Hey, you don't have to talk about it anymore to anybody. We took care of it. It's handled. He will never call you or set foot in this office again."

"How?" she asked, suddenly alert.

He hesitated a moment, then said, "I can't disclose that. You'll just have to trust me on this one. But you do have my word that he will never, ever come around here again."

"But I want George to take care of this. This is personal, and I think it's our business how we handle it."

"Hey, it's done! The company has already handled it, and there's nothing left for you or George to do. Trust me: It's handled. At this point, involving George will only make things worse." He took a deep breath. "You have our support and sympathy. Take as much time as you need, but I've already told everyone here that if it ever comes up again or if anyone talks about it they'll be terminated on the spot. What else do you want?"

She sighed. "I guess what I really need is to have it go away and leave me alone, so I can get back to being myself and put it behind me."

"Well then, what better way to do that than to get yourself involved in something—like work and a promotion? You do still want the job don't you?"

"Yes, I do."

"Then why prolong the situation and upset yourself and George all over again?"

She stared at the ceiling, thinking Tom was probably right. There was no point moping around at home. "All right, you win. I'll see you tomorrow."

\*\*\*

Jackie did go back to work, and she focused on her job, closing every possible deal in an effort to prove she was the best choice for the promotion. Still, she was nervous and jumpy for a couple of weeks, still trying to overcome her fear about what had happened. She decided to let it go and not involve George, at Tom's urging.

Three weeks later, as they were preparing for a series of pending sales promotions, Dexter hired a new salesman. Another female employee informed Jackie that the new guy was hired on at a rate considerably higher than her own salary, though he was young and had no experience. Jackie immediately confronted Tom and Dexter.

Tom said, "Dexter, since Jackie's doing all this extra work to get ready for the promotion, why don't you just pay her what you're paying this new guy?"

Dexter agreed, but Jackie interrupted him, pointing out that giving her a pay raise at this late date wasn't the solution. She wasn't the only female employee being cheated, and they needed to raise the wages of all the women in order to be fair to everyone.

Tom nodded. "Okay, we can do that."

Dexter screamed, "What the hell are you saying, Tom? You can't override me!"

Tom held up his hand toward Dexter. "No, she's right. You can't determine by sexual preference who gets paid more and less. We'll handle this, Jackie, and thanks for bringing it to our attention." He smiled and ushered her out of the office.

She felt confident that the issue was an oversight that would now be resolved, and the other female employee, Sydney, would also be compensated properly. Later that afternoon, Dexter announced the corporate office was sponsoring a training session the next week at the home office and the staff would split up so everyone could attend one day. He then teamed everyone up and assigned a group to attend on each day. Of course Tom and Jackie were scheduled together, and their scheduled training day was Thursday. Sydney's assigned date was Tuesday, and she mentioned that was her scheduled day off and she'd already made plans for the day.

"No problem," Dexter said. He moved on with the agenda without further addressing the issue. However, when Tuesday rolled around, Dexter made a 9 a.m. phone call to Hillary, his Corporate Connection, to take roll call, and she advised him that Sydney wasn't there. He tried to call Sydney at home and got no response. Then, a couple of hours later he got a phone call from Hillary informing him Sydney had in fact arrived, but was three hours late. Dexter instructed Hillary to send Sydney to his office right away.

Once Sydney arrived at the office, she expected to fill in for the others who were in training and assumed she'd be going into the next training session, but Dexter fired her on the spot, under the watchful eyes and ears of Tom, stating it was inexcusable for her to be late for the training. She reminded him about her other plans and the fact that she'd told him about them, but this meant nothing to Dexter. He instructed her to sign the termination form and pick up her belongings, telling her she needed to find employment elsewhere.

Sydney was furious, vowing revenge as she cleaned out her office and hastily left the building. As she left, she added, "I know you fired me because I complained about the pay issue. You haven't heard the last of this, you little prick!"

Dexter chucked as he watched her walk across the parking lot, climb into her car, and speed away. Then he and Tom did a high five, and Tom said, "See, we pulled it off. I told you it would work, and there won't be any repercussions because you handled it like I said."

## CHAPTER TWENTY-THREE

With the only other female salesperson gone, the language around the office became worse, and the atmosphere was "anything goes," as Tom bordered on psychotic with his comments and outbursts. He often shouted "Penis!" or "Suck a dick!" for no apparent reason.

Finally, the service manager demanded that he either stop or she was going to quit, for the eighth time, and get an attorney. Well this would NOT look good for Dexter since the service manager is his sister-in-law. So, after her threats, he counseled Tom and instructed him to knock it off. This lasted for a short while, until Tom figured a way to avoid the service manager and still use foul language. He simply waited until she was on the phone or out on the lot. He'd ask, "Is Connie here?"

Someone would answer, "No, she's off today," or "She's outside," and he would shout out "Penis!"

His actions bordered on insanity and fueled similar actions from several other male employees. Jackie was growing weary of the day-to-day struggles. She didn't seem any closer to the promotion she'd been promised and was carrying an extra workload with no compensation. She called Sam at his new place of employment to discuss how he was doing and see if there were any job opportunities there. Sam was delighted to hear from her.

"They still giving you a hard time around there?" he asked. "I thought by now you'd have them whipped into shape."

"Well, it isn't that easy," she replied. "When you're outnumbered by idiots ten to one, it's hard to change things. As a matter of fact, I'm thinking about finding another job."

"Really? They pissed you off that bad, huh? I still get the stats, and from what I've seen of you the last couple of months you're smokin' those guys."

"Yeah, but there's more to the job than selling. I'm at the point now where I can sell anywhere, and I need to get away from these idiots. I'm telling you, Sam, they never cease to surprise me with the crap they come up with. Some of it borders on criminal insanity, and some of it's just criminal."

"You're not telling me anything I don't already know. Don't forget, I worked there for several years. Those bastards are not just brutal—they're evil. Have you talked with Richard about this?"

"That works short-term, but then they come back with a vengeance!"

Sam sighed. "Damn, woman. You're too good to go to work just anywhere. You need a good company with decent work ethics where you can prosper, too. I don't have anything up my sleeve at the moment, but I'll make a few calls and get back to you."

She hung up the phone feeling slightly relieved. Perhaps there was hope on the horizon.

The next day at the office, Tom and Dexter called an afternoon meeting to announce there would be a mandatory get-together that night at Tom's house. It was Lucrezia's birthday, and everyone was "required" to attend. Tom passed out a list, outlining what each person was to bring to the party. As they examined the list, everyone looked around the room, but on one questioned anything.

Tom proudly asked, "Any questions?" Looking around the room holding his hands up, he added, "Great, I'll see you all there about 7:30." Just as everyone stood up, he announced, "Hey gang, just one more thing."

The group paused, waiting. With a goofy smile on his face, Tom shouted, "Penis!"

Most of the guys laughed, maybe out of respect for their boss, but Jackie was sickened by his humor, and Tom noticed the expression on her face.

Over the roar of laughter, he said, "Jackie, can I see you in my office for a minute?"

Entering his office, Jackie had a look on her face that even Tom couldn't ignore. He knew she was unhappy.

"So what's wrong?" he asked, propping his feet on the desk.

"You have to ask?" she snapped at him. "What the hell is this required meeting at your house, and we bring all the food. How rude can you get? Besides, I thought you and Lucrezia were separated. What do you have in mind, using us all for witnesses when she tries to kill you again?"

"Funny, Jackie. Real funny."

"I'm not trying to be funny, Tom. I'm being realistic. What do we have to meet about that can't be done in the office? She glared at him, waiting for an answer.

He shrugged. "Nothing. I just thought we all needed to get together after work for a little fun and visiting to smooth out the rough spots—that's all."

"Don't you think you might've run this by someone before you gave the command to show up. Hell, you run this place like you're a warden and we're prisoners. Think about it, Tom. We have rights."

"Okay, I'm sorry. I wasn't thinking right. Next time, I'll get your opinion before I plan anything." He smiled. "So, Jack. Will you help me out? I need you to pick up the kid from school and bring her over to the house with you and George. Will you do that for me?"

"I don't even know where George is working today. I think he's got his crew on a job for Alvin. You just do this because you know I can't resist that child," she said.

"And she loves you and George! She begs to go to your house, Jackie. And when she comes home she is always singing some little song you taught her and sporting her tiny little painted fingernails and toenails."

Jackie just fell forward her head hitting the desktop. "Tom, why do you do this to me? You use that child to get your way, and that's not fair! Who can resist her?"

"Nobody, so far," he said with a grin.

"You should be ashamed of yourself."

"I am," he replied, "but will you pick her up for me one more time?"

"I don't see how I can avoid it, Tom. This is a "mandatory meeting," and God knows I'd be the next one fired if I miss it."

"Great!" Next he handed Jackie the key to his house, saying, "You'll need this to get in. Maybe you can get there a little early and set things up."

"Of course," Jackie smugly replied. "What else would I be doing in my spare time?"

After work, she drove to the little nursery school to pick up Frankie Paige, who was so excited to see Jackie that she wrapped herself around Jackie's leg. "Can I go home with you today?" she asked.

"Looks like it," Jackie replied, bending over to pick up the little girl. Frankie clung to Jackie as though she hadn't seen her in months. Back at the house, she announced to Jackie that she was ready for Mama's birthday party.

"Oh, Really?" Jackie questioned.

"Yeah, didn't Daddy tell you? We're having a party tonight for Mommy."

At the get together that evening, people started showing up that Jackie didn't know. She assumed they were all friends of Lucrezia. Since they all seemed to have some class, they couldn't be Tom's friends. One particular woman looked familiar, although Jackie was sure they'd never met. She introduced herself as Juliette, saying she and Lucrezia had been college roommates.

The two women shared small talk and worked on getting everything set up before Tom arrived with Lucrezia. Jackie was still puzzled by her familiar face and finally mentioned it.

Juliette asked, "Have you ever heard of Edie Clark Fisher, the famous singer? She's my mom, and we look a lot alike."

"Wow! How exciting," Jackie exclaimed, setting a bowl of potato chips on the table.

"Maybe for you, Juliette said.

"What's she doing these days?" Jackie asked.

"I think she had a show in Branson, between her regular Vegas shows."

After an hour of work getting everything set up, someone shouted, "Here they come! Hide!"

Three hours into the celebrating and partying, Jackie decided to question Tom about the impending meeting. "Hey, Tom, I'm really tired and past ready to go home, so when are we gonna have that meeting we're all here for?"

Tom replied, "It's late now. We'll just go over it tomorrow at the office."

When she grabbed her coat and exchanged looks with George, he knew she was ready to go home. Driving home, she muttered, "Mandatory meeting, my ass. He just wanted us to put the party together for him."

"And it worked like a charm," George chuckled, steering the car through late-night traffic.

"You know, something about Tom seems really strange to me," Jackie said, leaning her head against George's shoulder.

"Like what?" He laced his fingers through hers.

"I don't know, but I'll figure it out and let you know. I'm too tired to think about anything but sleep right now, and it's already past my bedtime."

## CHAPTER TWENTY-FOUR

The next day at work Lucrezia stopped by the office and personally thanked each and every one for participating in her party. Jackie mentioned to her that she hadn't seen Crystal there at the party.

Lucrezia said, "Yeah, she's off doing her own thing right now. I'm really afraid she'll lose Hanley if she isn't careful."

"What do you mean, lose him?"

"I mean, she might lose custody. She's doing some stupid stuff, plus she has a new boyfriend who leaves very little time for Hanley."

"Wow, I hate that." Jackie replied. "Do you think she…" Jackie paused and then decided not to finish her sentence. "Never mind, it's none of my business."

"What?" Lucrezia asked.

"Nothing. Really, I don't want to stick my nose in." Actually, Jackie was afraid she'd let it slip to Lucrezia that Crystal and Tom had been seeing one another during their separation. Not wanting any part of that scene, she quickly changed the subject, asking Lucrezia about nursing school.

"Are you and Frankie Paige getting along all right?" She continued.

Lucrezia shrugged. "I guess. We're making it."

Jackie was curious about the situation with Tom, so she finally said, "I may be getting personal, but I have to ask: Are you and Tom getting back together?"

Lucrezia stared into the distance. "I'm not sure yet. He has some issues he needs to resolve first. Until then, Frankie Paige and I are just fine in our little apartment."

Jackie smiled and said, "Either way, I'm glad to see you. *Maybe it would be the best thing if she and Tom did get back together*, Jackie thought. *It might calm him down.*

Over the next couple of months, Lucrezia made her stops into the office on a regular basis, and sometimes Jackie suspected she was checking up on Tom. No one questioned why she continued stopping by until the day everyone was sitting in the main lobby during a sales meeting. Lucrezia strolled through the front door and directly into Tom's office without saying a word. She snatched Frankie's pictures off his desk and marched out the front door. Everyone was in shock as they sat in silence, awaiting Tom's response.

Moments later, he rushed outside. Tom and Lucrezia stood in the front parking lot, both screaming at each other as everyone looked out their windows in disbelief. However, this wasn't like a Hillary/Dexter argument, which could (and usually did) go on forever. This one only lasted a short time because Lucrezia kneed Tom and left him bent over, holding his family jewels as she climbed into her car and took aim, barely missing him as she sped off the lot.

As Todd went out to help Tom back to his office, Jackie remarked to Stuart Carlson, "I knew it. I knew he was using us all as witnesses when he held that mandatory meeting/birthday party the other day at his house."

Stuart chuckled as he left her office and commented, "I wonder what he did to piss her off so bad this time?"

Just then, it came to Jackie. "Oh my God! I'll bet Lucrezia found out about Crystal." Still looking out the window, she noticed George pulling into the parking lot. *What a welcome surprise*, she thought, as she left her office to meet him on the front porch. They chatted for a few minutes before Tom approached, saying, "So George, did Jackie tell you Lucrezia tried to mow me down in the parking lot today?"

George laughed, saying, "Tom you should never piss any woman off that bad! What the hell did you do to make her that mad? Never mind, don't answer that in front of Jackie. I don't want to give her any ideas."

Tom replied, "Nothing, but I want to ask a favor of you. I feel like Frankie Paige needs to know her own dad. He doesn't even know she exists. I want you to call him or go see him and let him know he has this daughter. He just lives in Fort Worth. Here's his name and address." He held out a piece of paper to George.

George backed away, refusing the paper. "I thought you were her father."

"No. I guess Jackie didn't tell you." He stuffed the paper into his pocket. "Lucrezia said he pissed her off so badly that she didn't tell him she was pregnant. Then we got together. But the more I think about it, for Frankie's sake, the more I think she needs to know her real father too. His name is—"

"Just then Jackie stepped in. Uh, Tom, I don't think this is a good idea. I don't want George to contact him for you. If you think it needs to be done, then you should do it yourself. Right now, I think you're just really pissed at Lucrezia, and you want George to drop that bomb for you. Why don't you make the call yourself?"

"Well, because Lucrezia will think I just did it in retaliation."

Jackie said, "Maybe that is why you're doing it. I think you should ask yourself some questions before you get someone else involved."

Tom stared at her for a few seconds and nodded. "Maybe you're right. I should be the one to make the call. I'll do it tomorrow." He walked away, leaving George and Jackie together in the parking lot.

As he walked out of hearing distance George asked, "What's up with him?"

"I told you there's just something strange about that guy. He gives me the willies with some of the stuff he comes up with. I don't want you getting involved in his problems."

George grinned. "Hey, you don't have to worry about that. I'll see you at home."

Later, as Jackie passed Tom's office, he motioned her to come in. Since he was on the telephone she wasn't sure why he wanted her to join him. As she entered, he put one hand over the receiver and whispered, "Shut the door and sit down for a second."

Not sure what was going on, she closed the door and took a seat across from Tom. As she listened, she realized he was on the phone with the corporate office personnel department, canceling the medical insurance on Lucrezia and Frankie Paige. Jackie assumed from this that he and Lucrezia were in fact splitting for good. Then he called IRS and turned her in for not disclosing the $500-a-day income she made from the bar where she'd worked when he met her. Obviously, Tom was really pissed at Lucrezia this time, but Jackie was shocked at the calm, cold, deliberate matter in which he handled these phone calls. In fact she suspected he'd had done this or something like it before.

As she sat there witnessing his revenge, she knew there had to be something else going on between the couple that she didn't have a clue about, other than Tom's carousing and playing around. She stood to leave his office, shaking her head in disbelief, but he held up one finger and whispered, "Wait a second."

Then he ended his conversation and hung up the phone, chuckling to himself. "Tomorrow, I'm calling the nursing school and telling them to revoke her scholarship!"

Jackie swallowed in fear and disbelief. Tom's revenge bordered on sadistic. "So, what do you think she'll do—or have done—when she finds out what you've done to her?"

"I Really Don't Give A Shit," he replied. "I'm tired of supporting her and her kid and being treated like this."

"Let me ask you something, Tom. Did she find out about you and Crystal, or is this about something else?"

Tom snickered, but he didn't answer. He picked up the phone and announced over the PA for everyone to resume the meeting in the lobby.

"So, Tom," Jackie continued, "Does it make you feel better to perform these acts of revenge in front of somebody? There's just one thing that I want you to promise."

"What's that?" he asked.

"That you'll give us all a heads-up when you see Lucrezia coming next time. You think she was mad today? When she finds out you called the IRS and had her school funds eliminated, this place will look like the Oklahoma bombing in a Texas hailstorm all over again. So why don't you go ahead and transfer to a different location while we're still in one piece around here?"

Tom laughed hysterically and rolled his chair through the door, heading for the lobby.

# CHAPTER TWENTY-FIVE

Jackie was so sure Lucrezia would seek revenge against Tom that she rearranged her office so she had a complete view of the parking lot's entrance and exit. She knew Lucrezia's wrath could come at any time, and she didn't want any part of the surprise attack if she could help it. From that day on, when she was in her office, she kept vigil over the parking lot.

Early one afternoon, the phone rang. Jackie answered, but before she could finish her introduction, Crystal cut her off demanding, "Let me talk with Tom!"

"Crystal, are you okay?" Jackie asked.

"I need to talk with Tom." Crystal didn't sound upset, but Jackie detected fear in her voice. "Hang on, I'll get Tom." Worried that something had happened but not sure what it was, Jackie immediately ran to Tom's office where she told him: "Take line two. It's Crystal, and she sounds like something might be wrong."

Tom snatched the phone up and then listened intently for just a moment, sitting motionless as a statue. Then he stood and circled his desk screaming, "God Damn, Motherfucker!" He slammed the door to his office and continued his phone call in private. But after just a few minutes he surfaced, looked around to see if everyone was gone to lunch, then screamed, "Jackie! Quick! Come Here!"

Startled by his shouts, fear ran through Jackie, and her chest tightened with each breath as she ran into his office.

He demanded, "Tell me—exactly what did she say to you before you gave the call to me?"

"What?" she asked.

"CRYSTAL!" he shouted. "What did she say to you before you gave me the call?"

"Nothing really—she just asked to talk to you."

"Was she crying or hysterical?"

"No," Jackie said, still puzzled by Tom's questions.

Tom burst out, "Motherfucker! I can't believe she really did it! She really pulled it off!"

Jackie demanded, "What are you talking about? What's wrong?"

Tom dug through his pockets and came up with his truck keys. "I've got to get to the hospital to get Lucrezia."

"Tell me what's wrong!" By this time Jackie was trembling, thinking Lucrezia had been involved in some sort of an accident.

Tom was hysterical as he stomped around the office, pounding his fists into the walls and throwing things around, mumbling something about $100,000 in insurance, all the while screaming. "That God damn cunt! That motherfucking bitch!"

Jackie slammed her fist onto the desk and shouted, "Either stop your insane cussing and tell me what's going on, or I'm going to pick up something and knock you out!"

She wasn't even sure Tom heard her. He just carried on, shouting if she EVER calls here again, you tell that Goddamn cunt I don't ever want to talk to her again! She killed that baby! She fucking killed that baby! I can't believe she really did it!"

Upon hearing this, Jackie grabbed Tom's arm and led him outside the office, away from anyone who might still be lingering in the office during the lunch hour. When they got outside and out of hearing distance, she demanded an explanation.

Tom said, "Me and Crystal were sitting around the other night chugging shots of Gold Schloggers and taking hits of nose candy and she started talking about what would be the perfect fraud against an insurance company."

"What does that have to do with the phone call from Crystal?"

Tom stood staring silently, and then swallowed before he answered. He began to tremble as the words caught in his throat. "Baby Hanley," he whispered. "He's dead! He just drowned."

"WHAT!" Jackie screamed.

"Crystal just found him on the bottom of the pool. Someone left the patio door open, and he wandered out and fell into the pool."

"Someone?" she questioned. "Who else was there?"

"I don't know," Tom said. "I'm just thinking I might have left the door open last night. I don't know right now. I just know I have to get Lucrezia and take her to the hospital where they're taking him."

"Hospital?" Jackie asked. "I thought you said he drowned."

"He did, but Crystal said they still had to try to revive him until a doctor pronounces him dead, and in order to do that they have to continue CPR until they get him to a hospital. They're taking him to Midway Park General Hospital."

Jackie was shocked. "You mean this is all happening right now, and she's this calm?"

"Yeah." "Look, I'm leaving to get Lucrezia and take her to Crystal. Lucrezia is his Godmother, and she needs to be there. You hold things together here until I get back."

As he walked away, Jackie stood in shock and disbelief trying to put the pieces of his story together and make some sense of this strange group of people.

Later that evening, before she left the office, Jackie received a phone call from Lucrezia, who told her that baby Hanley had in fact drowned, but there was something they needed to talk about.

"What's that?" Jackie asked.

"Well, Tom told me he flipped out when he got the phone call and he said some things that he shouldn't have said to you." Then she started going into details about the drowning and telling Jackie she'd talked to the paramedic, who stated the drowning was in fact an accident.

Jackie's take on this conversation was that Lucrezia wanted to convince her to ignore Tom's accusations against Crystal. Anyway, the baby was dead, and Crystal was $100,000 dollars better off. Jackie couldn't understand why any mother would insure an innocent child for that kind of money, but she never posed that question to Lucrezia. Instead she decided to observe from a distance and see what happened next. After all, perhaps the drowning really was an accident, and everyone was just acting crazy because of the grief.

Lucrezia then asked Jackie if she was coming to the funeral.

"Absolutely not!" Jackie replied. "There's no way I can handle that. No way. Just give Crystal my condolences."

Jackie hung up the phone, even more shocked as her thoughts ran wild about the whole situation. The next day Tom returned to work, subdued and acting somewhat normally for someone in a management position. He kept his composure well and conducted the ordinary business at hand. Whatever had happened between him and Lucrezia from the time he received that phone call from Crystal, no one else knew. But evidently their divorce was on hold.

Jackie thought it must have taken some serious begging and groveling on Tom's part to get Lucrezia to take him back, or else the two of them decided to protect each other and maintain what they knew with absolute silence. Whatever it was, it caused them to stop in the middle of the funeral planning to get with their lawyers and drop the divorce in its tracks. Jackie could tell that this incident really stirred something inside Tom when she saw a look of fear on his face that ran all the way to the core.

During the next weeks to follow, no one mentioned Crystal or Hanley Jaeger again. And whenever Lucrezia spoke, Tom responded. He was there for her every beck and call. He spent the entire day before the funeral making phone calls, trying to undo what he'd messed up when they separated, but he found the only way he could save face with the IRS was to pay Lucrezia's back taxes himself. Strangely, he didn't seem to mind this.

The next morning, Jackie opened the newspaper to read the obituary for baby Hanley. She looked at his picture there among the older folks and wiped away tears, as it all became a reality. She tried to focus through her tears. This was the exact picture she'd received a few weeks earlier, taken of Hanley wearing his favorite overalls. Jackie remembered the day she first met Hanley, and how she'd thought him such a loving child when he pressed his face into her neck and snuggled against her, almost melting into her as she held him. Jackie wondered if she should attend the funeral. But as she sat there looking at his picture, she decided against going, because she preferred to cherish the happy memories of the loving toddler she was so fond of. She could not imagine being in Crystal's position. Just the thought of it all sent pains through her, making it difficult for her to breath.

She took scissors from her desk drawer, cut the obituary from the paper, and folded it neatly in half before sliding it behind the same picture of Hanley she already carried in her billfold. She couldn't help but grieve openly for Crystal's loss as she closed the billfold with much the same feeling she felt as if she was closing a book after reading the final chapter.

As she put it away, something else occurred to Jackie. She pondered on just how unnatural it must be to bury your own child. Although it would be difficult to lose a parent, that is God's way of carrying life onward. But when a parent losses a child, they lose not only their past, but also their future.

## CHAPTER TWENTY-SIX

It's been said that death comes in threes. This group was no exception, because later that afternoon Jackie took a phone call that her grandmother had just passed away. Leaving the office to take care of the normal things one needs to handle at such a time, Jackie felt the next three days were almost a peaceful rest from the day-to-day crises around the office. She felt comfortable among family and friends during her time away, and she dreaded going back to the office when her grandmother's funeral was behind her.

But when she did return, she found that Lucrezia's mother had unexpectedly died. Jackie collected money from everyone to send flowers, although no one had done so for her grandmother.

What Jackie found to be most unusual was the fact that Tom was not going to the funeral. This was so strange to Jackie that she asked him. "Don't you think you should attend your mother-in-law's funeral?"

Tom shrugged. "No, not really. Her dad doesn't like me."

"Nobody likes you," Jackie said, "But that never stopped you before."

"You're really funny." Tom replied.

"Well, it's true. Why aren't you going, really?" Then it hit her. She smiled and said, "I know why. They don't know the two of you are back together, right?"

Tom just ducked his head as Jackie shouted, "I knew it! I knew they were smart people—and with class too!" She turned and walked away, calling over her shoulder, "They don't approve of their daughter running with the likes of you! If they only knew."

Tom followed Jackie into her office where he shut the door and sat down on the opposite side of the desk. "I thought I told you before, her dad is a CEO for a big government company."

Jackie snapped back at him, "You said you didn't remember any of that conversation on the plane? So Daddy doesn't approve of his little girl's husband. So what do you think he's gonna do when he finds out that you two are back together?"

"Nothing," Tom mumbled. "Maybe we won't be together when he finds out."

"Oh really?" Jackie turned and flipped the blinds open so she could see the parking lot. "Maybe I need to set up command watch again."

Tom said, "Nooo, it's nothing like that. We just may not be compatible with one another."

Jackie laughed. "You're the only two in the world who don't already know it. Tom, she's from M-O-N-E-Y. Anyone can see that. And you, you're from—who knows? Where the hell are you from?"

"What do you think?" Tom asked, draping one arm over the chair.

Jackie tapped one finger against her head. "Well, let's see. When you're sober you're from Minnesota, but when you're drinking you're from the Bronx. And that's when you give me the impression you have some hidden Mafia connections or something. Is that what you really did in Minnesota? Or was it the Bronx? So, tell me, Tom, who are you—really?" She paused, staring at him. "And you really wanna know what I think? I think you're working here under some police protection program while hiding your true identity. Am I right? Because I've always been a pretty good judge of character, and from some of the drunken conversations I heard from you, that's the only thing that would make sense of this whole situation."

Several minutes into this conversation, Jackie realized that Tom wasn't participating. She paused as *Oh, My God!* screamed inside her head. She stared at him, waiting for him to tell her that she was wrong... but he didn't. Instead she noticed the color had drained from his face. He was now chewing on his lower lip like he always did when he was nervous, waiting for her to finish ranting and raving. Just then, she experienced the same life-threatening fear she'd felt when she was being attacked. Except this time something inside her screamed SHUT UP! The light came on as she realized she was probably right about Tom.

Now, she desperately needed to somehow recant everything she'd said and convince him it was a joke. Her timing was the most important thing here, and she sensed that from deep inside. She added, "And yeah, I'm marrying the Pope!"

But she was so full of fear that the delivery didn't come off exactly as she'd hoped, so she tried to act all involved in something else. Tom simply stood, without uttering a word, and walked out of Jackie's office closing the door behind him. Jackie was so tense, and yet relieved, that she had to stand and bend forward to get her next breath. Then she sat down and placed her head on the desk for a few minutes, trying to gain her balance and get control of herself so she could get up enough nerve to open the door and face everyone without giving away her feelings.

As she pondered on it, she realized that if she'd guessed right he would never in a million years confess it to her, but the feeling in her gut was so strong that she knew she'd have to disprove her suspicions to herself before she could ever move past it. That meant that in order to seek the truth she would have to somehow remain involved and keep an open mind, neither judging or questioning, until Tom felt comfortable enough to let his guard down and confide in her. Jackie was scared of the truth, yet she was even more scared not to know the truth. She asked herself, *does the company know? How could they not know?*

Then the realization hit her. This is crazy! I must be really paranoid from what happened before with that Neal guy. What's wrong with me? She'd jumped to a huge conclusion with no real evidence to confirm it, and she felt that she owed Tom an apology. After all, Tom had handled the problem for her with that Neal creep, and now she was having paranoid delusions about him. She now felt not only stupid, but also guilty. She left her office to go apologize to Tom for her thoughtless remarks.

As she stepped into his office, he looked up at her without saying a word. She said, "Tom, I'm sorry. I guess I'm still paranoid about what happened with that creep Neal and I just flipped out and said that stupid shit to you. I'm sorry. I know you're here because of a bad divorce. I don't know what happened to me to say those things to you." She stopped for a breath. "I only hope that you can find it in yourself to accept my apologies. I feel like an ass after you handled that incident for me, and then I acted so stupid toward you during this time of your wife's loss."

Tom held up a hand. "Okay, okay. Just shut up and forget about it. I accept your apologies. Goddamn, now I know how you felt when I made an ass out of myself in the airport that time. We're even! No more! Leave!" he shouted. "Just get back to work and close my door on the way out!"

## CHAPTER TWENTY-SEVEN

The holidays were just around the corner, and business was slowing down. Jackie's thoughts centered on that previous conversation with George when he gave her the beautiful diamond ring and said, "Whenever you're ready, I hope it's me you choose."

She'd started daydreaming about a wedding and realized it was time to accept George's proposal. Not certain just how she'd break the news to George, she devised a plan. Since she had a grown son and daughter from a previous marriage she decided to visit with them and share her plans before moving forward with the wedding. She called right then and reserved plane tickets to California, which was where her son Brian was living. She bought a ticket for Regina to come up from Houston, where she lived with her father, so she could accompany them to California from Dallas. Jackie knew she wouldn't back out on her plans once she'd bought and paid for the tickets. With that in mind, she also made reservations for the restaurant where George had proposed to her. She thought this would be a nice surprise and assumed George would pick up on her intentions as soon as he heard about the reservations.

The day she planned to surprise him, she called George to make sure he'd shut down his crew a little early. George eagerly agreed as he always did, but this somehow caused Jackie to develop butterflies. She hung up the phone with her palms all sweaty and could hear her own heart pounding inside her chest. Just then Dexter knocked on her door. When she looked up at him, he asked, "Are you okay? You look a little pale."

"I'm fine," she replied. "What's up?"

Dexter said, I need you and Tom in my office to go over some deals and make some decisions."

She and Dexter mulled over the files for several minutes while waiting for Tom to finish with a customer. Jackie kept checking her watch, and finally Dexter asked, "Are you expecting someone? You keep looking at the time."

"No, I'm just a little nervous. It's nothing, really." At his questioning look she added, "Okay, I'm having a private dinner with George tonight, and I'm a little nervous, that's all.

"You act like—Oh, I know. You're gonna take him up on his offer! You're gonna say Yes! You're GONNA GET MARRIED!" he shouted.

"It looks that way, but keep your voice down. I don't want anyone to know just yet."

But Dexter butted in with his lame opinion, "Well personally, I don't think it would be a good ideal for you to marry outside "the family," but you do whatever you want. I will tell you this: IF you marry George, your chances of ever getting a management job in this company are slim and none, and slim just left town. That's just something I feel I need to share with you."

Jackie snapped, "I don't appreciate your opinion and I'll thank you to keep it to yourself. This is MY personal business and I don't need any of your advice." Before Dexter could respond, she added, "And I'll marry whoever I want, not what best fits this company's desires. You got that? Besides what's wrong with George?"

Dexter held up both hands. "Do whatever you want, Jackie, but don't blame me if getting married costs you a management position."

Jackie was so mad she stormed out of his office to avoid a further confrontation.

Before she could close the door behind her, Dexter shouted, "She's a swallower, not a spitter, boys!"

Jackie could not believe what she's just heard. She spun around in her tracks and swung his door open with such force that the doorknob stuck inside the wall when it came to a sudden stop. She could almost feel the steam escaping through her ears as she shouted, "What did you say?"

Dexter chuckled. "That means you're—"

Before he could finish, Jackie scooped up a folder full of papers from his desk, threw them in his face, and shouted. "Don't you EVER make the mistake of saying that to me or about me again or I'll have George sitting in the middle of your chest as he drains the life slowly from your lungs. Now, I need to hear an apology from you and make it loud enough that everyone who heard your repulsive comment understands it will NOT be tolerated. And you'd better sound convincing."

"Okay, Okay. I'm sorry you heard me say it!" Dexter replied as he chuckled out loud.

Just then Jackie drew back her fist, intending to take Dexter out. As she began her roundhouse swing, someone grabbed her fist from behind.

"Dexter, she's right. You're bucking for a sexual harassment suit. I think you need to apologize to Jackie and everyone else, and I hope you don't think you can get away with talking to her like that."

Jackie was surprised and appreciative as she turned to see Stuart, who had stepped in and spoken up in her defense. Dexter was embarrassed by what Stuart said before he apologized for his remark while Stuart leaned over his desk staring directly into his face. Jackie was grateful that someone else felt the same way she did. She appreciated Stuart's actions, but she still felt upset as she left to go back to her office.

Before long, Stuart popped into Jackie's office. He told her he too was tired of all the crap around the office and had requested a transfer to another territory.

"Really? Where?" she asked.

"Well, my father-in-law is also in management with the company. Not many people know that. I think I'm going to transfer into his district and take over management of a brand new lot."

"Wow, that's great! When are you going?" Jackie asked.

"In a couple of weeks," he replied. "And I'm wondering about something. You're obviously not happy here either, and I was wondering if you and George would like to transfer with me? I've already talked to my father-in-law, and he's been watching your stats and knows how good you are. I know you aren't prepared to make a decision right away, but please talk it over with George, privately of course, and get back with me as soon as you can."

Jackie was stunned, but impressed with this offer. "I might just take you up on that. But of course I do need to discuss everything with George. I'll let you know soon."

"Great!" Stuart said. "But promise you'll keep this just between us. I don't want anyone to know until I'm ready to move on it."

"Sure, Stuart. And by the way, just who is your father-in-law?"

"Peyton Gathers," he replied.

Stuart left her office and Jackie thought, *This explains why Stuart's always so involved in his own world.* Curious, she pulled out her company directory, searching for Peyton's location and position on the corporate food chain. "My, my," she mumbled. Stuart's father-in-law was in the same position of authority as regional president Richard Spaniel. But why hadn't Stuart gone to work for his father-in-law in the first place? Dismissing her questions for the moment, she decided to focus on whether or not she could manage to somehow leave this ungodly den of iniquity, move to another area, and still maintain the pay structure she was accustomed to. Stuart's offer was definitely worth serious thought.

Jackie decided that maybe it would be best if she had Brian and Regina come to Dallas to visit her and George, so she called and changed the ticket reservations from her and George flying to California to Brian and Regina each flying into Dallas. She figured that if she and George did decide to accept a job transfer it might start in a couple of weeks, and she had much to accomplish in that time.

Just then she took a phone call from George, who began with an apology, "Honey, I'm sorry, but I'm about 150 miles outside of Dallas. I'm having truck problems and if I can't get a mechanic out here to fix it we may not be able to make our reservations tonight. Can we go at a later time or reschedule for another night? What do you think?"

"I'll call the restaurant and reschedule. We'll see what happens," Jackie replied.

"What does that mean?"

"Oh, nothing," she said. "We'll talk whenever you get home."

With that, George set out on a mission to find a mechanic so he could get home.

As the evening faded it was obvious that George would be very late. About 9:00 p.m. she'd decided to fix herself something to eat and settle in for a night of TV. Just then she heard George pulling into the drive.

As she was putting leftovers in the microwave, George rushed through the door, apologizing. "What did we need to talk about?" He asked, giving her a bear hug.

"The kids are coming to see us." She wiggled loose so she could see his face.

"Oh, really? What for?" George peered into the microwave.

"I thought it would be nice to have them here for the wedding."

George froze. "Wedding?"

She stared at him for a few moments. "I was planning to accept your offer tonight over dinner at that famous restaurant in Las Colinas, but you stood me up, and now I'm not sure what that means."

"It means I had truck trouble and I'm really sorry I was late."

When he finally realized what Jackie was saying, George sank onto one knee and took her hand. "If I ask you again, right now, to marry me, would you accept?"

"I don't know. I'm kinda outta the mood now," she jokingly replied.

"Give me a break!" He shouted.

"Okay, okay, I accept!" Jackie bowed her head in a bashful-schoolgirl way.

"Are you serious? You're finally ready?"

"I think so," she whispered.

"FINALLY!" George shouted. "After three years, I get a 'Yes'! When do you want to do this?"

"How about two weeks?"

"Great! We'll get the license tomorrow and send out invitations. How many people are we going to invite?"

"Not many. I'd like to keep it simple, so we'll just ask family and friends—nobody from work."

Every spare minute of the next three weeks was spent rushing around: reserving the hall, fitting a tux for George, and shopping for just the right flowers and wedding dress. Then on December 31, 1995, Jackie Weatherby and George Kennard stood before God and thirty-five of their friends and family members as a woman judge married them, offering her suggestions for a lasting marriage. She said, "I can almost guarantee everyone here that at some time in the future one or both of these two people will want to end this marriage. I'm not basing that on anything I personally know about either of these two, but that's based on divorce statistics that show that one in every two marriages don't make it. I've thought about that a lot because I perform many weddings, and I've decided the key to a good and successful marriage is not so much *finding* the right partner, as *being* the right partner. So please keep that in mind as your life journey begins with the vows you are both about to take, and promise one another you will work to be the right partner. George, do you have a ring to offer?" George took the ring from his pocket and held it up for her to see.

The judge acknowledged this with a tilt of her head and began the reciting of vows. "I, George Kennard, take thee, Jackie Weatherby, as my lawful wedded wife."

As George repeated the words he looked directly into Jackie's eyes. Then it was Jackie's turn. The judge asked, "Jackie, do you have a ring to offer?"

"Yes," she replied, pulling it off her thumb from under her bouquet. Then Jackie expressed the same vows to George, repeating them as instructed by the judge.

The judge announced, "I now pronounce you husband and wife. And now, George, you may kiss your bride!"

And with that, George and Jackie became man and wife. Everyone clapped and threw birdseed on the couple, taking them by surprise as they departed the chapel. They held the reception at an area club with all their wedding party and several hundred other people in attendance. Their honeymoon trip to Cabos San Lucas wasn't scheduled until the coming month.

Everyone loves a wedding, and there were lots of well-wishers among the New Year's Eve crowd. Every time they returned to their table from the dance floor someone sent over drinks. Just before midnight, George took Jackie by the hand, still wearing her wedding dress, and led her onto the dance floor, but this time he carried with him a chair where he sat Jackie down. Then he circled around her before he knelt down, kissing her. He slipped the garter off her leg and stood with it spinning round and round on his finger, holding it above his head as the crowd cheered and the single guys gathered round him hoping to be the one to catch it as George let it sail through the air. There was a scramble, and after what seemed like eternity someone jumped up shouting, "I got it! I got it!"

Everyone was anxious to see who caught it, but no one could believe their eyes when Brian arose victorious, waving the garter his own mother had worn in her wedding! He grinned ear to ear and everyone roared with laughter as he replied, "Oh well—I'll take all the luck I can get. Maybe I'll find somebody now. Who knows?"

Jackie just shook her head in disbelief as she laughed at him. Then, with George's help, she climbed onto the chair and threw the bridal bouquet into the crowd. By this time, there were probably a couple of hundred ladies eager to catch that bouquet. She looked around the dance floor before circling it over her head. Every woman was screaming, "Throw it to me! Toss it over here." Then one shouted, "I need all the help I can get—just hand it to me!"

With that, she turned and tossed it over her shoulder into the screaming crowd. The ensuing riot was something to behold; several women shredded the bouquet into parts as they literally fought to claim it for their own. Just then, the countdown to midnight started, and the whole crowd took up the shouting—8-7-6-5-4... George whisked Jackie down from the chair while held her there in his arms until they finished the countdown. They kissed, and then he carried her in his arms out the door, taking her home to begin the New Year and their new life together.

## CHAPTER TWENTY-EIGHT

Jackie returned to work after the wedding refreshed and eager to talk more with Stuart about their plans to transfer with him to his father-in-law's, Mr. Gathers', lot. Because they didn't want any complications from Dexter before things were worked out, they talked in private and only when Dexter and Tom weren't around. Although Jackie and George had discussed it and decided it was what they both wanted to do, they still needed to work out the details with Mr. Gathers, and they planned to visit with him in a few days.

But before Jackie got to talk with Mr. Gathers, Dexter and Tom called her from Dexter's office and told her they needed to discuss something with her. Fearing they knew something of her plans, she prepared herself for the worst. As Jackie stepped into the office, Dexter just sat looking at her, not saying anything. Feeling even more nervous, she was certain someone had let the cat out of the bag.

"Why are you staring at me?" she asked.

Dexter didn't reply. Jackie then turned to Tom and asked, "Is there something you need to talk to me about?"

Still silent, Dexter slid a paper across the desk toward Jackie.

She looked at the paper, lying face down and then looked up at Dexter and Tom. "What is it?"

"Just something you need to take care of," Dexter replied, maintaining the blank stare.

Now Jackie was really curious as she picked up the paper and turned it over so she could read it. The paper was titled Internal Revenue Service, which really caught her eye. Both Dexter and Tom knew Jackie had previously received a letter from the Internal Revenue regarding some back taxes owed by her ex husband. She thought perhaps the problem had surfaced again and this notice was in reference to setting a payment. By now, her attention was focused entirely on the paper, which read:

To Male Taxpayers. Regarding Increased Tax Payment. The only thing the Internal Revenue Service has not taxed is your penis. This is due to the fact that 40% of the time it is hanging around unemployed; 30% of the time it is pissed off; 20% of the time it is hard up; while 10% of the time it is unemployed. But it operates in the hole. Furthermore, it has two dependents, and they are both nuts!

After January 1, 1996, your pecker will be taxed based on its size, using the "peckercracker" scale below determine your category. Insert the additional tax under Other Tax page 13 part 5 line 61 of your standard income tax return.

| Scale | 10" to 12" | Luxury Tax | $30.00 |
|---|---|---|---|
| | 8" to 10" | Pole Tax | $25.00 |
| | 6" to 8" | Privilege Tax | $15.00 |
| | 4" to 6" | Nuisance Tax | $5.00 |
| | 1" to 2" | Todd | $1.00 |

Do Not Apply For An Extension.
Note: Males with peckers in excess of 12" should file under capital gain.

Refusing to show any expression that either of the two sick bastards might take as amusement, Jackie remained calm and steady as Dexter asked, "Well, are you finished reading?"

Jackie looked at him with complete disgust on her face, but before she could respond, Dexter stood up and unzipped his pants, reached his whole hand inside, feeling around while rolling his eyes back and forth. He took his penis in hand and stated, "I need you to measure Kujo for me so I can pay my taxes."

But instead of his penis, he pulled out a live 14-inch-long snake from inside his pants! Jackie screamed, jumped to her feet, and ran out the door. Behind her, she heard Tom's hysterical laughter. Completely freaked out by this and scared out of her wits, Jackie ran into her office and slammed the door. Meanwhile, both Tom and Dexter continued howling.

Jackie sat at her desk, breathing hard. They had now stepped over the line. She had no other choice than to take action elsewhere up the management line. The next day she drove to Richard's office to visit with him about the snake incident and other problems. However after she arrived, Hillary met her just inside the entry and proudly informed Jackie that Richard was too busy to talk with her—then or any other time.

Jackie smiled and said, "That's fine, Hillary. I'm off today, so I can just sit in the front office all day. When he comes through here and sees me waiting all day he'll probably want to talk with me, or at least set an appointment." She knew Hillary was stalling until she could talk to Dexter and find out why Jackie was there. So Jackie took up residence in the front office with her magazine, a sandwich, and a soft drink that she'd packed away in her backpack. She waited it out, exchanging strained smiles with Hillary every time she walked through the office.

After a couple of hours, Richard stepped out and asked. "Jackie, what's going on?"

"I need to schedule an appointment to talk with you about some issues."

"Like what?" he asked.

"I'd rather not discuss them here in the lobby," she replied, looking toward Hillary's office.

"That's fine, but I'm booked today. How about I meet with you next Thursday?

"If that's the earliest you can see me, then I guess it will have to do." As Jackie left, she looked down the hallway directly into Hillary's office and they locked stares. Jackie didn't like the idea of having to meet with Richard, but Dexter and Tom left her no other choice with their stupidity and outrageous behavior.

The next day when Jackie arrived at work, she got the cold shoulder from both Tom and Dexter. They must have agreed to say nothing, which suited Jackie fine until she found that someone had posted a horrible picture of a shriveled up rat on the door of her office to greet her. This was again an attempt on their part to stop her from complaining to Richard.

She spent the entire day catching up on contracts and paperwork, staying mostly inside her office away from everyone else. However, she could tell she'd caused quite a stir among the group because they kept to themselves, never bothering or calling her all day long. Almost like a standoff. But Jackie had made her decisions: she was going to see Richard, and she was going to transfer. She didn't care if Dexter and Tom crawled to her begging and groveling, she was through taking their crap. The snake was the last straw!

A few minutes before she was scheduled to go home, Dexter called on the intercom and asked her to come to his office. She refused.

"What do you mean, 'No way?'" Dexter shouted.

"Just what I said. I'm not coming into your office."

Dexter hung up the phone and bolted through Jackie's office door with an attitude that said, *I'll show you! You aren't going to be disrespectful to me in front of my employees.*

But Jackie, like everyone else, was unimpressed with his outburst of authority when he slammed the door and shouted, "I thought I told you to never go over my head again! What do you mean going to Richard's office and refusing to leave?"

Jackie looked up at him, barely batting an eye.

Again, Dexter shouted, "Are you gonna answer me or not?"

"OR NOT!" she shouted back at him.

"Then I have no choice other than to fire you!"

Jackie shrugged and replied, "Okay. But first let me make sure I understand you, Dexter. You were the one who unzipped your pants pulled out a live snake, insinuating it was your dick, telling me to measure it. You were the one who put out a $50 bounty for one of my pubic hairs."

Dexter's expression changed.

Waving her finger back and forth, "Ah, you didn't know I knew about that one, did you? Weren't you the one who gave me that funny shaped vibrator and told me to go satisfy myself? You also told your wife we were 'fuck buddies' and were having an affair. You instructed Todd to drop his pants and moon everyone in front of me at a sales meeting. You told me that if I married outside the "family" I would sever my chances of ever getting into management with this company, yet I operate at management capacity daily—although I don't get management pay benefits."

Rolling her eyes, tapping her index finger against her mouth. "You were the one who shouted your announcement to everyone about me that—and I quote you, 'She's a swallower and not a spitter.'"

"All right, all right," Dexter said.

"Oh no, it's not all right. Please, let me finish." Jackie shouted. "You were the one who unzipped your pants in front of other employees, and offered to "lubricate" my throat the time I had laryngitis. You were the one who opened my office door, stuck your butt in, and farted before slamming the door shut. You were the one who announced for all to hear, 'I may be a little guy, but I've got a Big Dick' before you unzipped your pants and reached in as you asked me, 'Wanna see?'

"You're the one who refers to your dick as Kujo and threatens me that IF I don't do things your way, you'll sic Kujo on me. You told the paint contractor I would sleep with him if he'd lower his prices for you. Like I was yours to offer!"

Jackie paused to take a breath before she continued. "Now please, allow me just a moment to understand you. Are you going to fire me because I went to Richard or because Richard told you to after I went to his office?"

Dexter again shouted at Jackie, "Like I told you before—he told me to!"

"Great! If you do that, I'd appreciate it, because then I can go straight to a lawyer and past the regional president's office. I think I'd like that better anyway. Why don't you just go ahead and fire me?"

Then Dexter shouted again, so that everyone could hear, "I've already talked with Richard and he instructed me to do that!"

"Okay," Jackie replied. "If that's the way you want to do it, that's better for me. Either way, I'm going over your head—again—and if I have to go outside this company and over Richard's head to gain the right to a decent work environment, then so be it. Now, you can tell Richard I said that or I'll tell him myself. I really don't care, but I have the right under the law to a safe and healthy working environment and that's the L A W. So if you'll excuse me, I'm off the clock and I'm tired of giving my time away to someone who abuses it. I'm leaving for the day."

With that, she left her office and turned off the light, leaving Dexter sitting there in the dark. Jackie could tell he hadn't thought out his plan and was a little shaken by what she'd just said to him, enough that he probably feared for his job. But she was tired of the abuse in the name of job training. Jackie had come to the conclusion that she was not going to tolerate any more.

Before she could leave the office, Tom asked her to come into his office and talk with him for a minute. She sat down in front of his desk, thinking she could at least hear his input. Tom was cautious with Jackie and careful with his words as he offered to work something out that would allow her to keep her job.

She responded, "That's mighty gracious of you, but I don't think I'll be the one losing a job."

"What do you plan to do?" Tom asked.

"I'm not sure yet. I'm going to hold off on a decision until I've talked with Richard."

Just then Dexter bolted through the door and said, "Jackie, please accept my apology. I've said and done some things that were hurtful to you."

"What is this? The old rehearsed standard apology between you two? No, not this time."

Dexter shouted. I'm just not comfortable with your threats all the time. I never know when you're gonna explode and go running to the bosses just because you're pissed off."

Jackie laughed. "What the hell do you mean, 'whenever I get pissed off?' Think about it: The only time I get pissed off is when one of you two do something stupid to me like that episode with the snake or the story about Hillary thinking that we're 'fuck buddies.'"

Tom said, "Hey, Jackie, consider yourself fortunate. The last time he did that IRS skit he threw the snake on the guy from across the desk."

Jackie shook her head. "You're both sick, and neither one of you has a clue about how to manage people. I don't give a shit what Richard thinks about my decision, but I'll guarantee you both that if I don't get the results I want, I'll go outside this company and I *know* you won't like what happens then."

Dexter's face turned red, and he held a dramatic pause before he jumped up and shouted, "Do whatever you want, Bitch. You're gonna anyway!" With that, he flung the door open, impacting the knob into the wall directly beside Jackie's head. He turned looking over his shoulder before he screamed, "Fuck you!" toward Jackie as he stomped out of the office.

Jackie remained in the chair too shocked to move. She just stared in at Tom, but he, too, couldn't believe what he'd just witnessed. Then to make matters worse, Dexter started throwing things across the office lobby, breaking everything he picked up as he bounced it off the walls.

After several minutes, Dexter came back down the hallway and Jackie made a hasty exit through the front door to escape his most bizarre behavior yet. As she got in her car and started the drive home, she again felt as though she'd just stepped out of a pressure cooker.

Knowing that she was about to put all this behind her and move on made her feel somewhat better. Although they'd discussed these problems in the past, it was apparent that she now had both Dexter's and Tom's undivided attention because of her promise to conference with Richard and John Turner.

In spite of it all, Jackie was determined to make that evening a pleasant one as she and George spent it together with Brian and Regina. Or maybe just having the kids there just took her mind off all the office problems. Whichever way, she thoroughly enjoyed herself when they were together. Since Brian had to go back to California the next day, everyone focused on having a good time together. It was after 10:00 p.m. before they got home, so Jackie took a quick shower before settling in with the family. Just as she stepped out of the shower, she heard the doorbell ring.

A few seconds later Regina shouted "Mom! Can you come downstairs? You have a visitor?"

"Who is it?"

Regina replied, "I think it's Tom."

Jackie wrapped herself in a robe and hurried downstairs where she met Tom standing in the entry foyer. Tom politely said, "Jackie, I'm sorry for stopping by without notice, but can you spare a minute? I need to talk to you."

She could tell from his slurred speech that he was drinking again. Jackie replied, "Actually, Tom, I was just going to bed."

"This won't take long. Richard called me tonight. He told me that you came to see him and refused to leave until you had the chance to talk with him about some things. He instructed me to talk with you and see if I could get the problem resolved before next Thursday."

Jackie chuckled. "What if you're part of the problem?"

"Then I need to know it," he replied.

"I think you already do know it," Jackie snapped.

"Tom paused, and then stated in a begging tone, "Jackie, I've said some things and done some things that you probably found offensive, but they weren't meant to harm you in any way. I truly apologize to you and hope you can forgive me. Look, Richard basically told me under no uncertain terms that if he has another legal complaint against him it's going to be someone's ass in the sling along with his, and I can't afford for it to be mine."

"What are you referring to?" Jackie asked.

"Well, I can't talk about it here, in front of your family." Tom stared at Regina, who sat watching TV, ignoring the conversation.

Jackie replied. "Really, Tom why don't you try to find your way back home and maybe we can discuss this tomorrow sometime. Okay? I only have a few hours left with my kids before they leave, and I'd rather not spend this time discussing our office problems."

"You're right," he responded. He bowed his head in sorrow then quietly added, "I really did come over to apologize. I hope you can accept it Jackie."

She walked toward the front door, expecting Tom to follow. However he just stood there in his own stupid way, looking at Regina. Jackie had to raise her voice to get his attention, "Tom!"

He looked toward her as she stood there holding the door open for him to leave. He said, "Oh, sorry." Then he walked toward the door, but his body language said he wasn't ready to leave yet.

"Good night," Jackie stated as he stepped out the door. She closed it behind him, locking it before returning upstairs. Just then George was stepping out of the shower, "Was that Tom? What did he want?"

Jackie shook her head in disbelief as she replied, "I think he wanted to cover his ass and keep it out of any more trouble. But it didn't work."

"What kind of trouble?"

"Oh, nothing I feel comfortable discussing with you just yet, but I have to report something to Richard, and Tom's afraid he and Dexter are going to suffer some pretty serious repercussions."

"Oh well," George replied. "They shouldn't have done it, whatever it was."

"If you only knew," Jackie mumbled.

George and Jackie both went downstairs to be with Regina and Brian and watch a little TV together before going to bed for the night. But before the 10:00 news was over, the phone rang. Jackie quickly snatched it from the cradle and answered. She could NOT believe her ears. It was Tom!

He just started talking, "Well, I'm not supposed to say anything about it, but actually you know the guy. I think you even used to work for him."

"What the hell are you talking about?" Jackie questioned.

"Oh, um, that guy up in Oklahoma. I shouldn't even be telling you this, but I know you won't say anything to anybody. Okay? But he masturbated on one of his employees, a girl, and she filed a grievance against him."

"WHY ARE YOU TELLING ME THIS?" Jackie screamed. "Because they just settled the case out of court. And now Richard is all scared you're going to do the same thing. He just called me and told me to fix it, so that's why I'm telling you all this."

Jackie could not believe what she'd just heard, but there was more.

"Also Richard knows you want to go with Stuart, but he doesn't plan to approve it. He said either you work for him in his organization or nowhere, so he won't approve your transfer to Austin."

Tom then stated, "And by the way, you don't need to call Sam to talk to him about anything else again either. He doesn't need to know our business and I hope you keep it that way."

"I don't believe you!" Jackie shouted. "I'm going to end this conversation and pretend for now that it didn't happen. But I'm still going to talk to either Richard or John Turner, and if I don't get the results I feel are best for me and my situation, then I can and will go outside this company. You got that? Now good night!" With that, Jackie hung up the phone.

Brian said, "Mom I don't like that guy. Something about him isn't right."

Jackie replied, "I know. I feel the same way, and I've said the same thing, but he's my boss so I have to tolerate a certain amount of it."

George then looked at Jackie with a puzzled expression on his face. "Did I hear you right? Was that Tom again? What did you mean about not approving the transfer?"

"I'm not sure," she replied. "He's about plastered and I'm not going to hang my hat on anything he says when he's like that."

George leaned over in Jackie's direction and in a low voice said, "Honey, I know that something's going on and I still honor the promise we made to stay out of each other's working issues, but is there something I need to know about?"

"No," Jackie replied wearily as she stared at the TV. She was still in shock and could not believe what Tom had just confided, but she didn't want to discuss it with George or in front of her children.

Jackie was still angry the next day, but when she got to work neither Dexter nor Tom was there. Thinking they were both running a little late, she questioned Tammy, who told her neither of the men would be in because they were attending a managers' meeting.

"That's strange," Jackie said. "I didn't know anything about a meeting today. I wonder why I'm not supposed to be there?"

Tammy shrugged her shoulders and shook her head. "Don't ask me. I just work here. That's what I was told after I got to work today."

Later, a problem arose on a job site, requiring Jackie to leave the office. While she was gone, apparently Tom or Dexter or Richard tried unsuccessfully to call, so Tom called George and asked him to relay a message to Jackie that there was a meeting tonight at his house and she was required to be there. But when George relayed this to Jackie, her only reply was, "AGAIN? Do I have to bring the main course this time or just a bag of ice?"

George chuckled, as he replied, "He didn't say to bring anything. He just wanted me to let you know."

" Are you going, too?" Jackie asked.

"No," George said, "Tom specifically stated this is for management employees only, and that does not include me. In fact, Tom was very specific and asked me if I'd drop you off. He said he'll give you a ride home, since your car's in the shop."

"Why don't you pick me up?"

"Oh, didn't they tell you? I'm being sent out of town tonight. I have to be on a job by 7:00 a.m. and it's about 140 miles south."

"No, they didn't tell me anything about it," she replied. "Was someone supposed to tell me?"

At first Jackie thought this was at least peculiar, but then released it as just another coincidence of mismanagement. Either way, she had an uncertain queasy feeling in the pit of her stomach about the meeting. She pondered for a moment and then asked, "George, did he say what it was about?"

"No, he just said it was important that you be there, and I told him that I'd get you there. From the way he acted it must be pretty important because he asked me twice if I was sure that I could have you there."

"Did he say who else would be there?"

"Honey, I didn't ask," George said.

"Okay, okay," Jackie replied as she pondered on the situation.

# CHAPTER TWENTY-NINE

It was already dark when George pulled into the driveway at Tom's house to drop Jackie off. She felt uneasy, but she told herself it was just insecurity about being left there without her own car. George offered to walk her to the door, but he needed to get on the road. Besides, Lucrezia's car was there, so Jackie told herself she had nothing to worry about. She made her way to the door while George watched from his truck.

As Tom opened the door, he shouted "Jackie, Jackie, Jackie! I'm so glad you could make the meeting tonight."

"Where's everyone else?" She asked, looking around.

Tom grinned at her. "There won't be anyone else. Richard called and specifically requested I meet with you and get everything worked out between us."

"Oh yeah? Well, I don't think it's your place to work out my problems, and I think we just need to end this meeting right now, because my plans are to start with Richard and go up from there."

"You're making a big mistake," Tom said. "We really do need to get this resolved before it goes any further."

Jackie sensed heavy tension in the air and didn't like the tone of Tom's voice or the way he looked at her. She never heard that tone in his voice. Now completely uncomfortable, she started toward the door.

Tom's 130-pound rotweiler dog was lying against the door, and as she stepped closer, the damn thing raised his head and growled from deep within his chest, causing Jackie to stop in her tracks.

"Where are you going?" Tom asked.

"I'm leaving," Jackie stated.

"And just how will you get home?" He smugly inquired.

"I guess I'll walk," Jackie said. "Or else I'll use your cell phone and call George to come get me. He can't be that far away yet. She started for the kitchen, remembering the phone on the wall.

Tom followed her and leaned on the bar that separated the kitchen and dining room. When she picked up the receiver, Tom came up behind her, took the phone in hand and ripped its cord from the wall. Jackie was petrified with fear, not knowing what was about to happen next. She had no idea what was going through his mind.

Lucrezia was in the dining room feeding Frankie Paige, who was sitting there in her high chair like nothing was going on. Lucrezia didn't even look up.

"I'll take you home," Tom said. "But first we need to have a little talk and come to an understanding. Please, just hear me out. One time you mentioned something to me." He paused to gather his next thought before he spoke. You said you thought I am here working under some police protection program and that my real name isn't Tom Kerakasco. What made you say that?"

By now, Jackie could hear and feel her heart pounding so loud within the walls of her chest that she thought it would explode. She stood there in a daze, not sure what to say but trembling and shaking her head back and forth as she shrugged her shoulders.

Before she could answer, Tom continued, "Well, I don't know how, but you hit the nail on the head. I really am in the witness protection program. However, you cannot, I repeat NOT mention this to anyone." He shouted in her face, "You got that?"

Jackie was still frozen with fear, unable to say a word as he continued.

"I spent most of my adult life in the pen. I testified in a very high-profile case back in New York. There were eight defendants, and because of the high security they sent me here and changed my identity."

Jackie glanced at Lucrezia to get her reaction to this story Tom was telling. Just as they looked at one another, Lucrezia smiled and nodded her head. She continued feeding Frankie Paige as though Tom were talking about the weather. Lucrezia then added, "Why do you think we have different last names?"

Jackie was stunned and could not begin to think of anything other than getting the hell back home alive, as it became apparent that her worst fears were correct.

Tom said, "Jackie you need to understand something. I can't be uncovered; it would cost me my life and possibly put my family's in jeopardy. Both of them. I'll do whatever you need me to do in order to help you further your career, but you cannot implicate me in ANY legal issues. As a matter of fact, you owe Lucrezia for even being alive today. You see, the day you figured me out, I came home and told her I was probably going to have to knock you off. She spent four hours talking me out of it."

Lucrezia added, "We kinda like you. You're such a good person that it's a good idea to keep you around. She smiled at Frankie Paige and asked, "Isn't that right Frankie Paige?" Frankie Paige giggled with innocent agreement.

Tom said, "I will NOT lose my family over some stupidity that Dexter did to you. I hope you can understand where I'm coming from."

Jackie felt herself becoming faint, and she asked for a glass of water. Lucrezia said, "Sit down, honey. I know this all sounds crazy, because it did to me to the first time that I heard it. But you have to understand we live under the microscope every day and we can't take any chances. I hope you understand. We're trying to have a baby together, and I want him here to help me raise the children."

Tom added, "Just one more thing, Jackie, before we let you go home and think about your decision. We know a lot of people in a lot of areas, and if you and George want to maintain your careers—and your lifestyle—then you'll keep our little secret just between us. Believe me, I'll know if you tell ANYONE, so I suggest that you keep your mouth shut! You got that?"

Jackie nodded yes, still unable to speak.

"By the way, how old is your daughter, Regina?"

Jackie shouted, "You fucking better leave Regina out of this! Do you understand me? I'll fucking kill you over one of my kids!"

Tom just chuckled and in his smart-ass tone replied, "Then you know exactly how I feel. So I take it we've reached an understanding."

"I don't have a choice, do I?" Jackie asked. All the time she was thinking, *say anything to get the hell out of Tom's house and back home alive.*

"Sure you do," he replied. "But just remember it may not be at the price you're willing to pay. Come on, I'm taking you home." He took her arm and steered her toward the front door.

Jackie was terrified, but as she climbed into his truck for the six-mile drive to her house, she knew that in order to keep her life and protect her loved ones, she needed to prove to Tom that he could trust her. Just a few blocks from his house he stopped for gas. This made Jackie even more nervous. She wondered if he was planning to drive somewhere and do something stupid to her. Then she decided that if his story were in fact true, he'd be the first one suspected if she went missing—especially since George had dropped her at the house and would be able to tell the police. If Tom's outrageous story were true, then he certainly wouldn't want that.

As they drove down the road, Tom burst out with his insane laughter before he confided that it really felt good to talk to someone who could understand what kind of hell his life had been and how he liked being able to tell the truth for once instead of living the fantasy witness protection life.

Jackie asked, "Tom, why were you telling me this?"

"Because I like you, and like I told you, if you go forward on your threats and there's an investigation, I'll be in grave danger. So I'm going to make sure everything gets taken care of before it goes in that direction."

"What do you mean taken care of?"

"Just what I said. I'm going to transfer to my own lot when they promote me to general manager status, and I've requested they transfer you with me as my assistant."

"Your assistant! What the hell are you saying? I don't want to work with you!" Jackie screamed.

"But Jackie," Tom replied, "You really need to accept it. This is how it's going to be. Now that you've uncovered my past, I have to make sure it's kept quiet, and the only way to ensure both our lives are safe is to be where we can watch over one another. Otherwise, if you decide to leave... well, let's put it this way. I'll just hunt you down. And don't think I can't." He parked just down the street from her house and continued.

"Think about it Jackie. I won't need to hear back from you, because your next move will determine my course of action. But you need to understand something, Jackie. I testified against some Really Bad People. Don't think I ain't capable of knocking you off. I've killed before. And if it means the difference between life and death or freedom, don't think I won't do it again. The last motherfucker who planned to rat on me ended up with his brains all over the wall before he could make it to city hall. I can wait. Believe me, you can't keep your guard up forever. That motherfucker let his guard down just one time, and I was there. Right when he stepped off that elevator our eyes locked and we stared at one another, frozen in time, looking down the barrel of my gun. He knew he was mine! I shot that motherfucker in the head five times, and then I shot him in both eyes just to make sure I was the last thing he saw before God!" Tom snickered.

His disgusting snickers make Jackie cringe at the thought of what he was telling her. She longed to jump out of the truck, but Tom had locked both doors.

"Believe me, you don't want to know who I really am. I can make a phone call and make people go away just like that." He snapped his fingers in the air. "So, if you plan on staying healthy and alive, then I suggest that you change your plans and EXCLUDE ME FROM YOUR IMPLICATIONS!"

Jackie was hysterical as she held her hands over her ears and screamed, "Take me home! Shut up and take me home now! I don't want to hear any more!"

"I am taking you home!" he shouted back at her. "But I promised George I'd see that you got safely inside, so I have to go in and look around for you."

"The hell you do! I don't want you inside my house, now or ever. I have security and all I have to do is hit the panic button and police are here in less than three minutes. So I suggest you just drop me off and be on your way."

Tom put the truck in gear and cruised in front of her house. Jackie unlocked the door, opened it, and was ready to jump out even before he came to a stop.

"Just a minute," he shouted. "Don't jump yet!"

"Real funny," she snapped to him. "Just fuckin stop here!" When she leaped out of the truck, she thought she was home safe until she heard Tom's door open and close immediately after hers. She was now in full stride, running toward the door to let herself in. As she fumbled with the key in the lock she said, "I hope you don't plan on coming in."

"Well, I did make that promise to George. Besides this is fun—kinda like the fox getting to watch the henhouse."

"Get the fuck back or I'm hitting the panic button!" Jackie stepped inside, and the entry alarm began ringing.

Tom didn't know that was normal for the home security system, and he quickly recanted, "Okay, I'm leaving, but if anything happens to you, I'll have to tell George you refused to let me search the house!" And with that he turned, obviously afraid the police were about to show up, and hurried back to his truck. He stopped beside the vehicle and turned to look at Jackie before she closed the house door.

Immediately, she ran upstairs and into the closet where George kept his gun, fully loaded, all the while wondering why she didn't have the security system monitored. She was panting and shaking as she held the gun in both hands, making sure that it was loaded before she locked herself in her bedroom and crawled fully dressed under the covers. Time slipped away as she sat rocking back and forth for hours, trying to comfort herself from the terror she'd just gone through.

The ringing phone brought her back to reality. She threw back the covers to look at the clock to see that it was just before 11:00 p.m. She answered the phone, desperately hoping it was George.

"Honey, we finally made it. Did you have a good evening?" He asked.

Jackie remembered what Tom had said about not telling anyone. She replied carefully, "Well, I made it home alive."

George chuckled. "Did Tom check out the house like I asked him to?"

"Don't ever ask him to do that again. I don't feel comfortable with him in the house without you around." They chatted for a few minutes and Jackie tried to hide her fear. Just hearing George's voice made her feel better.

Still, after they hung up, she sat up in bed all night, trying to comfort herself and figure out her game plan so she and her family would come through alive. How could she handle the situation without ever telling what was really going down? Realizing her only option was to stay near Tom, she burst into tears and beat the pillow with her fist.

## CHAPTER THIRTY

The next day Jackie didn't plan to go into the office, but sometime around midmorning she got a call from Dexter. "Are you sick?" he asked.

"No, why do you ask?"

"Well, because you didn't show up for work today."

"Oh," she sighed, "I'm still waiting for Regina to get here with my car, she spent the night with a friend."

"Don't bother," Dexter snapped. "Just show up whenever you feel like it." He slammed down the phone.

Jackie wasn't sure what he meant, but she really didn't care. She walked downstairs to fix herself something to drink just as Regina pulled into the drive and rushed in the back door.

"Mom, I'm sorry I'm late! We stayed up all night reminiscing. Do you want me to take you to work or something?"

"No, baby," Jackie said. "Don't worry about it. I'm scheduled off today. Besides, I have a megaheadache again."

"Why don't you get that checked out?" Regina asked.

"I probably need to." What Jackie didn't tell Regina was that she'd already been to the doctor with headaches several times, and they were unable to find anything wrong—the pain was probably caused by the stress of her job. "I think I'd like to just take the day off and do a little shopping if you'll come with me. Then I'll bring you back home so you can get some sleep, and I'll go in to the office for a few minutes to check on things."

"Sounds like a great plan!"

Regina and Jackie went off to separate bathrooms to get ready. Jackie planned to pick up a tape recorder while she was out so she could record what had happened between her and Tom. She knew no one would believe her when she finally did come forth with the story, so she planned on getting something on tape from him that she could use to convince the authorities when the time was right. Not sure yet when or how she would do this, Jackie felt having his confession on tape was her best hope.

After lunch, Jackie stopped by a Radio Shack where she picked up a voice-activated, hand-held recorder. She couldn't have picked a better time to start recording, because no sooner did she get home than the phone rang and she heard Tom's voice.

"Hey, Jack, when did you plan to have the Davis house delivered?" he asked.

"I'm not sure. Why?"

"Well Dexter and I are looking at the delivery schedule and need to know, that's all."

"Tom, I'd like to enjoy one day off. I'll have to take care of it when I get back to the office. Don't worry, I'll call the delivery company myself and arrange it."

Jackie meant nothing by that remark, but before she could finish, Tom shouted, "The hell you will! I am THE ONLY ONE who arranges deliveries. You got that?"

"But I can call the delivery company…"

"No, you can't!" Tom shouted. "Even if we do own the delivery company, you CANNOT call in deliveries. So don't try it because they won't take your instructions. Dexter and I are the ONLY two they take delivery schedules from." He paused for a moment to catch his breath and added, "By the way, Jackie, did you get the notice that we're all going to be to fingerprinted?"

"Yes, I did, but I haven't yet had time to get mine done." Then it hit her: *If Tom's story were true, then what would he do about getting fingerprinted?*

"Well, there's something I need to talk with you about," he stated. Without hesitation he asked, "What does George's background look like?"

"What the hell are you insinuating?" she demanded.

"Oh, I'm not insinuating anything. I just need you to get George's fingerprints for me."

"He can get his done when I have mine taken," she replied.

There was a pause before Tom replied, "I'll call you back later," and abruptly hung the phone up.

Before Jackie could even leave the room, he called again, saying, "I couldn't talk because Dexter walked in, the nosey fuck."

Jackie was looking frantically around the room for the tape recorder as Tom continued talking in his crazy way. "Like I was asking you before we were so rudely interrupted, what does George's background look like?"

"Well to be perfectly honest…" She paused and then said, "What difference does it make?"

"Like I told you, I can't give 'em MY fingerprints, so I'll need you to get George's prints and bring his to me so I can use them for mine. Otherwise, we're both fucked!"

"Hang on!" She laid the phone for a moment while she retrieved the tape recorder from a table just outside the bedroom door. Returning hastily, she snatched the phone receiver up to get this confession on tape. As she picked up the phone, she started talking immediately to Tom. "You can't use George's fingerprints. He was military police in Vietnam, and his prints are on record with the government." There was no response from Tom. "Hello… Damn him!" she shouted as she realized that he had already hung up, and she had missed a perfect opportunity to capture his confession on tape and was simply talking into a dead phone. Just then she turned around as she heard George coming upstairs. She quickly hid the recorder in a dresser drawer.

"What's up, honey? Who were you talking to?" he asked, giving her a hug. "Why are you shaking? Is something wrong?" He pulled back and looked at her face. "What's wrong with you?"

"Nothing." She broke away from George and secluded herself in the bathroom, locking the door behind her.

But George worked his way through the locked door with some lock picking and his knife, then demanded, "Jackie why won't you tell me what's wrong? Did I do something?"

"Why do you always have to ask me that?" she shouted.

"Because I feel like I've done something wrong when you won't talk to me. If you would only tell me, maybe I could help you fix it."

But this thought only made Jackie tremble more in fear. George noticed her shaking as he grabbed her and said, "I'm sorry, I've only made it worse. I wish you could tell me something. Why can't you tell me what it is that's bothering you?"

"Because it's about my work," she said, and then burst into tears. We made a vow not to involve each other in our problems at work.

George perched on the side of the tub and pulled Jackie onto his lap as he consoled her, saying, "Honey, there is *nothing* you can't tell me. I know we made a promise about—

"No, I'll work through it myself," she said, hiding her face against his shoulder.

George shook his head. "I do believe you're the most stubborn woman I ever met."

"Thank you," she replied. "I'll take that as a compliment." She wiped away the tears and tried to smile.

"Well, that's not always a good thing," George stated. "You need to learn to share once in a while so we can communicate and work through problems together."

She sighed. "I know. But this one is mine, and I'll deal with it in my own way."

"Oh Woman!" He said. "I do believe you are part... never mind. Just think about it and try to share some of your needs with me. Please."

"I will, but not about this one."

George shook his bowed head and said, "You're impossible!"

Jackie wanted to tell him, but she knew that wasn't a good option. There was no telling what George might do when he found out Tom had threatened her. Besides that, George had seven employees with families to support, in addition to their own family, and if she blew the whistle before she had all her information together it would mean complete devastation for all of them.

So she kept a low profile, feeling she would need absolute proof before she told George her story. Even though things at work were often unbearable, Jackie worked through, determined she would find the truth and still stay one step ahead in the whole situation. But she could not have foreseen what happened next.

## CHAPTER THIRTY-ONE

Regina had decided to stay awhile longer with Jackie and George since his two boys would be away visiting with their mother all summer. The house was pretty much hers during the day, and she welcomed the relief from her father's constant arguing with her about everything she did or said. Although she was only fifteen, Regina was very mature for her age, and everyone she met always thought of her as much older.

Jackie was talking with Regina on the phone from her office about getting a job when Tom walked in and made himself at home, lounging in one of the chairs in front of the desk. Glaring at Tom, Jackie said, "Regina someone just walked into my office, so I've gotta go. I'll see you later at home." She waited for Tom to say something, but he just sat there, almost like he was in a trance.

Finally, she asked, "Tom, what exactly brings you into my office this time? What do you need now? My first born?"

"That's real funny," he replied. "Actually, my son would really like Regina."

"DON'T EVEN GO THERE!" Jackie shouted. "What the hell do you want?" she asked again.

"Nothing. I just stopped by to see how you were doing."

"When did you ever give a shit about how I'm doing?"

"No, really, I do. But I see you're busy right now, so I'll catch you later."

With that he excused himself, leaving Jackie to ponder just what the hell he was up to. She had an appointment scheduled at a job site and expected to be away from the office for several hours, so she called Regina back and asked if she'd like to ride along. However, Regina wasn't dressed yet and declined the offer.

Jackie was gone longer than she expected, and when she got back to the office she tried calling Regina, but there was no answer at home. Thinking Regina might be in the shower, Jackie had just decided to call back later when she looked out her office window and saw Tom's car pulling into the parking lot. Regina was sitting in the front seat beside him. Jackie dropped the phone and ran toward the lobby, arriving just as Regina stepped through the door with Tom right behind her.

"Hi, Mom!" Regina said.

"What's going on?" Jackie demanded.

"Oh, I called up here and Tom told me you were gone. He offered to come get me, but I didn't expect him to take me to lunch. Since we both hadn't eaten, he offered and I accepted." Regina looked around the room. "And guess what? He gave me a job house-sitting and baby-sitting for him and his wife while they go on vacation for a week. Look, he already paid me!" Regina held up a handful of money."

"I think we should have discussed this first," Jackie said. Tom stood behind Regina, smiling that disgusting smile of his.

Regina looked puzzled. "I'm just going over there to take care of the dogs and the house and keep Frankie Paige."

"Great," Jackie replied. "Would you wait for me in my office, please. Tom can I see you in your office?"

"Sure, come on." He escorted her inside and closed the door behind them.

"What the fuck are you doing? What do you mean paying her up front and doing all this without asking me?" Jackie was so angry she could feel the veins in her neck throbbing.

"It's no big deal," Tom drawled as he shrugged his shoulders toward Jackie. "I just needed a baby sitter while Lucrezia and I are on vacation.

What's wrong with that?"

Jackie stood up and leaned over right in Tom's face as she replied. "Don't go near my house again, and do not pick up my daughter EVER. I don't have to answer why. You know perfectly well why! Do Not FUCK with my daughter! You got that?"

Tom just stared directly into her eyes. "Jackie, you need to remember something, too. You should never underestimate me or my abilities."

"What does that mean?" she demanded.

"Just that," he answered.

They glared at one another in silence before Tom continued. "By the way, did you get those prints I asked you for yet?"

"You ask him yourself." She turned and stomped from his office, slamming the door behind her.

Jackie went directly to her office and locked the door shut, trembling with rage. Sitting beside the desk Regina asked. "Mom, is something wrong?"

"No, baby, not with you anyway."

"Well, what going on?"

"I just wish that Tom had asked me first about having you house sit."

"Well, I already spent some of the money, or I'd give it back," Regina replied.

"Just how much did he pay you to do this job for him?" Jackie leaned back in her chair, trying to look normal so she wouldn't scare Regina.

"Um, I think he gave me $450."

"Four hundred fifty dollars! For what?" Jackie demanded.

Regina curled the strap of her purse around her fingers. "House sitting, dog sitting, and baby sitting for a week."

Jackie sighed. "I don't like the idea of you staying alone in their house for a week. Tom has a lot of strange friends, and I don't want you involved."

"Well, can I keep Frankie Paige at our house and just feed and water the dogs every day?" she asked.

"Let me think about it," Jackie replied. Before she could draw her breath from that last statement, someone knocked on her door. Regina turned and opened it. It was Lucrezia with Frankie Paige.

Lucrezia smiled at Jackie. "Hey, Regina, I heard Tom hired you to take care of things while we're gone. I want to thank you. You don't have any idea how much Frankie Paige is looking forward to this. Aren't you, honey?" She pushed the hair away from Frankie's face. Frankie Paige shook her head yes and smiled, holding out her arms to Jackie.

The night after Lucrezia and Tom left for their trip, Jackie went over to their house to get some things Frankie Paige would need for her visit with Regina over the next few days. As Jackie was packing the baby's clothes, she heard a telephone ringing in the back room of the house. She paused, straining to hear where the sound was coming from. Then she heard a man's voice with a heavy East Coast accent. The sound of his voice startled Jackie, and she walked down the hallway so she could hear better. The voice said something about "the truck has made the delivery." Jackie figured this was the owner of their delivery company calling and her curiosity was aroused—why would he leave a message on Tom's private phone line? She went into the room with the telephone and hit the play button on the answering machine to hear the message in its entirety.

The man said, "Hey, T. Just to let you know the shipment came in and the stuff was transported into the Eastside warehouse. I'll make contact later."

Jackie wondered what it was all about. Looking around the room, she saw Tom had a complete home office with maps, a police scanner, and a copier, fax machine, desktop scanner, and a computer. She wondered why he needed all that, since he didn't have a home business. None of this made sense to Jackie. As she stood there deep in thought, the fax line rang, startling her. She gasped and clutched her chest as it tightened in fear.

She leaned over the machine and read the fax as it came in: The Colombian Eagle arrived today—stored in warehouse on East Side awaiting distribution. Do you know yet if we are going through Mississippi, Alabama, Florida, or Texas?

Suddenly everything came together. There was no doubt in her mind: Tom was dealing drugs and using the mobile homes to transport them. The voice on the phone was a drug connection confirming a shipment. No wonder Dexter and Tom didn't allow anyone else to handle the home deliveries!

She sank into a chair, almost overwhelmed as the pieces of the puzzle came together in her head—conversations she'd overheard, things she'd wondered about, the lack of discipline in the office. But now that she knew about the operation, how would she convince George or the police? She knew she had to keep this to herself until she could put it all together. But how in the world could she prove anything? A fax coming from an undisclosed location with no signature didn't implicate anyone. How clever. The possibility of this "deal" being traced back to Tom's connection would be impossible. And since there was no phone conversation, how could the FBI trace the call or tap the phone line? Only the person it was intended for would actually know the meaning of the message.

Jackie was scared just being in the house, so she quickly gathered what she needed for Frankie Paige to stay one night at their house with them. There was no way in hell she would let Regina house sit, dog sit, or even set foot inside this house. They had no choice about keeping Frankie Paige since Tom and Lucrezia were already off to the Bahamas. But Jackie would NOT let Regina set foot inside the house. And she did have control over that.

# CHAPTER THIRTY-TWO

On the sixth day of baby-sitting they received a call from Lucrezia. "How's she doing?"

"We're getting along just fine," Jackie replied.

"Are they making it okay over at the house?" Lucrezia asked. "I tried calling there but didn't get an answer."

"That's because I felt better having them just stay with us," Jackie replied.

"Oh, that's okay. Can I talk with Frankie Paige?"

"Sure," Jackie replied and called for Frankie Paige to come to her. The little girl talked to her mama for several minutes before Frankie handed the phone back to Jackie.

Lucrezia said, "You don't know how much I appreciate everything you've done, Jackie. I can't wait to get back home. I've had a good time but I'm ready to come back."

"I am, too," Jackie said.

"I know you must be really tired. We should be home in about twenty-four hours, and I'll pick her up just as soon as we can get there."

The group arrived the next afternoon, apparently sooner than they anticipated. Lucrezia walked into the office with Frankie Paige and Tom about 3:00 p.m. Lucrezia had brought Jackie a gift and wanted

Frankie to deliver it to her. Jackie was nice and thanked them for their thoughtfulness, but she breathed a sigh of relief—now she could get back to a somewhat normal life without a toddler in the house.

Lucrezia didn't stay long, saying she needed to get home and unpack. Just as she was leaving Jackie's office, Dexter came in. "Hey, Jackie, what's up? How did things go today? Can you fill me in on everything before you leave tonight? I've got something important to do first, and then we'll get together." He stepped into the men's room.

Tom called out, "Hey, Jackie!"

She listened for a moment before she responded, "What!"

"Can you come here?" She was already walking toward his office. As she stepped through the door, Tom whispered, "Sit down."

Tom wasted no time as he began to brag, "I was in close contact with a lot of higher ups on this trip. I'm not meaning to rush you, but I need those prints as soon as you can get them—like tomorrow. Can you arrange that?"

"Like I was trying to tell you on the phone before you so rudely hung up, No, I can't," she replied.

Tom bit his lip as he stared into her eyes. "What do you mean, no? You have no choice. If you don't get me those prints I'll have to get another flooring contractor, and I know George sold off his other business to take on this account. How many people does he have working for him now? Five or six, am I right? Don't they all have families relying on this account?"

"Are you threatening me?" Jackie questioned.

He shrugged. "Looks that way. If that's what it takes to get you to do what I need, then I guess I am."

"I'm not going to stand for this!" She stood and started to leave the office.

"You don't have to," Tom said. "The choice is yours. Just bring them in to me tomorrow, and George can keep the contract. Otherwise, I've got another guy who's willing to give up his fingerprints for the contract." He grinned at her. "Oh, by the way, I checked, and the company currently holds approximately $78,000 to $80,000 of your money, between George's outstanding invoices and your commissions."

Jackie came back to her seat and slammed her hand down onto the desktop. "You sleazy bastard. You'd fuck your own mother! I'm not going to stand for this. You wait until I tell George. You'll be lucky if he doesn't rip your fucking head off. Then I'm going straight to the top of this company, you can bet on that!"

Tom shrugged his shoulders as he replied, "That's gonna be fun to watch, because the top guy really took a liking to my wife on the trip, and I don't think he'll believe you over me."

Seething, Jackie immediately left his office in search of Dexter to see if she could talk with him about this. But before she could even begin to ask Dexter what was happening she walked in on him finalizing a "deal" with the new carpet contractor. As she turned and left, she fought an incredible urge to get a gun and take both these sleazy bastards out.

Jackie was pissed. Things had gone too far—there was no turning back now that they were screwing with her family and George's employees. She knew it was time to come clean and spill the truth, and she wanted to tell Richard first. When she got home, she placed a call to Richard Spaniel, anticipating an immediate return call. However there was no reply, so she paged him again. Again, there was no reply. He returned her call later that evening and advised her to be in his office at 8:30 the next morning.

Finally, she felt satisfaction was on the horizon. The next day Jackie went straight to Richard's office to settle things permanently and tell him her fears and findings about Tom and Dexter. However, it seemed as though he was already under the impression of something totally different. When she stepped through the door, he had one of those stern looks that expressed that he was not happy as he greeted Jackie in the foyer.

"Take a seat. I'll be back to get you in a moment."

She knew this would not be an easy interview, but she had no choice. A million things ran through her mind as she awaited him to call her into his office. After several long minutes, it was now her time to talk. Richard entered the lobby to escort her back to his office.

"Exactly what the hell is going on with you?" he asked?

Obviously he already knew something. She replied, "Well, I'm not sure myself, but to start with there are some things that need to be investigated and looked into going on at the Midway Park location."

Before she could say another word, Richard interrupted holding up one hand to stop her. "Jackie, let me say something. You're done at Midway Park. D-O-N-E. That location is no longer any of your concern. In light of what you did in the absence of the principals of this company, you're lucky to still have a job, but you will not be working at the Midway Park location again. You can work for Alvin or Stan, but you'll have to report to me on a regular basis, and George's contract is officially revoked as of today also. Now, you need to go to the Midway location and pick up your personal belongings and return back over here in one hour."

Jackie could not believe what she was hearing, but Richard continued, "That is, if you want to be paid on those outstanding deals of yours. You know company policy: You have to be actively employed to be paid commission. We will cut George a partial check and hold the rest for ninety days until we're satisfied that his work is satisfactory."

Tears welled up in Jackie's eyes and she started trembling as it all sank in. "What are you saying? You're wrong!"

"Jackie, I got a call from Dexter and Tom last evening telling me you hadn't taken care of the business while we were away. Tom said when he confronted you, you blew up and threatened them with George. Well, let me tell you, I won't stand for you threatening my employees and placing them in a fearful situation. Just because your husband is a contractor does not give him or you special privileges."

Jackie could not believe what she was hearing, but she knew she had been betrayed in the worst possible way.

## CHAPTER THIRTY-THREE

Jackie was completely devastated. She didn't know how she was ever going to explain this to George. Again, she tried to talk to Richard, pleading with him to just hear her story. She tried to explain that something very wrong was happening at the Midway Park location, but he refused to listen. His mind was made up.

At one point he shouted, "You're done, finished, released from your job! Don't you get it? There's no reason for me to listen to you. Because of the fact that you refuse to get along with Dexter and Tom, you are no longer an employee of the Midway location. Therefore, you can go back there only to clean out your office." He paused, glaring at her. "I mean it, Jackie. I don't want you, or George, having contact with ANYBODY over there. You should have never threatened my employees with your husband. And if you intend to be paid on any of the deals you've closed over there, then you'll have to transfer over here under my watchful eye. Only you'll have to start over—low man on the totem pole."

Realizing there was absolutely no reasoning with Richard, Jackie stood to leave his office, trying to get outside before she started crying, but she couldn't hold her tears as she stumbled from his office. She was crying so hard that she stumbled over Hillary in the hallway.

Hilary gleefully announced. "Jackie, I have your termination papers. I need you to sign these before you leave."

Jackie was still so grief stricken that she couldn't do what her first instinct told her to. Richard interrupted, "That's okay, Hillary. I think I want her to come to work over here instead."

Jackie leaned onto the wall in the narrow hallway to steady herself while making room for Hillary to move past her. She tried to hold it together until she could get to the front door, all the while refraining from acting on her inner desires to just bitch-slap Hillary until her hand wore out. She was thinking, *I've got to do something. I can't let them to get away with this.*

There was quite a lot of money at stake for Jackie and George—more than $70,000—and they couldn't afford to just walk away without it. As Jackie drove back to the Midway Park location to clean out her desk, she considered a lot of things. But mainly she thought of ways to get even with the two bastards who'd just thrown her to the wolves. She cried so hard that at one point she couldn't see to drive and had to pull off the roadway to get control of herself.

She wanted to leave and never go back, but with the money owed them by the company she had to do everything she could to keep her job—even if it meant working near Hillary at the other location. When Jackie finally made it to the Midway Park location and walked into the office, there in the front lobby sat Lucrezia with Frankie Paige. Jackie just walked past them like they weren't there. Lucrezia immediately followed Jackie to her office and closed the door behind her.

"Jackie," she said. "I heard what happened. I'm so sorry."

Jackie at first thought she was being sarcastic, but once they looked at one another she could tell that Lucrezia was genuinely serious. But how much did Lucrezia know? She just continued in silence, packing things from her desk into a cardboard box.

Lucrezia said, "Jackie if there's anything that I can do for you, will you let me know?"

"Like what?" Jackie questioned.

Lucrezia shrugged. "Like anything. Frankie Paige and I really like you a lot, and we think what Hillary and Dexter did to get you fired is unacceptable."

Jackie wasn't sure what the hell she meant by that comment, but apparently Lucrezia thought Tom was an innocent bystander.

"Where are Tom and Dexter?"

"I'm not sure," Lucrezia replied. "I think Richard called them over to his office for a meeting."

Jackie didn't respond. She just kept dropping things into the box. The more she thought about it all, the more she realized she had to find out exactly what Lucrezia knew. She stopped packing and turned to Lucrezia to ask her a question that would determine whether she knew the truth or was just putting on a front to cover Tom's tracks. "Well maybe there is one thing you can help me with."

"Sure, whatever you need, just name it." Lucrezia said.

Jackie took out a pen and note pad and asked, "Do you know a good lawyer?"

Lucrezia set Frankie Paige on the edge of the desk and picked up the pen. "I sure do. My dad has a friend who handles high-profile cases, and their office is where I'd start if I were you." She jotted a name on the pad. "Now they may not handle this type of case, but they can refer you to someone else." Lucrezia handed Jackie the number and patted her gently on the shoulder.

Jackie realized Lucrezia was in the dark about why she'd lost her job.

"What are you gonna do?" Lucrezia questioned.

"I don't know right now. I've got to take some time and think this thing out," Jackie said. "If you don't mind, Lucrezia, I'd prefer to be alone with my thoughts right now."

"Sure, I understand." Lucrezia hugged Jackie before picking up Frankie Paige and leaving the office.

At that moment the events of the day had really taken their toll, and Jackie felt sick in her stomach. She sat down at the desk holding her stomach while rocking back and forth, hoping the feeling would go away. She ran toward the bathroom as the urge to vomit increased with each step. Jackie had never had such stress as she did from all this, but she was shocked when she realized she was vomiting blood. Something was very wrong, and she needed to get to the doctor.

The doctor sat down to talk with Jackie for a few minutes to try to figure out why she was back in his office again. "Jackie," he asked, "have you been having family trouble or marital problems."

"No sir," she replied. "Why do you ask?"

"Well, this is the eighth, no ninth, time I have seen you with stress symptoms in the last twelve months. Is there something you want to talk about?"

"No sir," she replied.

The doctor sat quietly looking at Jackie, but she stayed silent. "I promise I won't reveal what you tell me to anyone." He added.

"It's nothing I can't handle," she replied, fearing what might happen If she did tell. She felt it was best not to trust anyone.

The doctor paused and drew a deep breath before taking Jackie's hand in his. "I'm sure you can handle anything, Jackie, but I'm not sure your body can keep up with it. You came dangerously close to having a heart attack, and I'm going to put you on a sedative for your stomach. You have to take this medication, but only as the instructions indicate. This what I usually prescribe to chemotherapy cancer patients to calm their stomachs from all the medication. Then, I'm placing you on bed rest for at least ten days. After that, I want to take a blood test and make sure you're strong enough to return to work before I release you." He scribbled something on a prescription pad. "Here's a note to your employer. Don't take this lightly, Jackie—bleeding ulcers have been known to cause heart attacks if not properly treated."

"Okay," she replied. "I hear you. I'll take a few days off, but I'm not sure about ten days."

He sighed. "I'll look into reducing the recovery time if you will come back in four days and let me test your blood again. But you really need to go home and go to bed for now. I'll call your employer from here and let them know. I'm on their preferred doctor list."

"I know," Jackie replied, thinking, *and that's why I'm not confiding anything to you.*

A couple of hours after Jackie had gone home to rest, the doorbell rang. She climbed out of bed, put on a robe, and made her way downstairs, wondering who was at the door. She certainly wasn't expecting anyone. Looking through the peephole in the door, she saw and elderly woman with silver hair standing on the porch. Jackie cracked the door squinting her eyes as she tried to focus on woman's face.

"Jackie? Jackie Kennard?"

"Yes," Jackie replied as she opened the door wider. "I'm Margaret Box with Rest Haven Funeral."

"What!" Jackie's heart was pounding so loudly in her chest that she could hardly hear what the lady was saying.

"Can I come in? I believe your husband ordered this. Is he here?"

With that statement, Jackie felt the tightness leaving her chest. "No, as a matter of fact he won't be home until later tonight."

Mrs. Box smiled, "Then why don't I just leave these papers with you. You and your husband can look over everything, and if you have any questions, just give me a call."

Without looking at the papers, Jackie put them on a shelf in the closet. George could explain things when he got home. Exhausted and still sedated from the medication, she just wanted to lie down, but as she started back up the stairs toward her bedroom, the phone rang. She answered quickly, expecting to hear George's voice.

It was Tom. He said, "Jackie, did Mrs. Box get by there yet?"

Jackie was so stunned by the question she couldn't answer. She didn't know what to say.

Tom continued, "I just want to make sure you understand that I mean business. Therefore to prove my point, I went out and selected a couple of plots for your possible future needs. I even paid the first premium. I just want to make sure that you understand that there will be consequences if you don't keep your end of our bargain. And I hope you do keep our agreement. I know you're planning to transfer, but I wanna to make sure that you don't talk to anyone about anything. I even know that George plans to go to work for Alvin, but I'm not sure that's a good idea. I have to work all that out with Alvin, myself."

Jackie interrupted him. "Tom, I went home today because I was throwing up blood. That means that I have a bleeding ulcer or something else really bad wrong with me. Either way, I'm going to have to be off work for a few days. You can rest assured, I'm not going to be talking to anyone. You have my word on that. Now if that's all you have to say, let's cease this conversation and let me get some rest." Jackie was terrified every time she heard his voice, but something told her that no matter what he said or insinuated, she had to appear tough on the outside. If she let him see how terrified she really was, it would only make him worse. So without allowing him any further time to terrorize her, she hung up the phone, trembling uncontrollably. Immediately she ran to her purse and dumped it out on the countertop. She scrambled through all the receipts and papers, looking for the phone number Lucrezia had given her for the attorney. Jackie's hands were shaking as she dialed the phone.

The phone rang twice before Jackie heard a woman's voice answer, "law office." Immediately, she replied in a shaky voice, "Hello, my name is Jackie Kennard and I need some legal advice. May I talk with an attorney?"

"I'll need to ask you a few questions before I can just put you through to an attorney," the receptionist explained. She advised Jackie that once they completed the questions she could immediately consult with one of the attorneys. If they feel the situation merits followup, one of them would call her back.

"Please!" Jackie begged. "My life has been threatened, and I need advice. Can't you at least just put me on hold until you've talked with one of them?"

"I'm sorry ma'am, but if I just put everyone through, then the attorneys couldn't get anything done. I'll try to get back with you myself if one of them can't call you, but that's the best I can offer."

"Thank you." Jackie replied, wiping tears from her face. She'd barely hung up the phone when one of the attorneys called her back.

"Jackie, this is Christine Cox. My assistant told me about your employment problems. Do you have a minute to go over some things with me?"

Jackie almost jumped through the phone, "Yes! Ms. Cox, I really appreciate you calling me back. I think I'm in a serious situation."

"Sounds like it." The attorney stated. They talked briefly back and forth as Jackie took notes on everything the lawyer told her to do.

"First, I want you to go to the police. Too bad you don't have these threats on tape."

"Well, actually I do have several of his conversations on tape."

"Really? That's good," Ms. Cox continued. "You need to go file a complaint immediately. Second I want you to go to EEOC—Equal Employment Opportunity Commission—and file a complaint there also. Nothing ever goes to court without a Right To Sue letter from the EEOC. This certainly sounds bad enough that you need to file with them right away. Also, be aware there is a time limit for filing your claim." She paused to speak to someone in her office. "Now, if your employer doesn't do an investigation and come to the realization that you mean business, call me back and I'll meet with you then. Good Luck!"

"Thank you so much, Ms. Cox."

Jackie immediately got dressed and went to the local police station, where she asked to meet privately with someone about what was going on with her employer. After discussing a few things with a police officer, Jackie was taken directly to the chief of police, where she told him her story. She told him about the fingerprint episode and the fact that this creep claimed to have killed someone in another state and got away with it. She also divulged the threats Tom had made against her and her family, plus the information about Tom being in the witness protection program. The Chief listened intently to Jackie's story, never interrupting or making a comment. But he did state that he had no knowledge of anyone within his jurisdiction in the witness protection program. He pondered silently for a moment, then asked, "Is this guy covered in tattoos or is his hair real long?"

"No, neither one," Jackie said.

"Hmmm," The chief responded. "I'd like to help you, but I can't just go around arresting people for telling wild stories. And I guarantee that this guy is just making up a story as he goes. No one under witness protection is going to blow his own cover. Maybe we can pull him over for outstanding tickets or some other minor offense and bring him in for fingerprinting and check out his background that way. But first he has to be speeding or something—we can't just go over and knock on his door and ask for his fingerprints." He stared out the window for a moment, intertwined his fingers, and added, "I think you really need to work this out through your company."

To Jackie, it was obvious the police chief had never heard a story quite like this before, and she could tell he had no intention of making out a report or even checking on her story. Finally, he handed her his card and told her to consult with a lawyer and go to EEOC because there was nothing he could do.

"From where I sit," the chief stated, "this is more of an employer-employee problem."

Jackie thanked the chief for his time and shook her head in disbelief when she left his office. From there, she went back home, intending to call the EEOC to start the process rolling. When she finally made contact with a counselor and explained her situation, he gave her directions to his office and requested she come down immediately to talk with him and file a complaint.

## CHAPTER THIRTY-FOUR

The closer she got to the EEOC office, the more scared Jackie felt. But she knew something had to be done because if things went bad, she'd need someone with authority to document what was actually going on.

At the EEOC office, a receptionist asked her to fill out a form explaining what was going on and why she felt the EEOC should become involved. Jackie hit the high spots, mostly describing the fact that she was fired and then told she'd have to transfer to a new location and take a lower paying commission rate in order to get the money owed her by the company.

She had hoped that during the interview process she could explain more about her fears and the threats she received. Once the investigation started, she felt the EEOC would be able to uncover the rest of the story and find out what was true and what was a lie to scare her into submission.

As she waited for someone to call her in, she realized she wouldn't have much time to explain her case, because it was almost time for the office to close. Finally, at 4:25 p.m., five minutes before closing, the counselor himself came to get Jackie and escort her back into his office.

He introduced himself as Mr. Jones and briefly described his position with the EEOC. "Mrs. Kennard, I can go into a company, no matter how small or large, and if I find violations that merit, I can and will shut them down on the spot." Then he explained the reason he'd kept her so late was because he wanted to get his other issues out of the way so that he could devote his undivided time to her complaint. He went on to explain that he'd been on the job for fifteen years and could always read between the lines and could tell which complaints were filed in retaliation and which ones merited serious investigation. He added, "And I'm sure your claims merit our investigation, so that's why I kept you for last. Now, let's start from the beginning and go over things one at a time."

The discussion went on for over three hours, and things flowed from Jackie until she broke down crying. She trembled, telling Mr. Jones about how she was verbally mistreated on a regular basis, assaulted by a customer, cheated on her commissions, and still not paid as much in commission as the male employees.

"I feel so ashamed, like I allowed them to get away with this, but you have to understand I can't just walk away from all the money that they owe us! We've worked so hard. We can't just walk away. What will we pay our bills with?" Mr. Jones handed her a tissue, and she wiped her eyes. "We have other people who rely on us for this income, not to mention our children, and I just can't let them down." She sobbed so hard that Mr. Jones excused himself from the room and returned with a glass of water and more tissues.

"Listen, Mrs. Kennard, I'm going to do an investigation myself, and I'll rush this along so we can get it behind you. In the meantime, here's my card. I suggest that you just go to work like nothing is happening and let me handle it from this side. If you think of anything else, give me a call. It's almost 8:00 p.m. If you will give me a moment to make a phone call, I'll ask a security guard escort you to your car."

"Thank you," Jackie said, offering her hand. "I really appreciate this. I feel better just knowing someone in authority understands the situation."

As she drove home, Jackie thought, *This is how it has to be, they gave me no other choice.*

George met her in the driveway as she pulled in. "Honey," he shouted, "Where have you been? I was worried sick."

As she parked the car and stepped out, George could see from her face that she'd been crying. "George, we need to talk," she replied. "Let's go inside."

George's face was pale with fear as he walked to the house and unlocked the door. "Honey, please tell me what's the matter," he said, pulling her into the living room where they sat together on the sofa.

Jackie drew a big breath. "George, there is something that I have to go over with you that involves my job and your contract with Midway." She paused, trying to think how to begin.

"I'm waiting," George said. "Just tell me."

"Okay, I've just come from EEOC office where I filed a grievance against the company on behalf of myself. As a result, I am probably going to lose my job, and your contract will be dropped."

"Well, I don't have to work for them," George said. "Alvin has been dying for me to come to work for him."

"No, George, neither one of us will be able to work for the company anywhere."

"Why?" He asked, frowning.

"Well, there are some things you'll just have to trust me on here and let me work through. But I want to make sure you understand that I did this because I have no other choice. Please, just give me a few days to get this thing settled and we'll probably just take our money and leave. In the meantime, why don't you just hang out around the house and not go into the office or call anyone at the Midway Park location."

George looked puzzled and shook his head.

"Just seven days, that's all I ask," she said.

"Jackie, aren't we married for better or worse?" he asked.

"I think so," she replied.

George put his arm around her. "Then when are you going to accept the fact that we're a team and not just married for the sake of a piece of paper to hang on the wall? I realize that we made an agreement before we married not to get involved in one another's careers, but I have a feeling that this thing is bigger than the both of us, and I can't be of any help until I know what's going on."

Jackie swallowed hard, thinking, *This will probably destroy my marriage or cost us our lives if I tell him now—and I just can't cope with that, too.* "Please George, just let me handle this. I really don't want any more people involved right now."

"I don't think so," George replied. "Let me guess. I'm supposed to just sit here for seven days doing nothing."

Jackie shrugged, not knowing how to answer.

"So when do you think that you can fill me in with these major missing parts that go along with this story?" he asked.

"Whenever EEOC completes their investigation," Jackie replied.

"And in the meantime, what the hell am I supposed to do with myself and my employees, Jackie?"

"I guess sub them out somewhere," she replied.

"Great! But I don't think I can just sit here for a week waiting for someone to make a decision about my future and not have any input. You'll have to be a little more specific here, Jackie."

"George, just give me forty-eight hours. That should produce enough for this to come to a head. That's all I ask. Then if something doesn't happen, I promise I'll sit down with you and go into detail. But for now, this is all I can say." She hesitated for a moment. "This is one of those times I wish we didn't work together. Not because of you or anything you've done, but because of something I uncovered."

"I don't have a choice, do I?" George asked. "As usual it's your call. But after those forty-eight hours, we're going to sit down and completely renegotiate our original agreement. I have way too much money sitting out there outside my control to just sit around waiting on someone else to call the shots. If it was anyone besides you, Jackie, you know what the answer would be. But, because I trust you, I'll agree to your request."

"Thank you!" she replied, followed by a deep sigh.

Jackie was really stressed, but the medication she was taking seemed to help her stomach. She hadn't mentioned the medical problem to

George either—she just told him she'd requested a few days off to spend with him and catch up on her rest.

After a few days, Jackie decided for herself that she was ready to go back to work. She reported to the manufacturing location, where she was assigned an office. Her new quarters were being used as a storage closet and she had a lot of work to do before she could put it to good use. Even though this was humiliating, Jackie reminded herself of the conversation with Mr. Jones and told herself she could endure until he completed an investigation. Then she'd collect her money and go somewhere else to work.

Several days later, a letter from EEOC arrived, outlining the details Jackie had discussed with the counselor about her complaint against the company. Jackie was called into the business manager's office and questioned about why she'd filed the complaint.

"I think that it's self-explanatory," she replied.

"Well then, you're just gonna have to meet with Stan about this," The office manager remarked in a hateful tone.

"That's fine," Jackie shrugged her shoulders and walked away.

Within a few minutes, Stan called her to his office where he had papers laid out on his desk. "Close the door," he said.

As she stepped in, she could see the EEOC letterhead on the document. She quietly sat down, waiting for his response.

"Jackie. I interviewed you to come to work for this company, and during that interview I learned that you were an honest person... maybe even found you to be one of the most honest people I've ever met. Then this shows up. Can you tell me what this is all about?"

Jackie looked into his face and back down as the tears flowed from her eyes. She felt ashamed. She tried to talk to him without emotion, but she couldn't hold it back. She told Stan about some of the cruel things that Dexter and Tom had done and said to her. About how they had treated others and offended every man woman and child who entered the doors at the Midway location.

Stan listened for several minutes without interrupting, mesmerized by Jackie's story. His face turned beet red when she told him how Dexter had shouted to everyone that she was a swallower and not a spitter. And how Dexter tried to make his wife jealous telling her the two of them were "fuck buddies." Stan held up his hand and shook his head no as he told Jackie, "I've heard enough. This explains a lot to me. As a matter of fact this explains EVERYTHING. Please give me a few minutes to make a phone call. No, actually, you can go home and I'll call you there. Give me your home phone number."

"Am I fired again?" she asked.

"No, but I just don't think you can work through this right now and be on the floor selling. Just go home, and I'll be in touch with you later."

A couple of hours after Jackie arrived home, she received a call from Stan asking her to come to the office the next day for a meeting with Richard Spaniel.

Jackie responded, "No thanks. I've tried to talk with Richard on several occasions, but he refused to listen. I'd rather not set myself up for another letdown."

"Please, Jackie, try once more," Stan said. "I talked to Richard myself and explained the situation. I think he's willing to listen to you now."

Jackie paused, trying to decide what she should do. "Stan, I'll do this, but only because it's you asking. I still want the EEOC to investigate."

"Oh, I agree," he replied. "I want them to look into the situation myself, but I also want you to be able to feel comfortable working here."

The next day, as Jackie had agreed, she arrived at Richard's office expecting to have a conversation with him one-on-one about the issues between her and the Midway location. Jackie was immediately led to Richard's office where he stood to greet her and motioned for her take a seat. She didn't acknowledge his greeting or say anything. She just quietly took a seat as she prepared herself to hear whatever he had to say. Jackie fully expected to hear an apology, but once again she'd given him more credit than he deserved. Richard told her he felt uncomfortable discussing the issues brought forth to him by Stan and preferred she talk with a woman he'd selected. He said he thought

Jackie would feel more comfortable and could be more open with another woman.

Jackie slightly raised her hand. "Can I ask you something?" When Richard nodded, she asked, "Is she an attorney?"

"No, she's simply an impartial middle person we feel can tell us how to best handle the situation. Her name is Marion Littleworth. She's waiting for you now in the conference room upstairs. If you'll go up there now, she'll talk with you, and I'm sure we can work this thing out."

Jackie just looked at Richard, awaiting any further instructions. He paused for a moment, watching her. She just sat there silently staring into his face. The silence was deafening. The two of them locked eyes for what seemed an eternity. This obviously was very uncomfortable for Richard—he wrung his hands together and clenched his jaw. Then, for no apparent reason he asked, "So, Jackie, how many kids do you and George have?"

She was somewhat stunned and offended by the nature of his question, knowing he was trying to distract her from the problem and gain control. She glared at him as she leaned toward him across the desk, "Richard, why would you ask about my children at this time?"

"Oh, no particular reason, I just wondered," he responded.

She shook her head no without answering, then stood to leave his office. Turning back she responded. "My children have nothing to do with this, and my children are none of your concern. So, I'll thank you to leave them out of this ugly situation."

In the conference room, Jackie introduced herself to a woman who seemed to be trying hard to make a good first impression, but there was something odd about her. She had a large nose, black hair, and a mole on her chin that should have been removed decades ago. Jackie thought, *this woman gives a whole new meaning to the word ugly.* Before she sat down, she took a moment to scan the room to see if there was a broom parked somewhere in the corner that the woman used for transportation.

Then, as Jackie got closer she knew she would have a difficult time sitting just across the small table looking directly into her face. The woman had more facial hair than most men, especially on her top lip. It was just extremely distracting. In an attempt to keep her mind off it, Jackie just tried to focus on the computer sitting in between them. Then Ms. Littleworth asked, "Would it be all right with you, Jackie, if I take notes about our conversation on my personal computer?"

"I don't mind," Jackie replied.

Once the conversations started, Mrs. Littleworth asked general questions and Jackie answered. Then as time went on, the questions became more detailed. Jackie was beginning to feel uncomfortable with the way some of Ms. Littleworth's questions were coming out and at one point even asked her. "Are you an attorney, Ms. Littleworth?"

"What makes you ask that?"

"Your line of questioning, that's what. Plus the fact that Richard Spaniel stated that you're a disinterested party who will see that this matter is straightened out."

"Then that's what I'm here to do," she replied.

"Do I need an attorney?" Jackie asked.

"Why?" Ms. Littleworth responded.

"Because I believe from your questions and the impression I now have from you that you aren't at all what Richard insinuated you are."

Ms. Littleworth stared down at her computer keyboard as she replied. "Look, Jackie, I'll level with you. This is not my first encounter with Dexter on this level of misconduct. But we really don't want that published, because we don't want to bias your report. We simply want to get to the truth, and we feel the best way to do that is for you and me to meet face-to-face and have an open discussion."

That seemed fair to Jackie, and she agreed to continue answering questions. But after four hours of questions, Jackie began to tire and felt she was being interrogated. She even told Ms. Littleworth that she really didn't want to discuss the issue any further. At this point, Jackie purposefully began withholding information because she wanted to see whether or not she could trust this strange woman.

Ms. Littleworth said, "I assure you I'll conduct a thorough investigation and get back with you in a couple of weeks. Until then, why don't you take some time off, with full pay of course, until you get your ulcer under control? I'll see to it that a medical leave is taken care of for you. You don't even have to go to the office. I'll call Stan myself. Just go ahead and go home from here. Call me in a few days to let me know how long you will need to be off. Here's my card with my office number."

As Jackie took the card and read from it, she felt immediately that any trust that had ever existed between them was broken. The card read, Attorney Marion Littleworth, Specializing in Employee-Employer Rights. As soon as Jackie looked at that card, she knew Ms. Littleworth and Richard Spaniel had lied and deceived her. She now had confirmation that neither one of them could be trusted. She knew their way of resolving this situation would only favor the company and their own needs.

Without commenting, Jackie put the card in her purse and glanced at Ms. Littleworth, as she was rolling up the cord on her computer. The smirk on her face was enough to tell Jackie she was proud of herself and couldn't wait to report to Richard that she had pulled that one off. Again, Jackie felt deceived because she had been lied to and taken advantage of. She left the conference room with a gut feeling that they would meet again.

The four-hour meeting between Attorney Littleworth and Jackie must have sparked something in Tom, making him nervous, because he or Lucrezia started called Jackie at home on a regular basis. One evening they made so many calls to Jackie's phone that the caller ID just shut down. Regardless of which one of them initiated the call, Tom always ended up on the telephone with Jackie at some point every day, questioning her. Then at some point during the conversation, either he or Lucrezia would switch to other points of interest, almost like it was scripted. Jackie didn't always have the recorder close at hand, so she learned to carry it in her pocket because their phone calls became a daily occurrence.

Jackie felt very uncomfortable talking with them since she'd filed a grievance against the company. However, she knew the only way she could prove her story was to have a recording of Tom's harassment, so she listened to them talk and would ask a few leading questions whenever she could. Then the calls became more frequent—sometimes even six to eight times a day, or more. Jackie knew these weren't social calls. They was meant to let her know who was in control. Little did they suspect that Jackie "allowed" them to be in control, all the time recording parts of their conversations and confessions along the way? Tom called Jackie very late one night and she could tell from his slurred speech that he'd been drinking heavily. He was on a real confession trip and just laid his sordid affairs out on the table. Jackie knew this was something worth recording, so she snatched the recorder and placed it against the phone receiver. All the while, Tom never suspected she had the recorder on.

He said, "You know we have our managers' meeting at Richard's house. A couple of those guys are pretty heavy into that nose candy. A few of the guys were outside smoking a crack pipe and I guess they got a little loud and pissed one of the neighbors off. Anyway, someone called the cops. It was funny as hell. You should've been there and seen those bastards scatter. Anyway, someone showed up with that new date drug. Ecstasy. Have you ever tried it?" he asked.

"I don't think so. I don't do drugs," Jackie replied.

"Well I wanted to try it out, but first I wanted to hear from someone who'd used it. Anyway we were trying to get someone to just experiment with it, but everyone was chicken. I think Alvin wanted to, but he was afraid his old lady would find out and then be really pissed as him. Jackie, you better NEVER repeat any of this stuff I'm tellin you."

"Oh, you don't have to worry about me repeating any of this, Tom." Jackie said, still holding the tape recorder. Her comment really boosted his confidence, and he crossed over into another taboo subject, bragging about all the women in the company he'd "fucked" and even going into details about one particular woman. He described in intimate detail how he picked her up at their arranged meeting place, and as they were driving down Highway 75 he told her to take off her panties, and then he threw them out the car window. Then he described how she started masturbating and how he fingered her while she had a couple of orgasms. Then he bragged that she gave him a blow job in the restaurant parking lot for his birthday present before they went in. Tom remarked, "I think that's where all women need to be, on their knees in front of a man giving head."

He went on to describe how she claimed to have a "dark side" to her that she didn't want her family or anyone within the company to know about. Then he said, "I think they were part of that Southern Baptist holier-than-thou bullshit movement or something."

Jackie interrupted his story. "Tom, I really don't have time to discuss this with you, and I don't really care to hear about your wet dreams, so if you'll excuse me I have better things to do than listen to your vulgarity."

Tom laughed that disgusting laugh again. "Well, did I ever tell you about the time that manager friend of yours masturbated on one of his employees?"

"TOM!" she shouted! "Cut the bullshit."

"No really," he said. "I saw the court papers she filed on him." He could hardly talk for laughing.

Jackie replied, "Tell me later, but not right now."

## CHAPTER THIRTY-FIVE

The next month proved to be very stressful both on and off the job, making it difficult for Jackie to work around all the problems the investigation had created. She was such a nervous wreck that she often felt completely out of control and unable to cope. It was difficult to sleep or eat, and she had frequent headaches and episodes of uncontrolled shaking. After waiting for weeks for the investigation results to come back from the EEOC, she couldn't take another minute—she just had to get away from things and take time to think. So, without telling anyone, she drove to the airport and purchased a one-way ticket to LA, where her son, Brian, lived.

After she boarded the plane, Jackie realized she should at least call Brian to let him know she was on her way. She called from the plane, and luckily he was home and delighted to have her visit. She thought, *I'll just have a nice quiet weekend with Brian, take a long walk on the beach, eat some good seafood, and clear my head and catch my second wind. Then I'll set my directions toward ending this employee-employer relationship and move on.*

When she arrived and met Brian, he said, "I'll go to baggage claim and get your bags."

"No need, I don't have any," she replied. "I just decided last-minute to do this and really didn't plan it."

Once they were inside Brian's car, driving to his home, he looked over at her and said, "So, Mom, do you want to tell me what's going on, or are you gonna make me pull it out of you?"

Jackie stared out the window and spoke quietly. "Not yet. Give me some time. First I need to make a phone call and let George know where I am."

Brian looked surprised, but he didn't say anything for a while. Finally, he couldn't stand the suspense, "Mom, is there something wrong? You just aren't yourself. I know there's something wrong, but when are you going to tell me what it is? Is Regina okay?"

"She's fine," Jackie said. "As a matter of fact, I sent her off to school in Spain."

"Spain!" Brian shouted.

Jackie took a deep breath. "She's going as a foreign exchange student. Can we at least wait to talk about it over dinner? I'm starved for some good seafood."

He sighed, "I guess I don't have much choice."

Jackie stalled at every opportunity. She wasn't sure she needed to tell Brian what exactly was going on, and she didn't want him involved in this crazy situation. Over dinner they both hardly said anything. Brian was holding out for an explanation, and Jackie held out for fear of what he might say or want to do.

Finally he put down his fork and glared at her. "Mom, what is going on? Are you going to tell me or am I going to have to call George to find out? Are you two having problems or something?"

"No, nothing like that. There is something I need to talk with someone about—something very serious. I need you to promise me you'll keep it in strictest confidence before I can tell you."

"Depends on what it is," he smiled.

"No son, I'm serious. You have to keep this to yourself. Only if something happens to George or me do I want you to disclose what I'm about to tell you to anyone. I can not stress enough how dangerous and serious this is."

It was the hardest thing Jackie had ever done, telling her son what she knew. But she desperately needed him as a sounding board to help her decide what to do next. Over the next hour and a half she told him about Tom and exactly what he'd disclosed to her.

Brian's eyes flashed, "I told you that time he came to the house there was something about him that I didn't like. Have you gone to the police?"

"Yes, but they didn't believe me."

"How do you know that he isn't just bullshitting you, Mom?"

Jackie twisted her napkin. "That's what is so scary about this. I don't know anything for sure. I don't have any proof, and I can't just call up and ask someone if he's on the witness protection list. In the meantime, all I can think to do is continue recording the phone calls he makes to me and try to gather anything I can to put his story together."

"Mom, do you have an attorney?" Brian asked.

"I talked to one over the phone, and she suggested I contact EEOC right away and file a complaint. Which I did, and they are investigating. However, I didn't tell them about this side of it. I hope they'll find out about him during their own investigation. In the meantime, I want you to take this and keep it in a safe place. Only if anything happens to myself or George, do I want you to open it." She removed an envelope from her purse and gave it to Brian.

"What the hell is this?" He turned the envelope over.

"Just some things that I think would be helpful in an investigation.

"I'll keep it locked inside the glove box in the car." Brian said.

"I don't care where you keep it," Jackie replied. "So long as you know where it is and can get to it, should you have a need to."

"Does George know you're here, Mom? Does he know about all this?" Brian leaned back and sipped his coffee.

"No, I kinda just left town without telling anyone. And he does not know anything because Tom threatened me about telling anyone."

"Mom, you really do need a good attorney."

"I know. I intend to get one when I get back to Dallas." She sighed. "Let's go to your house so I can call George."

Brian lived within a few miles of the restaurant, and during the short drive they continued discussing various aspects of the problem.

He was genuinely concerned and strongly suggested she tell George the entire story. But Jackie wasn't comfortable taking the risk that George might get angry and do something he shouldn't. She preferred to handle the things on a legal playing field. As she nervously made the call to George back in Dallas, she thought, *Maybe I should tell him what the hell's going on. He deserves to know so he can make his own decisions about things.*

Just then he answered the phone. Before she could explain where she was, George said, "I've been trying to find you. I have some bad news."

Immediately Jackie sank down onto the arm of the chair. She didn't want to even think what it might be. "What's wrong?"

"Well, I made an appointment to go talk to Alvin about working exclusively for him."

"What!" she shouted. "George, you promised not to do anything like that."

"Listen to me, Jackie," he demanded. "When I got to his lot there wasn't anyone there. So I sat in my car and waited for a good fifteen to twenty minutes before someone showed up. The yard guy told me Alvin was found on I-35, sitting out beside his truck—dead."

"My God what happened to him?"

"I was told he had a heart attack, but there's evidently more to the story. The media report mentioned foul play and some drugs present, indicating a possible drug-induced heart attack."

"Jackie slid down into the chair, clutching the phone with both hands. "George, what did you do before you made that appointment with Alvin?"

"Oh, not much. Tom had called earlier and said that he needed me to measure to install carpet in his new house."

"Did you go?" Jackie asked as she panted with fear.

"Yea, I went over there for a while. I figured that would give me the opportunity to talk with Tom about my contract. Then after I measured for his carpet I fixed a couple of cabinet doors and the disposal for him and Lucrezia. Why do you ask?"

Jackie's heart was pounding in her chest. "Did you tell him that you were probably going to work for Alvin?"

"Yeah, we talked about that," George said.

Jackie bowed her head gritting her teeth to keep George from detecting any emotions. She now knew she could never allow George to know anything about what was going on. She was certain that if he knew, then one or both of them would be killed.

"Where did you say you are, Jackie?" he asked.

"Oh, I'm spending the night at Linda's. I'll be home tomorrow. I really needed to get away for the evening, and we decided to go out for a late movie. Since it's so late I'll spend the night here. Is that okay with you?"

"I guess so," he replied, "but hurry home because I miss you."

"I'll see you tomorrow," she replied.

Jackie and Brian sat up most of the night talking. Near the end of their conversation, Brian said, "Mom I want you to promise me something, too. I want you to promise you'll find a good attorney once you get back to Dallas. Then I want you to call me and tell me his or her name so that I can keep up with this."

"I promise," she replied. The next day Jackie boarded the plane back to Dallas, feeling even more distress than when she arrived. So much so that she broke down and cried uncontrollably. The person sitting next to her offered condolences, thinking someone close to her had died. Jackie just shook her head yes in appreciation. As the plane got closer to Dallas, she felt more and more agitated. Finally on the ground, she wondered if she could even drive herself home. She sobbed all the way from the airport to the house.

When she got home, George questioned her about the movie and other things. Jackie shouted at him, "Please leave me alone! I don't feel good!"

"Honey, what's wrong with you?" He asked.

"NOTHING!" she shouted.

"Then why are you yelling at me?" he asked, looking confused.

"I told you, I just don't feel well." With that, she started crying again and ran into the bathroom, locking the door behind her. As she sat there crying and shaking out of control she came to the conclusion that she needed professional help before she cracked up.

The next day Jackie called a therapist to set an appointment. The doctor must've detected something in her voice, so she set an appointment for Jackie to come in that evening. Once they were together inside the secluded office, Jackie used an entire box of Kleenex to dry her tears as she tried to explain her fears and concerns to the doctor, who listened intently.

"Jackie, let me ask you some important questions first. Do you have an attorney?"

"Not yet," Jackie said, dabbing at her eyes with the tissue.

"Well, let me suggest you obtain one as soon as possible. Number two, have you talked to anyone else about this?"

Jackie was afraid to involve Brian, so she said, "Absolutely not."

"Don't you think that you should at least tell your husband?"

"No! If I tell George he could be in grave danger."

"Okay," the doctor replied in a soothing voice. "I recommend right now that you take a sedative and get some rest, talk to an attorney as soon as you can, and then I want to see you again tomorrow. In the meantime, we'll spend as much time as you need working through this until you feel comfortable enough to go home tonight."

The next day the attorney Jackie had originally contacted called the house and left a message asking Jackie to call her back. After Jackie made contact with her, she was informed by Attorney Cox that she wanted a second attorney to hear Jackie's story, and he would be in Dallas in a couple of days. Ms. Cox inquired if Jackie could come into the office to discuss a few things with them together. Jackie agreed, and the appointment was set. Things now appeared to be moving faster. Struggling with her thoughts about what to tell George, Jackie determined she needed to include him in this meeting. She simple asked George to come with her, telling him only that it had something to do with the claim she'd filed with EEOC.

So, together they went to the law office, which was located in an industrial area. Without the precise instructions she'd gotten from Ms. Cox, Jackie wouldn't have found the office. The building looked like and abandoned warehouse from the outside, with no signs indicating an office. Jackie had been told to honk the horn twice as she drove past the front door to let them know she'd arrived. As they walked up to the door, she and George had to get through a buzzer, a microphone, and a camera, along with an automatic door lock system that took some time to get through. The place was like Fort Knox.

Once inside, Jackie was impressed with the elaborate decorations. They were from the Ming Dynasty. They were immediately led down a hallway to a back elevator and up a few floors and introduced by Ms. Cox to Mr. Max Mulligan—an attorney from DC. They spent a few minutes getting acquainted and going over the high points of the situation before Jackie requested a few minutes to enlighten George about what was going on. Without disclosing any of her personal issues on the case, she began telling him what had happened. As she discussed the issue about the fingerprints, George looked at her in shock.

"Honey, I know I owe you an apology for not telling you sooner, but I thought I should keep things to myself until I could figure out what to do. After struggling with it, I came to the conclusion that you were safer not knowing. Besides, Tom has more to lose than we do—especially if he's telling the truth about the witness protection program."

Attorney Mulligan added, "And there's a good possibility Tom's telling the truth. He certainly fits the profile." He turned to George, "I don't always agree with keeping someone in the dark, but I believe in this situation Jackie's actions were right."

Just then there was a knock at the door. Ms. Cox excused herself and stepped outside and immediately returned to tell Mr. Mulligan the press was there, awaiting his interview.

Jackie and George looked at one another, wondering just what was going on.

Mr. Mulligan held up one hand and apologized, saying, "I need to make a statement to the press about something else. Please wait for me right here, and I'll return shortly."

As they patiently awaited his return, they could hear the reporters outside the door firing questions at Mr. Mulligan. Jackie looked around the office while they waited, scanning the dozens of pictures on the walls. She gasped, "George look! He's not gonna touch my case outside this office. I'll bet you anything he'll only take my case if Clinton is innocent, but I'm betting Clinton is guilty and he knows it."

"What makes you say that?" George asked.

"Look!" She pointed to an 8 x 10 glossy print of Attorney Mulligan and President Clinton holding their hands raised in the air at the Democratic Convention." As Jackie looked around the room, she figured it out, shaking her head in disbelief. "This attorney who's office we're sitting in, is the chairman of the Democratic Committee. Don't you see? He and Bill Clinton are buds. I'm thinking that if Clinton is guilty of the Paula Jones accusations, then Mulligan can't take my case."

"Why?" George asked, frowning.

"Conflict of interest!" Jackie stated.

Just then the door opened just enough so Ms. Cox could slide inside. "I apologize for the interruption, she stated, but we had to meet with the media about a high-profile case here in Dallas. You probably read about it in the paper—the priest who supposedly accosted several altar boys."

"Yes, I read something about that," Jackie replied.

"We now represent the young men. It looks like it's going to court, so the media is having a field day. Anyway, I apologize for the interruption."

"That's quite all right," Jackie replied. "I'm just admiring the surroundings."

"Well, Ms. Cox stated, "I wanted Mr. Mulligan to hear your story and offer his advice. Have you heard from EEOC yet, or received your Right to Sue Letter?"

"No, not yet," Jackie said.

"Well, that's what we're waiting for at this point. Let me give you my card, and I'll be back in touch within a few days." She handed Jackie her business card. "In the meantime, just keep a low profile."

George interrupted, "Ms. Cox, I want to ask you a couple of questions. Since I am just now hearing about all this for the first time, don't you think we need to do something to protect Jackie while all this investigating is going on?"

George then turned to Jackie, "We'll finish discussing the rest of this when we get home." Attorney Cox shrugged her shoulders, "What would you suggest, George?"

"Well," he replied as he sat in thought for a minute. Then he replied, "I'll just take care of it myself."

Attorney Cox interjected, "Don't go and do anything stupid."

"Oh, I'm not going to initiate anything stupid," George confessed, "but I will do what I have to when he comes around my house again."

"All right then. I'll expect to hear from you when your letter comes in from the EEOC," Attorney Cox said as she offered her hand and stood to see them out.

Before they left the office, Jackie had to know one more thing. She paused inside the door. "Ms. Cox, just what is the connection with Mr. Mulligan and the President."

"Oh, Max is his Campaign Chairman and a good friend. Why?"

Jackie replied, "Well, it's not every day I get to meet someone who's that close to the President."

Ms. Cox smiled. "I think the Prez stays at Max's home when he comes into Dallas. They're pretty tight."

"Is he representing the President in any of his legal battles?"

"I'm not sure," she replied. If they do discuss things, I'm not privileged to any of those conversations. Those probably take place on the golf course away from the rest of the world. Or at Max's East Texas ranch."

Jackie really didn't care for the current President or his lifestyle, but this was not the time or place to make that known. Jackie thanked Ms. Cox and told her that she'd get back in touch when she received that letter from the EEOC.

In the meantime, Jackie tried to wait patiently for the EEOC to make their move. After several days she decided to inquire, just to keep herself one step ahead of the investigation. Much to her surprise Mr. Jones advised her that'd just mailed a letter to her.

"Since I have you on the phone, I want go ahead and discuss something with you," he added. "I sent them a request to meet with us and settle this issue. We were a little shocked when we received their reply. It states you do not work for that company."

"WHAT!" Jackie shouted. "How can they say that? I have a check stub to prove it."

"This is just a ploy to try to slow us down, but it won't work. I'm about to reissue the form and address it directly to the corporate office so that it doesn't have to go through anyone else's hands. I assure you, Mrs. Kennard, this is just a minor setback. Don't let it bother you. We'll get it handled. However, I suspect this will be the beginning of many frustrating attempts to get this matter peacefully resolved."

That evening Jackie went back to the therapist for another session. This time, Jackie was better able to control herself and she talked with the doctor in depth about her situation. The doctor recommended that Jackie stay focused and allow the legal system to work. They talked for another two hours, and at one point the doctor said, "This Tom guy and the situation he created is classic mob behavior—a girlfriend on Friday and Saturday nights and a wife during the week. However, I think this guy has it reversed and sees you in the girlfriend position during the week. You need to be VERY careful dealing with this man. I think he may be telling you the truth about his past." She paused, looking into Jackie's eyes. "For some reason he feels comfortable around you—perhaps because you remind him of someone from his past that he trusted. For whatever reason, he confides in you almost like a confession to clear his conscience. Don't ever judge or scold him, because if you do he'll probably eliminate you."

"Oh, that's just great," Jackie said.

"I think you really need protection, like maybe police surveillance. Do you have a security system in your home?"

"Yes," Jackie said, clenching her hands together.

"I'm not trying to scare you any more than you already are. I know that you're already terrified, but I want to say for the record that you need to be very cautious. I'd like to see you again in a couple of days."

However, the next day Jackie received a phone call from the doctor advising Jackie that she'd received a call from the corporate office HR department advising her that she could no longer treat Jackie.

"Why?" Jackie asked.

"I don't know," the doctor replied. "They simply told me I could no longer treat you." She paused. "But I'm willing to continue seeing you, and I'll address this issue with the insurance company directly. Or I can bill you separately and you can try to get your money from them at a later date."

"I'm really sorry for this inconvenience," Jackie said.

"It isn't your fault. We'll get through this. You just need to know someone's on your side. Why don't you come back tonight so we can further discuss other things that need to be addressed? I'll see you around 7:00 p.m."

Over the last several months, a therapist, an eye doctor, a neurologist, a chiropractor, and a stress management coach had treated Jackie. Yet she still experienced severe headaches, sleepless nights, uncontrollable trembling, and inability to function or control her emotions. She was still vomiting up blood and losing weight.

Finally, she received a phone call from the CFO of the company, Marvin Singleton, who wanted to fly into town and have a one-on-one meeting with her. Jackie knew she was screwed when she walked into his office and the conversation started.

He peered at her from behind a massive teak wood desk. "I have a letter for you from our attorney, Marion Littleworth. She has completed a through investigation. She came to the conclusion that this issue is resolved."

"How so?" Jackie asked.

"It's none of your business," he said. "Our attorney advised that I am under no obligation to disclose that information to you."

Jackie sat quietly, waiting for his next earth-moving statement.

He then requested in a demanding tone of voice that she respond. "I'd like to hear your response to this and know what you're thinking or planning to do."

Jackie had no intention of giving him information the company could use against her. She sat staring at the top of his desk.

Singleton slammed his hand onto the desk, making a loud sound that caused her to jump. "Damn it, woman, I want to know your thoughts on this!"

Jackie stared directly into his face pondering if she should say what she was thinking. She couldn't resist—she had to know. She leaned forward and quietly stated, "I just have one thing on my mind, sir." She continued in a voice so quiet that he had to strain to hear her. "Did you handle this like you would've handled it for your wife or daughter?"

Singleton's face turned bright red and he pounded his fist on the desktop. "Damn it, woman, if you think I'm gonna throw a bunch of money at you, you're crazy! You're lucky you still have a job! Now get yourself the hell out of here and back to work!"

"No, thank you!" she replied, "but I would like to have my letter now."

"What letter?" he barked.

"You know, the one that you said you had for me."

He opened his briefcase, retrieved a letter, and tossed it onto the desk in front of her. She picked it up and walked out without another word. Just before she reached for the doorknob, he said, "Jackie, you'll be sorry if you try to pursue this!"

She stopped dead in her tracks, refusing to turn and look at him.

He continued, "It just wouldn't be healthy for you. I know a lot of people in this business, and I'll see that you never work in this industry ever again."

Jackie almost laughed as she replied with a one-sided smile, "Really, Mr. Singleton? What makes you think I want to?" Then she opened the door and slammed it behind her.

Jackie immediately went into her office and wrote out her letter of resignation, which she turned in to Stan, citing that internal threats, obstacles, and business problems had not allowed her to perform her job to the best of her ability.

Stan read it and looked up at her. "Are you sure?" he asked. "I thought Mr. Singleton was here to get this thing settled with you."

"Maybe that's what he thought," she replied, "but it didn't happen." She offered him her hand. "Stan, I appreciate everything you did for me, but I really can't see me here any longer. My health simply won't take any more."

"I'm sorry," he replied. "You're a damn good person. Do what you've got to do to resolve this." As they shook hands, he added. "I wish you luck, Jackie. I wish it could have turned out better for you. I have a feeling we'll be seeing each other under legal circumstances in the future."

"Probably," she replied as she left his office.

Jackie made a couple of phone calls, and before the day was over she had two interviews set up with other companies. The first one hired her on the spot and wanted her to start right away. Jackie knew the sooner she started the better she'd feel, especially with a regular paycheck coming in.

She was in her new employer's office late one night just before closing when she heard someone knock on her window. It was already dark outside and she couldn't see who was knocking. She got up to open the front door, expecting to see a customer, but just as she unlocked the door someone jerked it from the outside, pulling her off balance. Jackie stumbled and caught herself just in time to see Tom and Todd. "What the hell?" she exclaimed.

As usual, both men had been drinking. Tom yelled. "Hey there, Jackie. I really do need to talk to you, in your office." He grabbed her arm and led her down the hallway. Obviously he thought she was alone as he took her into the first office, which just happened to be hers. He closed the door behind them and started asking questions.

"So, Jackie you been good? I mean, you been talking to anybody about anything?"

She shook her head. "Of course not."

He took a pencil from Jackie's desk, held it up inches in front of her face, and snapped it in half. "Don't forget, I can have this done to you if you don't keep your mouth shut about what we talked about before."

Before she could reply, her new boss came busting through the door. "What the hell is going on here? What are you doing here? Who are you? You need to leave now, or I'm about to call the police."

"No need," Tom replied, "I was just leaving. I'll see you again, Jackie."

Just then Todd came into the room and announced that he was there looking for a job. Howard said, "Well you aren't going to find one here. Now if you will excuse us, we were locking up to go home."

Before Tom walked out the door he looked back at Jackie and said, "Be good. I'll see you later."

"What the hell was that all about?" Howard asked.

"An intimidation tactic from my former employer," Jackie said.

"Well, it worked," Howard said, wiping sweat from his forehead. "Those bastards scared me. I thought something bad was about to happen. If they come back, I'll call Richard and tell him to put them on a short leash. No, screw that. I'm calling him tomorrow morning. They have no business busting in here like that." He paused and looked at her. "Are you sure that's all it is, Jackie? That big one seemed like he was on a mission for something."

"I'm sure," she replied.

Just then they both turned their attention to the TV in the front office as the news highlights came on. Yet another woman had come forward naming President Bill Clinton in a scandalous relationship.

"Wow," Howard remarked. "Let's close up shop so we can get home to see what this is all about."

# CHAPTER THIRTY-SIX

The next day Jackie phoned Attorney Cox and requested an immediate appointment with her to discuss threats Tom had previously made about hunting her down. It was apparently clear he had intentions of carrying out his threats from the night before, and she believed if someone else hadn't been there, she probably would not be having this conversation right now. Attorney Cox advised that Jackie make a call to EEOC and discuss the situation with them, asking them to drop the investigation and immediately issue a Right to Sue Letter so the legal part could get underway. Then she could get a restraining order against Tom.

Howard was already in his office when Jackie got to work that morning. She wasn't sure if he heard her talking to her attorney or if he was still shaken from the previous night's incident, but he seemed genuinely concerned and called Jackie into his office to talk with her.

"Jackie," he said, looking into her eyes, "I've known of you within the industry and I'm really happy to have you as an employee, but I need to know what the hell's going on between you and those two goons who showed up here last night. I got the feeling the big one intended harm to you. Do you want to enlighten me on anything before I make my call to Richard?"

"Well," Jackie said, "As I told you during my job interview, I've filed a grievance with EEOC against Richard's company, and those two were named as perpetrators." She sighed and took a deep breath. "There are some things I don't feel comfortable discussing openly, but I can tell you I'm obtaining counsel and plan to go forward with this matter."

"Well, let me advise you—they're a large conglomerate. They own everything in the manufactured housing industry, from the material, to the delivery company, to the mortgage company they use to finance it all. They have some very heavy hitters, and they're known as a very a close-knit group. Hell, Richard lives next door to Wayne Marker."

"Who's Wayne Marker?"

"You know Wayne," Howard replied. "He owns and operates the delivery division of their operation. Personally, I'd prefer not to live next door to my delivery guy, or anyone else I do business with. I don't like to have work contacts around me when I get home." He drummed his fingers on the desk. "But Jackie, I just want to tell you I've had business dealings with these people in the past. They took over a factory that carried a line of homes I'd been buying for years. They tried to sue me and refused to provide me with any more housing inventory once they took over the operations. We settled the thing out of court, and as you can see, I'm still carrying that line of homes. I don't really give a big fat rat's ass if I ever sell one or not, but for them the issue was, 'We'll squash you because we're big and you're little.' However, they backed off after I obtained a big high-powered attorney and filed on them in federal court.

"Good for you," Jackie said.

"Yeah, but you should watch your back because they don't fight fair. At first I thought that encounter last night had to do with my past experience with them. I didn't realize your deal is such a big issue to them. I just don't ever want you being in here by yourself. And I never want you showing any houses after dark. I don't care who it is. I wouldn't put it past them to send a messenger. Just be careful. Take no risks."

"Thank you so much, Howard. It sure makes me feel good to know you're concerned about me."

For the first time in a long while, Jackie actually felt relaxed at work. Even the drive home wasn't as stressful. But when she arrived home that evening and listened to the message on the answering machine, she realized her problems were never far away.

"Heyyy Jackieee, you know who this is. Calll mee!" came across in an ominous-sounding whisper.

Though it was obviously Tom, she chose to ignore it and hit the erase button. Again the phone rang, and she just let the machine pick up. Again in was Tom's voice. He said, "Jackie, call me," and then hung up. She erased this message also. The phone rang again approximately twenty minutes later, and again she didn't answer. It was Tom again, and this time he said: "Jackie, I know you're in there 'cause I'm sitting in front of your house. Now Pick Up the God Damn Phone!"

She snatched the phone off the cradle and snapped, "What do you want?"

A moment of silence, and then he said, "I just wanted to talk to you, I miss you being at work and I want to make sure that you're goin all right. I don't like you working for that creep Howard."

"I'm doing fine," she replied.

Again there was a pause before Tom said, "Jackie, why don't you let me get you a better job at another lot? Just tell me where you want to work at, and I'll fix it so you can work there."

"No thanks!" she replied.

"Why not?" he demanded.

"Because I don't need or want you to get me a job. I prefer to work wherever I wanna work."

"Jackie, I'd feel better if you'd go to work somewhere else, like maybe for Shane Sturmer. He has his own lot now."

Jackie shouted, "Hell no! Are you talking about that filthy little bastard who worked at the Midway Park location when I first started there? The one who demonstrated fucking his wife over a chair? No way! Thanks, but no thanks. I'm just fine where I am."

Tom laughed. "You know Jackie, I don't think I've ever met a woman like you." He paused. "Well, maybe my first old lady. She was real tough too. I admire that in a woman."

"Leave me alone!" she screamed and hung up the phone.

Again, the phone rang. She snatched it up and shouted, "Stop calling me!"

George replied, "Why? Don't you still love me?"

"George," she said, "I'm sorry. Some creep keeps calling."

"Where are you?" she asked.

"Actually, I'm just finishing installing the new wood floor at Tom's house."

"Tom who?" She asked.

"You know, Tom and Lucrezia."

"George… are you finished?"

"I hope so," he replied. "I've been all day on this."

"Please come home now," she said.

"Is something wrong?"

"Yeah, kinda, but we can talk about it whenever you get here."

Jackie paced back and forth for the next thirty-five minutes until she saw George pull safely into their drive. She walked outside to let him know how much she'd missed him and how glad she was that he was finally home.

That evening over dinner she told him that the ties between them and Tom and Lucrezia had to be cut. Jackie explained that since she'd filed her grievance it probably meant she shouldn't have contact with anyone from Midway Housing and vice versa. Jackie felt it best to just leave it at that.

"Okay," George answered, "I'll do whatever you say."

After that conversation, Jackie realized she was going to have to change careers.

Otherwise, Tom would continue calling and trying to involve himself in all of her business.

The next morning when Jackie arrived at the office, she noticed no one else was there yet. She sat in her car for a few minutes before she decided *I'm just early. It will be all right.* As she entered the building she noticed there weren't any lights on, and she stumbled over something in the doorway of her office. She looked down to see all her personal belongings in a box. Lying on top of the box was a note that read, "Jackie, I'm sorry, but I can't take a chance on you. Good luck."

And with that, her sixteen-year career was ended. Nobody wanted to hire the person who'd go against such a giant in the industry. She didn't know what she was going to do, but she obviously needed to seek employment outside the mobile home business. Since the economy was doing very well, she had a large selection of jobs to choose from.

Knowing it was best to stay in a field she was familiar with, Jackie chose the financial side of the housing industry. There were as many opportunities out there as there were people to fill them, so Jackie prepared her resume and faxed it to several employers who'd recently run ads in the classified section of the newspaper. She received several replies and started interviewing the next day. She was surprised with the offers that started coming in and decided that this was the best thing for her to do in light of her situation.

One company where she interviewed had an excellent location. The main employee entrance was underground and required a special ID card to enter the parking lot and again to gain entrance into the building. Once inside, the picture ID card had to be used to move from floor to floor. This was truly a comfortable setting, and Jackie accepted the employment offer they extended to her. Seeing how she and George didn't have the money to celebrate Christmas, she welcomed the opportunity to start over and begin the new year with a new employer and a good base salary.

George was struggling with it all too. Even though he didn't know all the details about the situation, he knew that he had to keep trying to make ends meet while they awaited some word from the EEOC. Naturally, they hadn't received the money owed to them from Midway Housing. George wanted to reestablish his own business out of the house, but that required too much cash investment up front, and they just didn't have it at the time, so he decided to try something new himself. He went to work driving a truck. Unfortunately, the new job called for him to be away from home several nights a week, but he didn't have much choice.

Just as Jackie thought things were calming down, she came home to find an eviction notice posted on her front door. At first she thought it was some sort of stupid advertisement, but when she opened it, she realized it was not joke. The couple she and George had purchased the home from, Dexter's aunt and uncle had, out of the blue, decided they didn't want to sell the house to George and Jackie and were therefore filing eviction on them to be removed from the property, citing inability to make payments.

Jackie instantly knew this was a lie and a trick to cause them further damage because she had filed a complaint on Dexter and the company. Just then George arrived home, and Jackie shared the notice with him.

"Those motherfuckers!" he shouted. "I oughtta go over there and just beat the literal fuck outta that little bastard Dexter." George threw the notice on the table and asked, "What do you wanna do, Jackie?"

"I want to get a lawyer and see just what our options are," she replied.

George picked up the phone and called information, requesting a specific lawyer he'd done business with in the past. He got right through to his attorney, and when he heard the problem, the lawyer asked them to come to his office immediately.

The attorney instructed them on something called Vernon's Law, which covered legal issues involving renters, tenants, and landowners. He explained, after looking over their agreement, that the owners had no grounds for issuing an eviction notice. Immediately the attorney composed the letter to them, which Jackie and George both signed. They gave the couple one chance to resolve the issue, or they were going to go to court.

What a nightmare! Jackie and George didn't need any more hardships to deal with, but they realized this was a tactic to distract them from the other issues, plus get revenge. From then on it was something every day with the owners—they constantly harassed Jackie or George, making their lives miserable. After battling with these people for nearly a month, the truth came out. As soon as the attorney obtained a court order signed by the judge, they were able to contact the mortgage company where the house was financed to inquire about the account. Much to their surprise, they discovered that the couple George and Jackie had been making payments to had not made a payment on the house in six months!

George was pissed! He was ready to rip someone's head off. Jackie and the attorney convinced him there were better ways to handle the situation. After George cooled off, he decided they needed to focus on the larger battle at hand—and the only way to do that was to move out of the house. Deep down, Jackie knew he was right, but she struggled against losing all the money they'd tied up in the house. Still, they really had no other choice. They put most of their belongings in a storage building and kept out only what they needed for daily life.

They rented a one-bedroom apartment in the upstairs of an old converted house. The quarters were cramped, but after talking about it and preparing themselves for the expected legal battle ahead, in addition to the monies still being withheld by the company. They decided to scale down their living arrangements for a while. So they said their goodbyes to the neighbors and moved. Some of the neighbors still kept in contact and later confided in George that since the owners had moved back into the house the husband fell ill, and neither of them had been able to work. Consequently, the original owners, Dexter's aunt and uncle, were facing both bankruptcy and foreclosure on the house.

# CHAPTER THIRTY-SEVEN

On June 12, 1997, some eight months after she initially filed her complaint, Jackie received her official notification from the Equal Employment Opportunity Commission in the form of a Right To Sue Letter. In fact, because Jackie had filed on multiple charges, she was awarded three separate Right To Sue Letters. The first was for discrimination, the second for discrimination and constructive discharge, and the third was an amended charge of discrimination and violation of Title VII of the Civil Rights Act of 1964. This was actually amended in 1991 and later became the Texas Commission on Human Rights Act, or TCHRA.

Immediately, she called Mr. Jones at EEOC to thank him for his help in initiating a closing to this situation. He apologized for the delay and explained that the process had taken so long because the Dallas office of the EEOC received more than 15,000 complaints from June 1996 through June 1997, and each one of these had to be looked over and evaluated during this time frame. However, out of those 15,000 complaints, only 200 Right To Sue Letters were issued, and three of those were hers. He went on to wish her the best of luck, and he hoped she'd some put the problems behind her.

Little did Jackie know, this was only the first step in a legal battle that would take place over the next three years. Without knowing what awaited her, she was thrilled to finally receive those letters. She immediately called Attorney Cox and made an appointment for the next day.

The only thing Jackie could think was, *FINALLY! After two years, something positive!* Jackie could hardly wait to see Attorney Cox and deliver the letters from the EEOC. She felt an inner glow of hope for the first time in a long time.

The next morning, after Attorney Cox welcomed Jackie to her office, she opened the discussion by saying, "Before we begin, I'd like to go over some expectations. What do you want or expect to come out of all this?"

"Well," Jackie said, "for starters, I'd like my job back. I'd like to be compensated full commission for all the mobile homes I closed and funded but wasn't paid for." She hesitated briefly. "You know, I'd really like to see Dexter, Hillary, Tom, and Richard lose their jobs. Then, I'd like to be reinstated at the management level they promised me and put on my own lot somewhere as the GM."

"Is that all?" Attorney Cox asked, smiling.

"No. I'd also like to know the truth about Tom's background and whether he did kill that man like he told me he did. Then I'd like to see justice done with that."

"Is that all? Ms. Cox asked again.

"I believe that's it," Jackie said.

Then Attorney Cox leaned forward, looking directly into Jackie's face. "I'm sorry, but you won't get any of that. Why should they fire those two idiots? They were only doing everything demanded of them." She paused, fingering her pen. "Jackie, think about it. You're the only one who refused to conform to their way. You were too high-maintenance for them. They did what they set out to do, and that was to get rid of both you and your husband. It was just a matter of time before one or both of you stumbled on something they couldn't explain away. So accept it. No matter what it is you want, they are not going to give it up. Therefore you have to get their attention through their pocketbook."

Jackie opened her mouth to speak, but Ms. Cox held up one hand and continued.

"Unfortunately, most people, once they get going and start making big bucks like this company has, quickly forget how and who got them there. They operate off green backs and greed. Think about it, Jackie. They don't have ANY intention of EVER employing you again—or any of your descendents for that matter. You can forget that request. From this day forward, they cease to be people with names. To us, they become a six-figure cash amount on a demand letter. Get that through your head and accept it. They thought this was over for them the day you left. So, you now have a new career, and that career is to make them pay, and pay big! The question is, are you ready for the battle?"

"I don't know," Jackie replied. She thought about how she'd worked hard all her adult life for everything she'd earned. What she was hearing something was hard for her to understand. "Ms. Cox, you'll have to be patient with me. I'm just not the kind of person motivated by greed. I don't know how to deal with what you just said."

"That's okay," she replied. "That's what lawyers are for. It's my job to prepare you for battle. But first I brought you down to talk with you about something I really wanted to discuss face-to-face."

"Okay, I'm ready," Jackie replied.

"Well, you met my partner the other day, Max Mulligan. He's very involved with someone in Washington DC right now. After meeting with him about your case, we think it best if we don't handle it at this time. Its not that we don't feel you have an excellent case—it's just that with Max supporting this well-known politician in Washington on a similar case, we feel it will be in your best interests to use another law firm. It's called a conflict of interest. He would have trouble explaining to the media when they found out—and believe me they would—how and why Max can represent a case from the opposite side of the same issue he defended his well-known political friend through. She paused looking at Jackie, waiting for her reply.

Jackie knew Ms. Cox was referring to President Clinton and his sexual harassment cases. Since Paula Jones' law firm was located in

Dallas, although Max Mulligan didn't directly represent the President, it made perfect sense that the President used Max as a friend and advisor—plus Max was near the courthouse for any necessary quick filings to offset the Paula Jones' legal team.

Jackie didn't know what to say. She was paralyzed. She questioned in her mind, *Is this it? All this effort for nothing?*

Then the attorney added, "Jackie, I've prepared a letter of introduction for you to three other attorneys in Dallas who specialize in this sort of thing. I have even briefed each of them on your case and they've all three agreed to talk with you. You can choose whomever you feel most comfortable with. Here are their names, addresses, and phone numbers." She held up an envelope. "I want to wish you luck, and I hope this gets resolved very quickly. I know it has created a huge strain on both you and your husband, not to mention your health and family concerns. I hope the next time I hear from you you'll have brought these bastards to their knees."

Jackie continued sitting with her head bowed for a moment, and then replied, "Thank you Ms. Cox," as she took the envelope.

# CHAPTER THIRTY-EIGHT

Jackie took the letter of recommendation then went directly home to make the phone calls to determine which of the three lawyers she wanted to use. After making the initial call, she waited for each of them to call her back. As she talked with them one by one, she determined she'd go with Jackie Bernard and set their first appointment for the next morning.

They discussed the case and signed a contingent agreement contract, outlining settlement fees to be split between them when the case settled or went to trial. By this time, Jackie felt more comfortable with the lawyer-client thing and was able to openly discuss her issues with Ms. Bernard.

Ms. Bernard told Jackie she'd compose a demand letter and send it to the company's attorney right away. Once they had received a response, they would determine where to go from there. Ms. Bernard predicted this Fortune 500 Company would ditch the idiots who were responsible and make a hasty settlement.

"I don't want this case just settled," Jackie stated.

"What do you mean?" The attorney asked.

"A murder was committed, and I want this man brought to justice as part of my terms to resolving the case. I don't want them to just write a check, seal my case, put it in a file somewhere, and forget about it. Settling the case just further stuffs the truth. I'd rather not go into a business relationship with you if that's all you plan to do about this."

Looking surprised, Ms. Bernard said, "Well, we have to start somewhere, so let's send this demand letter and see how they respond."

"And then what?" Jackie asked.

"We'll meet back here in my office and go from there."

The eight-page letter outlined every detail of Jackie's complaints, including allegations of sexual harassment, sex discrimination, and constructive discharge violations of Title VII of the Civil Rights Act of 1964. It went on to spell out details such as invasion of privacy, intentional infliction of emotional distress, assault and battery, negligence in hiring, supervision, training, and retention of employees, along with interference of business.

Page three described how Mrs. Kennard was a model employee and had often received awards for highest sales performance, company wide. The next several pages spelled out thirty-four different sexual harassment charges one by one, detail by detail, describing each incident and quoting the exact words used. For example: "Here's a vibrator go take a few minutes to fuck yourself" or the everyday classic, "She's a swallower, not a spitter." They also included Hillary's outburst insinuating Jackie was "fucking" her husband, Dexter. Then Tom's comment about how Dexter would look like a Chihuahua fucking a German shepherd if he ever were to ever mount Jackie. The pages went on and on, describing incident after incident, detail after detail.

Last but not least, the thirty-fourth incident described how Dexter called Jackie to his office for a meeting and then unzipped his pants and pulled a live snake out in front of her. Toward the end of the list was a paragraph detailing the conversation between Jackie and Tom where Tom discussed his involvement in the witness protection program, confessed to the murder he'd committed years earlier in another state, and his threat to Jackie should she ever reveal this to anyone. The letter included Tom's threat to "hunt her down" should she ever leave the company and his recent attempt to carry out that threat. The letter concluded with notification to file a motion to disqualify both the law firm and attorney Littleworth due to the fact that both she and Mr. Richard Spaniel completely misrepresented her and their intentions while conducting a four-and-a-half-hour deposition with Mrs. Kennard, making Ms. Littleworth subject to being called as a witness for the plaintiff.

The letter stated, in part:

Furthermore, I believe a jury would be extremely sympathetic, given her excellent job performance, the disgusting nature of the sexual harassment, the physical assault by a customer after she previously reported concern of his awkward actions around her, and that, despite her opposition, the conduct not only continued, but increased in severity over time. If Mrs. Kennard does not obtain the position from which she was discharged or an equivalent position along with front pay, back pay with interest, as well as award for the substantial attorney's fees occurred in bringing forth her action filed, Mrs. Kennard will also be entitled to recovery of compensatory and punitive damages for her Title VII and TCHRA claims.

Mrs. Kennard has already suffered severe emotional distress due to the discrimination and harassment and for her constructive discharge. She had to seek medical and psychological treatment and continues to suffer extreme anxiety and depression, in addition to medical attention for a bleeding ulcer. The emotional devastation caused to Mrs. Kennard by all this will certainly support a large compensatory damage award. (Since we are filing our case in the Federal Court please be aware unlike District Court there is no cap on damages that a jury can award in a case such as this.) Midway Housing Corporation's obvious disregard for the applicable laws and the outrageous threats to her physical safety if she reported all the discrimination conduct will also support a large punitive damage award. I am representing Mrs. Kennard and have advised her of the strengths of her case should she proceed to litigation. However, she has instructed me to advise you of the advantages of resolution of this dispute, should you be willing to resolve this matter in the early stages of this conflict. Accordingly, if Midway Housing wishes to resolve this matter short of litigation, Mrs. Kennard would like to inform you what she would be willing to settle this now.

1. Payment in the amount of $750,000.00 in total resolution of her employment discrimination claims and tort claims.
2. Termination of employment for Dexter Kuykendahl, Tom Kerakasco, Richard Spaniel, Todd Hunter, and Hillary Kuykendahl.
3. Signing a waiver and release acceptable to both parties relating to all claims of discrimination claims and tort.
4. An agreement signed by both parties that no negative information regarding Mrs. Kennard will be given to anyone by anyone related to the company, either through current employment of any such person or after termination of employment from the company, with any information disseminated regarding the circumstances of her employment restricted solely to the following information:

a. Dates of employment
b. Description of job duties
c. Salary received
d. Letter of reference signed by CEO and CFO of Midway Housing Corporation

5. Removal of any/all negative information from Mrs. Kennard's file.
6. Provision of training on discrimination and harassment at the company by an outside consulting service specializing in such training, requiring everyone to attend and letters of completions to be signed by Mrs. Kennard for each of the named people to be displayed within their office at all times.

Otherwise we intend to file immediately in Federal Court for:

1. Economic damages for her invasion of privacy, assault and battery, slander and defamation, and interference with business relationships claims including back pay, front pay, reinstatement, retroactive seniority, pension benefits, promotions or other positions she otherwise would have been entitled, all other employee benefits including health,

disability and life insurance benefits to which she otherwise would have been entitled, and any other relief necessary to compensate her for the tort violations;
2. Compensatory damages for mental anguish, humiliation, loss of privacy, loss of reputation and emotional distress relating to her invasion of privacy, assault and battery, slander and defamation, and interferences with business relationships claims;
3. Special damages including compensation for lost earnings and medical expenses relating to her slander and defamation claim.
4. Pre-judgment interest at the legally prescribed rate from the date of violations until judgment as well as post-judgment interest is applicable.

See Pacific Mutual Life Insurance Company vs. Haslip 111 S. CT. 1032 argued 3 October 1990.

This offer is far less than what would likely be awarded at a trial of this severe nature, but it is a good-faith effort to avoid litigation and further choking the legal system. Should you decide not to accept this offer, Mrs. Kennard's amount will greatly increase should she be forced to litigate.

*I have also discussed with my client the possibility of early mediation of this matter and can ask the courts to assign a mediator right away for early meditation and resolution. If not, Mrs. Kennard intends to file her lawsuit in Federal Court and move forward immediately. Please be aware, and notify your employees, based on the threats and allegations relating to Mr. Kerakasco and his past, I am notifying Midway Housing that a protective order has been put in place to protect Mrs. Kennard and precludes Mr. Kerakasco from initiating any further contact with Mrs. Kennard either in person, writing, telephone, messenger, telegram, pager, answering machine, US mail, or fax machine. Please advise me whether Midway Housing Corporation wishes to accept this offer before the end of business on June 20, 1997. Otherwise, on June 21, 1997, this case will be filed in The Federal Court Northern District Dallas, Texas.*

Upon reading this, Jackie braced herself against the wall as she sank to the floor. Somehow seeing it in writing brought it all back to life. As she sat on the floor fanning herself with the letter, she was now more than ever scared of what the company might do to try to stop her. Though the demand letter contained a clause naming the company responsible for protective measures, she wasn't ready to stake her life on the company protecting her, since they'd never showed the slightest interest in her welfare—or in following the rules.

# CHAPTER THIRTY-NINE

For eight days there was no reply—not even a phone call, until finally Jackie couldn't stand the suspense. She had to call Ms. Bernard's office.

The attorney said, "No Jackie, I haven't heard a thing. As the demand letter stated, we'll go forward tomorrow if they haven't responded and let the court dictate to them their next move." There was a pause, and then she said, "Hang on a second. I think someone just delivered a letter from them. I'll call you right back."

A courier had delivered a message from the company. It read:

Dear Ms. Bernard;

In response to your letter, this law firm has represented Midway Housing in the past. However, the person you reference, Jackie Kennard, recently resigned our employment after an investigation into her complaints was settled internally. We do not now nor did we ever intend to submit to mediation or settlement in her claims after our investigation proved false accusations on behalf of Mrs. Kennard. Therefore, the answer to your question in regards to arranging a meeting to discuss mediation or settlement is unnecessary to proceed at this time, and we would like for it to stand for the record. Our response to this is absolutely, no. The allegations are completely unmerited and we are satisfied with our findings that support our conclusion.

Respectfully,<br>Attorney Marion Littleworth

Immediately, Attorney Bernard phoned Jackie to tell her the decision. "I pretty much expected this," the attorney added, "so I've already prepared a document called the Plaintiff's Original Complaint and Jury Demand. Now that I've formally heard from them, I'll file that tomorrow with the federal court, and we move forward from there. I'll send you a copy in the mail."

"Is there anything else I should do?" Jackie asked.

"Not really. I'll see if I can budget for a private investigator to start looking into Kerakasco's past to see if we can disprove his story. But I pretty much expect that will turn into a dead end. I've seen a lot of these blowhard guys who try to impress people, only to have it come out during the deposition that they were in fact lying."

"Don't bet on that," Jackie said. "You haven't seen or heard him yet. He's pretty convincing with his story. Also, don't forget, I have access to phone service worldwide with my job, I can make some calls myself."

"That's fine," Ms. Bernard replied, "But I don't want you doing anything they might use against us, so let me see what I can do from this side."

After she hung up, Jackie still didn't feel satisfied. The conversation had sparked her desire to find the truth on her own. The very next Saturday she started going to the library and reading whatever she could on court cases similar to hers. Then she studied the nature of what each case was about: Title VII and Involuntary Discharge. Jackie thought the more she knew about the process, the better she'd be prepared to handle it. However, she didn't necessarily have to go to the library to get an education on the subject because many of the issues she'd faced were splashed on every newspaper and magazine cover from coast to coast—in reference to President Clinton's legal troubles. Questions like: Should She Be Heard? referring to Paula Jones about President Clinton. Then there was the Jessica Flowers story to spice things up. Everyone everywhere received a daily dose, whether they wanted it or not.

Tired of being bombarded with all this in addition to her own situation, Jackie decided to try something new. She decided to search Tom's current name and see if she could find out anything about his prior life. Or did his name really come from a character in a book he'd described to her? Jackie searched throughout the library and finally found the book in the reference section. Reading through the list of characters in the show she remembered him talking about, she gasped and chills ran up her spine as she stared at the printed page and saw exactly what Tom had described in his drunken stupor. This was the exact name and the person he'd chosen to become! She had to take this to her attorney! This was proof! She made copies and immediately drove to Ms. Bernard's office to share the "find" with her.

The attorney smiled and shook her head. "This doesn't mean anything, Jackie. Anyone could have used this name—it's not a secret. It proves nothing. I guarantee you, whenever we get him in a deposition you'll see he's full of hot air and his story will deflate. Before we finish with him, you'll see he just a guy who likes to drink and brag about who he wishes he was."

"Okay," Jackie replied in a disappointed sigh. "I just thought... I was hoping." She shrugged. "I'm sorry that I wasted your time."

"That's all right," Ms. Bernard replied. "At least you're involved in the case, which is good. I'll keep you posted when I hear something."

"Thanks again," Jackie said, preparing to leave the office.

"Oh, before you go, I do have something we need to go over. Can you bring in that desk diary you mentioned—where you kept notes when you worked at the Midway Park housing office? Also, Christine Cox said you have some tapes. Do you know what I'm talking about?"

"I sure do," Jackie said. "I left those at Ms. Cox's office. I just assumed she'd sent them to you along with the other stuff."

"Oh really?" Ms. Bernard replied as she picked up the phone to call Ms. Cox. "I'll just call her right now, I'll let you know whenever I have them here. I'll need to familiarize myself with them first, and then I'll probably have some questions for you. I'll be in touch, probably in a few days."

"Great! Have a nice weekend," Jackie replied as she left the office.

That night George asked Jackie out for a quiet dinner, just the two of them, so they could relax and talk. They went to a local restaurant, which, like all the other restaurants on a Friday night, was packed. As they stood in the crowded lobby waiting for a table, George excused himself for a moment to go to the men's room. From where she stood, Jackie could see inside the bar. Scanning the room she noticed a couple of empty seats at the bar. Hoping to grab them so they could sit and have a drink while waiting for their table, Jackie started to move through the crowd. She felt George touching her elbow and turned around to show him the empty seats. Before she could say anything, he pulled her towards him and she felt him lean against her, his lips in her hair, about to whisper something into her ear.

But something just didn't feel right. As Jackie leaned her head toward him, she realized it wasn't George—it was Tom who had her by the arm! He whispered, "I can always find you in a crowd." Then she heard him say something about fingerprints as she gasped and jerked away from him, half running through the crowd toward the restrooms, looking for George. Again, she felt Tom grab her, this time at the waist. She swung around, intending to hit him then she realized instead of Tom, this time it was George.

"Whoo," he chuckled, as he pulled her toward him. Then he realized Jackie was trembling, "What's wrong, honey?"

"I'm ready to go!" she demanded, scanning the crowded room looking for Tom. "I can't take this crowd—I can't breathe in here."

"Okay," George said, "But don't you want to get something to eat?"

"I just want to go home," she replied, clinging to his arm as they hurried back to the car. From that day forward, Jackie refused to go out to eat for fear of what Tom might do since she'd come forward with all his dirty secrets.

# CHAPTER FORTY

At the next attorney-client meeting, Ms. Bernard discussed with Jackie how the deposition would proceed. Jackie remarked, "I'll be fine as long as George is there with me."

"I'm sorry," Attorney Bernard stated, "but George is the last person any of us want in that room—especially after what you've told me and the fact that he knows very little about the charges. I don't think this is the right time or place to bring him in."

Jackie agreed reluctantly, shaking her head yes.

Ms. Bernard added, "You and I need to become VERY familiar with one another. I have to know everything about you and your past—the bad and the good. I don't care how bad or how minor something now seems to you, I don't care how embarrassing it was, I have to know everything. They are going to conduct a deposition on you, and they'll drag up everything they can find from your past. I'm certain their attorneys plan to hit you hard and heavy. They'll look into every job you ever held, talk to every doctor who ever treated you. They'll dig and dig until they have anything they can use to discredit you and make you look like a liar. They may even call you a liar. Believe me, with this amount of money at stake, these people will come at you hard."

"I hadn't thought about that," Jackie responded as she sighed a deep breath.

"You just have to look them square in the face and tell the truth. No matter how hard or how deeply it hurts, you can't allow them to see your feelings or let them push your emotional buttons. Once an attorney finds those, he'll use them over and over to try to destroy you. So, I want you to go home and make a list of all the things in your past that you can think of that might become an issue." Attorney Bernard paused for a moment before she continued. "I know this is hard for you Jackie, and I really hate to ask you, but I'll also need a list of names of every man you've ever slept with."

"WHAT! NO WAY!" Jackie shouted as she shot out of her chair.

"I'm sorry, but due to the nature of your case, I know they'll demand it."

I am NOT providing them or you any such list!" Jackie demanded, sitting back down.

"I'm sorry, but due to the nature of many of your charges they'll try and make you look like a promiscuous…"

"Slut?" Jackie added.

"Well, yes, and I don't want any surprises."

"Why am I on trial here, when they're the bad guys?" Jackie asked. "Why don't we get to ask them such embarrassing questions?"

"Oh we will," Attorney Bernard replied. "Believe me, we can ask some personal questions also. But I want to make certain you aren't thrown off whenever they ask you these shocking questions."

Jackie turned her head downward as she rubbed her hand back and forth across her forehead in an effort to hide her embarrassment before she answered. "The list is short, and I'd rather not give it out."

Ms. Bernard replied in a low, calming voice, "I'll settle for that right now, but I can't guarantee it won't come up from the other side. We'll work on that later."

Jackie kept her head bowed as the attorney continued, "Soon you'll receive a questionnaire in the mail called an Interrogatory, asking you about different things. You will need to complete it and return it to their attorney before the stated deadline. If you aren't sure about any of the answers, leave them blank, make a note in pencil in the side margin, and ask for a specific explanation."

Jackie nodded her understanding as she looked intensely at Attorney Bernard.

"I've also made an appointment for a therapist who'll evaluate you." She held up a hand before Jackie could interrupt. "I know you've already seen a therapist, but this one will become your expert witness after she determines the severity of your damages. It's okay for you to discuss everything with her—if you can. You will need to set aside about four to five hours for your first visit because she's going to put you through a thorough investigation. I've set it up for next Thursday. Can you make that date?"

"I'll just have to," Jackie replied with the shrug of her shoulder.

"Okay, that's all I have for you today." Attorney Bernard stated. "We'll meet again after your visit with the therapist."

During her meeting with the therapist, Jackie became very agitated and unable to control herself emotionally. She cried, she trembled, and she found it often too difficult to talk about many of the incidents. She really struggled with her words and fought back tears as she tried to tell about the assault she suffered at the hands one of the customers. But the most disturbing to her was remembering the way Tom described in detail the murder he'd committed, and his threats against her if she decided to go forward. Jackie wept openly for several minutes while the therapist just sat and observed her. Finally she stopped crying enough to apologize and share some of those explicit details with the doctor. She confided the only way she truly felt comfortable was to go home immediately after work take a hot shower, go inside a closet in her bedroom, close the door behind her, and sit alone in the dark. Sometimes she would take a flashlight with her to sit and read inside the closet. At other times she took a Walkman radio into the closet with her and listened to music until she heard George pull into the driveway.

Jackie also admitted she was frightened of what George would do if he ever found out what had happened to her. Because of that fear, she'd kept most of it from him. The therapist assured Jackie her fears were unmerited and that if Tom were in the witness protection program, she'd be able to find out because she, herself, had a connection in Washington that would allow her to check that out. Then she assured Jackie that if Tom was in fact part of the protection program there were probably people looking for him and he wouldn't last long once his cover was blown.

The doctor adamantly assured Jackie she was safe and her fears were false and probably unmerited because she was suffering from post-traumatic stress syndrome and was not processing the incidents out or finding closure to any of them. Therefore, the doctor stated, "Your imagination is simply taking control of your thought process."

She then suggested that she prescribe a medication that would allow Jackie to get the mental rest she needed and clear the cobwebs in her head so they could then begin the therapy to get her on the road to recovery.

Jackie agreed, thinking, *After all, what do I know? I have post-traumatic something or another.* She wanted to believe the doctor's explanation and needed to control her fear in order to get on with her life.

# CHAPTER FORTY-ONE

After months of trial preparation, medical treatment, and more delays from the defendants' side, a letter arrived from the federal judge ordering mediation before the case proceeded any further. It stated:

This order, in addition to giving orders, is also meant to impart certain information and give expectations of this Court. Read It Very Carefully.

Counsels are directed to confer for the purpose of submitting a Joint Status Report in this case. This report is expected within 30 days following the date this order is filed. At this conference, which needs to be in person by both Counsels, we shall discuss the nature and basis of claims and defenses in this case and the possibilities for a prompt settlement resolution, saving both time and expense for both sides. Therefore, I am assigning a mediator and plan to give you both all that information at our next scheduled meeting. This Court strongly encourages using the mediator BEFORE proceeding to trial. However, make no mistake about it; this Court is both able and very willing to take this case to trial if they so desire a trial. If you choose to appeal, you will need to do so with the Fifth Circuit Supreme Court of Appeals In accordance with 28 U.S.C. & 636(c).

So Ordered: July 30, 1997
United States Federal Judge Northern District Court

Immediately following, the mediator the judge had assigned refused to mediate the case, citing inability to deal with the defendants' attorney and law firm as the result of a previous case in which things went badly. This caused another delay, and the judge had to interview the mediator before he could determine what to do next.

After the interview, a second mediator was assigned and a date set for them to all meet to hash things out. The two groups were placed in separate rooms, and the mediator worked back and forth between the two offices while taking notes, suggesting terms, and supposedly negotiating toward a settlement. The mediator's office was strategically located in between so she could stop and refocus on all her notes before continuing with the other side. To Jackie, it appeared to be more like score-keeping. Even though this meeting was ordered by the court, the defendants clearly showed no intention of settling the issue until just before the eight-hour time limit expired, when Midway's attorney sent an offer to the table through the mediator. Attorney Bernard hastily opened it, reserving her comments until after she'd read it. She didn't have to say a word. Jackie knew it wasn't good from the look on her face.

Then Attorney Bernard's face turned bright red just before she yelled, "What the hell? Do they think I won't take this to the judge?"

"What is it?" Jackie asked. She took the note from Ms. Bernard read the offer, and then threw it onto the table in disgust. The offer was $2,500. "Let's get out of here." Jackie said as she stood up. "Another wasted day with this scum." She picked up the note reflecting their offer and handed it back to her attorney. "Ms. Bernard, please take this note to the judge tomorrow. We'll see how funny he thinks it is."

The mediator asked, "Can I try one more time?"

"NO!" Jackie snapped, "I'm through, finished, done! I'm ready to go."

Just then the phone sitting on the end table rang, and the mediator answered. She said, "I'll be right there." After hanging up, she told

Jackie and Ms. Bernard, "Please wait here. They have another offer."

After another ten minutes the mediator returned and laid another offer on the table. This one stated, "We'll pay all legal fees accumulated to this date to Attorney Bernard and $2,000 to Jackie Kennard."

Jackie snatched a piece of paper and pen and started writing in big bold letters

F - U- C -

"What are you doing?" Ms. Bernard snatched the paper from Jackie.

"Giving them MY answer," she replied.

"You can't do that!"

"Really? Then you go to the judge tomorrow with MY answer, and you tell him them have no respect for him, for me, for his mediator, or the law. Then you tell him I want to go to trial—the sooner the better. And if you can't tell him, then you call me and I'll tell him. But I am not going to sit through another one of these all-day filibusters to be insulted and humiliated by those filthy trailer trash bastards AGAIN. I just wasted $900 dollars on a court-ordered mediator to sit here all day. And for what? To be further insulted!"

Jackie grabbed her purse and stood. "I'm leaving now. Don't try to stop me. And if you choose to remain my attorney, you'll leave with me. Otherwise you can accept their offer and stay here with them." With that, she marched out of the conference room. As she stomped past the office where the defendants were sitting, she could hear them laughing hysterically. Before Jackie reached the elevator, Attorney Bernard was standing by her side, assuring her she would be in the judge's chambers first thing the next day.

As Attorney Bernard stood before the federal judge explaining the prior evening's experience, she could see from the stern look on his face that he was not happy with the mediation outcome either. He immediately moved to set a trial date and ordered that Jackie be given official notice that the trial was scheduled for September 18, 1998, with pre-trial conference on September 14, 1998.

That date was thirteen months into the future and seemed like a lifetime away to Jackie. She knew part of the defendants' plan was to just wear her down and outlast her. So she decided to use the time wisely and continue trying to find out whatever she could about the witness protection program so she could nail Tom.

She wasn't quite sure how to do this, but the library downtown seemed the logical place to start, using their Internet connection. After spending every Saturday morning there for a month without success, she decided to try another avenue. She checked out numerous books from the library, but this didn't help either.

However, Jackie couldn't spend every free minute researching this because she had to finish the Plaintiff's First Interrogatories to Defendants, Instruction and Definitions For Interrogatories. The document contained page after page filled with over 500 questions and was as thick as a book. It took her the better part of a month to complete the answers while working on it every night. Some of the questions had absolutely nothing to do with her claim.

She and her attorney then spent the next four months completing a mountain of paperwork and filings with the district clerk's office in preparation for the trial. Finally, the deposition date was set and agreed upon by everyone involved.

November 14, 1997—the deposition day—had not come soon enough to suit Jackie. On that cold morning in mid November she could hardly wait to get to Attorney Bernard's office and get this thing behind her. As she sat with Ms. Bernard inside her office going over certain things and receiving last-minute instructions, Jackie watched from the window as the defendants drove into the parking lot of the office. She immediately began trembling. Just seeing them all for the first time and knowing they were outside made her chest tighten up. Ms. Bernard looked over her shoulder out the window and then turned to Jackie and affirmed, "Don't worry, I'll be with you through the entire thing. I can't talk to you or answer any questions, but you can ask for a break if you need to get a drink or something."

"Don't forget, I'm hypoglycemic," Jackie reminded her. "I'll need to break occasionally so I can get something to snack on or drink."

"That's fine," Ms. Bernard said. "We should get this thing wrapped up today. Since they've already questioned you for over four hours, there shouldn't be much left to ask you about."

Then Attorney Bernard got up, secured her office door shut, and gave Jackie some last-minute instructions: "Number one, they're here to question you, not me. Don't turn and ask me anything. Just answer the questions as simply as you can, and always be truthful and to the point. Put on a poker face and show absolutely no emotion or anger no matter what they say or insinuate. Should their lawyer and I get into it, do not say anything. Just sit there until I give you instructions. Got it?"

"Got it," Jackie replied with a forced smile.

"Always remember, those creeps already know your hot buttons and your weak points. Their attorney will use them every chance he gets. Be ready, and think about your answers before you respond. Never, never answer a question using the words *absolutely* or *without a doubt*. If you do, he'll use it against you later. Believe me, this new attorney of theirs is very good at making people look bad. He also has a reputation for making big cases like this go away before they ever get to a court room."

Jackie grimaced. "Can he make the truth go away? Cause that's what he's going to hear from me."

The attorney smiled and hugged Jackie, wishing her luck, before they left her office to meet the defendants in the conference room down the hallway. When the conference door opened, every eye inside that room focused directly toward Jackie. She quickly scanned the room to see just who all was there, hoping she didn't appear as scared on the outside as she was feeling on the inside. There were quite a large number of people present. In addition to Jackie's legal team, the defendants had their new attorney, along with Richard Spaniel and the court reporter. Plus, they'd brought two legal assistants just to take notes and observe. All eyes stayed on Jackie as she took her assigned seat at the conference room table.

The defendants' attorney further fueled Jackie's fear as he made an announcement that they were all assembled today because of her allegations. He then asked Jackie to raise her right hand, state her name, and be sworn in before the questioning began. As she began stating her name, Attorney Woodcock yelled, "Last name first!"

Jackie jumped from the unexpected outburst but obliged with the correct way. Then, he proceeded to introduce himself.

"Mrs. Kennard, my name is Ralph Woodcock, and I'm the attorney representing Midway Housing, the defendants in this lawsuit. Do you understand what a deposition is?"

"Yes sir," she replied.

"I'm going to ask you a series of questions about the incidents which form the basis of this lawsuit, and the court reporter will take down your response word for word. Therefore, it is very important that you give a verbal answer each time and not just a nod of the head or a grunt for an answer. Do you understand that?"

"Yes, sir."

After a few more preliminary questions, Jackie's attorney interrupted, stating, "I need to have put in the record that this testimony given by my client today will remain confidential and not be shared with anyone outside this room with the exception of the judge or jury. It is most definitely not to be shared with Dexter Kuykendahl, Hillary Kuykendahl, or Tom Kerakasco for the client's assured safety and well-being, as the current restraining order states."

Attorney Woodcock had no verbal reply. He simply made note on one of his many legal pads before he continued.

Jackie then spent the next few hours answering generic questions about her current and previous addresses, marital status, and history of jobs for the past twenty-five years. Then the attorney asked personal questions about her and her divorce. She answered as instructed by her attorney—short and to the point, showing no emotion. When the defendants' attorney asked about her children and their whereabouts, she felt uncomfortable and had difficulty keeping her composure. She looked toward her attorney, hoping to see or sense something to help her keep from answering. Jackie felt reluctant answering questions about her children because she feared the information would fall into Tom's hands. Still, she answered and tried to appear to stay cool, hoping they'd soon switch to another subject. Her answers seemed to satisfy the attorney and eventually he did move on. This time questioning something she felt was absolutely none of his business.

"Jackie, have you ever used the word F U C K?"

"Yes," she replied without hesitation.

"In what context?" he questioned.

"You," she stated, as she staring directly into his face.

"Are you saying fuck you to me?" He asked as he glared at her over the top of his Halston horn-rimmed glasses. Everyone in the room couldn't help but notice how embarrassed Attorney Woodcock was by that unexpected reply as the color red beamed from his normally pale face and he wiped sweat off his forehead with a handkerchief.

"Just answering your question, sir." Jackie replied in a most matter of fact way.

"Well, I don't like the way you answered it, ma'am." He shouted back before turning his wrath to Ms. Bernard. "Attorney Bernard you will instruct your client to have some respect for this table and answer me in a more respectful manner?" He shook his dangling finger from the end of his outstretched arm toward Jackie.

Attorney Bernard picked at her fingernail with a paperclip as she responded. "Actually, Attorney Woodcock, she did answer your question. Maybe you should have asked it in a different way if you didn't like her answer. Personally, I didn't see anything out of line with her answer. The way I see it, she just truthfully answered your question."

Without further response, Attorney Woodcock continued, "Mrs. Kennard, have you ever used the word FUCK outside of heated intercourse with a man or outside your private bedroom?"

Jackie was shocked by his question, yet she calmly replied. "Yes, I believe I have."

"Can you elaborate on that?"

"Not really. Unless you prefer to be more specific, I don't know what you're asking."

"Well, I'm asking have you ever fucked a man outside your bedroom? You know in any out-of-the-ordinary places?"

"Sure," she replied as she shrugged her left shoulder. Then she sat motionless, hands neatly crossed lying on top the table, awaiting his next question.

The attorney had expected she would elaborate without having to be coaxed. But Jackie just sat exchanging stone-face glares across the table with him. She planned to make Attorney Woodcock work for any and all information he got from her.

"Like where?" he asked as he hastily motioned with his hand as if to say, "out with it."

"Anywhere we wanted to," she smugly replied.

"Ms. Kennard, have you ever FUCKED another man while you were married to either of your husbands?"

"For the record," she replied. "I have but one husband and his name is George. I also have an ex husband. I just wanted to say on the record that your last statement made it look as if I currently have two husbands. Then to answer your question, have I ever FUCKED another man outside my current marriage..." She hesitated and appeared to search through her mind before she replied, "I've never had the time or desire. Neither my present nor my ex husband left me any free time in that department for another partner. They both were able to keep me satisfied sexually, if that's what you're wondering."

After that response, Jackie saw revenge in Woodcock's eyes.

Attorney Woodcock hesitated for a moment, appearing deep in thought, arms crossed in an arrogant sort of way, silently shaking his head up and down before he proceeded.

"Ms. Kennard, have you ever said, "suck a dick?"

"Oh, that was Tom's daily expression," she recalled.

Almost before she had finished with her answer Attorney Woodcock quickly asked, "Ms. Kennard, have you ever sucked a dick?"

That question blindsided Jackie. She sat silently mortified for a long time, probably two full minutes, as she quietly tried to decide how she could ever answer this question.

The silence was deafening until Attorney Woodcock smiled, leaned back on one arm clicked his pen and winked at Richard Spaniel, basking in what he thought was checkmate position as he smugly asked, "Ms. Kennard, did you not understand my question?"

Appearing undisturbed by his last remark, she remained deep in thought for several more minutes as she looked around the room and stared into the face of each of the defendants. They sat staring back at her, each one wearing on his face his own brand of smutty smirk. She thought how pathetic they each looked as they basked in the glory of being able to legally humiliate her. Then she drew a long breath before she replied.

"I answer your question with the affirmation that the marriage vow taken by a man and woman before God is both sacred and private. Whatever is shared or takes place between a husband and wife is strictly between them. Therefore let your record show that I am standing true to my wedding vows and will not to allow you to put asunder any part of my marriage by answering your question."

The defendants stared at Jackie. Even Attorney Woodcock was surprised by her answer and sat with his mouth hanging open. Richard Spaniel leaned over and whispered something to his attorney. The attorney grimaced, "Strike that question! We'll go forward and come back to it later." He continued.

"Okay, Mrs. Kennard, did you ever make the statement that Hillary kept Dexter's job for him by sucking Richard's dick on a regular basis?"

"Oh, no sir. That was Tom's assumption on Dexter's job security. Tom often made that statement when Hillary stopped by the office and threw her Corporate Connection threats around."

"Strike that! Nonresponsive!" Attorney Woodcock shouted. "Mrs. Kennard, did *you* ever make the comment that Hillary kept Dexter's job by sucking Richard's dick?"

"No sir. That was Tom's—"

"Strike that! Nonresponsive!" Attorney Woodcock yelled at Jackie.

Jackie was not sure what all that was about, but she sat quietly waiting for someone to tell her what to do. Then Attorney Woodcock switched and started his questioning in yet another direction.

"Okay, Mrs. Kennard, our records indicate you had a tax lien brought against you for back taxes. Could you explain to us what that was about?"

"Yes. I worked for a company outside Nashville, Tennessee, back in '88. They fell Out of Trust with their lenders and fled the country, taking a large sum of money and leaving all their employees penniless and stranded. Because they didn't forward a 1099 or W-2 to anyone, I simply estimated my tax base for that year to the IRS. However I later received a notice that I had grossly underestimated my income for that year and therefore IRS was filing a Tax Lien against me in 1995."

"Did you underestimate your taxes due?"

"No," Jackie replied. "How could I owe taxes on money I never received? Apparently the owners of the company forwarded false information to the IRS."

"Mrs. Kennard, what was the name of the company and please explain what Out Of Trust is, and who were the owners?"

"Out of Trust means they cashed in, or funded several home loans with their finance companies after the manufactured houses were closed and delivered. Then, they never paid the manufacturer for the original invoice due for the house, nor did they pay the vendors involved in the sale and set-up of the house. The company was Dryer Mobile Homes and the owners were DeDe and Dawn Dryer."

Everyone in the room couldn't help but notice how that comment had made Richard's head spin around on his shoulders. That statement definitely caught his full attention. These were his friends from the picture on the wall in his office that he and Jackie previously discussed when she interviewed with him. Richard and his attorney conversed in a whisper with one another on the other side of the table momentarily.

"Mrs. Kennard, is this the same DeDe and Dawn Dryer who now have a Midway Housing lot east of the Metroplex?"

"Yes," she replied, looking directly at Richard.

"Now, Mrs. Kennard. Please tell us how you took care of that little problem with your taxes."

"I paid them," she replied, "all 3,600 dollars they said that I owed, in order for them to drop the tax lien and interest mounting against me."

Attorney Woodcock then asked for a fifteen-minute break to confer with his client. Jackie and Ms. Bernard departed the conference room to retire to her office.

"How am I doing?" Jackie asked, before sinking into a chair.

"You're doing just fine. I was a little concerned with the way he started off on the sexual questioning. I commend you on the way you answered his question—you know the one I mean. They got all built up with that long drawn out pause, and when you answered, it just let the air out of their sails. Maybe he got it out of his system and just wanted to start with that to test the waters. I do think you've shown them you're straight-forward and won't back down. Just keep up the good face—don't get smart or cocky with him. Keep making him work for his answers. He'll eventually give up and move on to another line of questioning when he sees you aren't taking his bait."

Just then Attorney Woodcock tapped on Ms. Bernard's door before he opened it and stuck his head in, "My client wants to take a lunch break now. How about if we meet back here in two hours?"

"Let's make it an hour and a half," she replied.

Attorney Woodcock nodded his head in agreement.

Moments later, they watched from the window of her office as the defendants' legal team climbed into Woodcock's new black Mercedes and drove off the parking lot.

"What do you make of it?" Jackie asked.

Ms. Bernard shrugged her shoulders. "I think he's going to check out your story about the Tennessee people. Do they still work for the company?"

"Well, up until today they did. I think Richard had to know about it because he told me a long time ago that they were all friends. Or maybe he's going to warn them that the truth is out."

"Maybe so," Ms. Bernard replied. "Either way, it struck a nerve with Richard. Did you see his head spin around whenever you said that? He either didn't know you knew or was shocked that you told it." She shrugged and grinned at Jackie. "Let's take advantage of this downtime and grab a bite to eat."

Over lunch they discussed several things and highlights of the case. Ms. Bernard gave Jackie a pep talk and assured her things were going well.

Between bites of her salad, Jackie remarked, "I can't be certain, but I think I know Attorney Woodcock's father. I think my dad and his are friends from way back. Does that matter?"

"Not unless the two of you know each other and were to associate with one another on a personal level. Don't think about that right now. We have too much other stuff to focus on right now."

They were first to return to the office just under the agreed hour-and-a-half time limit, ready to get the deposition behind them. Ms. Bernard looked at her watch time and time again as the two sat patiently in the conference room awaiting the defendants' return. Finally, over an hour later, the defendants walked in and took their place at the table.

Ms. Bernard stated, "Let me state for the record, that we are just now moving forward after the defendants' two-and-a-half-hour lunch break. We had previously agreed to take a one-and-a-half-hour break after the defendants originally asked for a two-hour lunch, but compromised and agreed on one and a half hours. Let the record show the defendants are over an hour late returning."

Not to be outdone, Attorney Woodcock also made a comment. "Let me state for the record also. We were late because the plaintiff produced some information during the deposition that needed to be checked into. Therefore, we were working off record because the plaintiff chose to disclose this to us only during deposition."

Ms. Bernard quickly added, "Let it show for the record this line of questioning was not something introduced in the original Interrogatories. Therefore the defendants brought the subject to the table and opened the discussion with my client during the deposition."

Mr. Woodcock rebutted, "Let the record show that I have the right to question the plaintiff. The deposition is a fact-finding mission, and we will exercise our right under the law."

Ms. Bernard added, "I still want the record to show there was no professional courtesy shown by the defendants' attorney. They should have at least called instead of agreeing and then taking advantage of the situation by being over an hour late to return as agreed."

Jackie sat quietly, wondering if these two were about to climb on top of the table and duke it out. All the time, the court reporter was banging away on her little machine as the two of them argued back and forth while everyone else in the room sat silenced by it all. Then, as quickly as it had started, they dropped the matter completely, and the questioning resumed.

"Ms. Kennard, what is your height and weight?"

This line of questioning went on and on, obviously wasting time and dragging on about Jackie's boring life until everyone in the room was completely numb from their backside up to their brain. But why? Why would he ask these questions that had absolutely nothing to do with the charges? Jackie thought it was just to punish her attorney for putting something on the record about his being late from lunch. If this was the case, he was doing his job, as Ms. Bernard showed signs of fatigue with every question. The questions went on and on and until the 6:00 hour.

"Okay, Mrs. Kennard. Let's talk about profanity for a second. I take it that certain people would use profanity or slang words, and you found those to be offensive. If you could, please describe to me the profanity that you heard that you considered to be unwelcome or offensive to you."

"Well, Mr. Kuykendahl referred to me as, 'a swallower and not a spitter,' insinuating that I performed oral sex on him. Then he stated he was small guy, but he carried a big dick and offered to show it to me. There was really not any profanity that wasn't used in this office at some time by someone."

Mrs. Kennard, I take it by making that statement that you never use profanity."

"That's not what I'm implying, sir. There is a difference when someone uses profanity around you, opposed to directly at you."

This conversation went back and forth for over an hour before Attorney Woodcock stated. "Off the record. I have to catch a plane to Amarillo tomorrow. We'll need to finish this next Tuesday back here in your office, Ms. Bernard. Is that agreeable with you?"

"Not really, but if you have to," she replied. "However, I would like to state for the record that I do want this to be wrapped up next Tuesday. I, too, have other cases that I am working, and this should have been done in one day."

Attorney Woodcock replied, "For the record. Again, a deposition is a fact-finding mission, and I will take my time questioning the plaintiff. Thank you, Ms. Bernard. We will resume on next Tuesday. That is, unless your client wants to drop the charges against my clients?"

"Not a chance!" she chuckled.

Jackie followed Ms. Bernard's lead and stood to leave the room before the other attorneys had their books packed. Jackie could tell that Attorney Woodcock had truly pissed Attorney Bernard off as they walked together into her office where she slammed her door shut.

Jackie said, "I thought we weren't supposed to show them any emotion?"

"Well, they pissed me off!" she shouted, loud enough for them to hear.

Uncertain how she should respond to that, Jackie sat with Attorney Bernard, quietly watching through the window as Woodcock's assistants loaded their heavy legal briefcases into the back of his Mercedes and paused for a short discussion before they left for the day.

*November 21, 1997, One Week Later*
*Deposition, Day Two*

Again Jackie was in Attorney Bernard's office going over things as they awaited the arrival of the defendants' legal team. When the men finally arrived and stepped from their car, she saw they'd brought Dexter along on this trip.

"Why are they bringing him?" Jackie asked Ms. Bernard.

"I guess so he can hear your accusations against him," Ms. Bernard said.

"But I don't want him to have access to some of the information."

"Well, I'll put that on the record, or we'll have to have another court order issued," the attorney said.

Once again, they assembled at the big conference table, and the legal team for the defense announced they were ready to begin the second day of testimony with Mrs. Jackie Weatherby Kennard.

After Jackie was sworn in, the attorney said, "The last time we met, we discussed several things, and this time we're going to use a different line of questions. I remind you that you are under oath and should you not tell the truth, you can and will be held in contempt of court. Do you understand that?"

"Yes sir, I do."

"Then we will proceed. When we stopped last week I believe we were discussing the tax lien filed against you. So, if I may reflect back on that subject for just a moment…"

Jackie quickly responded, "Sir, with all due respect, we had already discussed and concluded that issue. When we stopped the deposition last week, we were actually discussing Dexter's accusation that I had performed oral sex on him."

Just then Dexter's eyes became so big she thought they were going to pop from the sockets. He turned red in the face and picked up his glass of water as his hands trembled, and he drank from it until there wasn't a drop left. Jackie stared directly into his face. There was no denying his part of the charges. While Jackie continued answering questions, she stared at Dexter as she recalled the ugly incidents and sexual innuendos she'd endured from him during her employment at the Midway Park location. She described the embarrassment she suffered so they could have a laugh and make a spectacle of not just her, but also every man, woman, and child who ever worked there or walked through those doors.

Jackie then told how Dexter and Tom had called her into his office and handed her a piece of paper describing how men should pay taxes according to the size of their dick, then Dexter unzipped his pants, pulled out a live snake, and asked Jackie to measure it for him so that he could determine how much he should pay.

Even the court reporter choked up on that one. She coughed and held up one hand for everyone to wait. As she got her breath, she asked. "Off the record. Sir, do you mind if I take a break? I need to step outside for just a moment. The reporter wasn't supposed to show any emotion, but Jackie's story caught her off guard, and she had to get a breath of air to be able to finish.

"Sure," Attorney Woodcock replied. "We'll take ten minutes."

When they returned, the defense attorney continued his questioning. "Mrs. Kennard, I'm showing you a piece of paper marked States Evidence No. 1. Can you identify this for me?"

"Yes, this is the form Dexter handed to me before he pulled out the snake from his pants."

"Mark this to reflect Exhibit No. 1."

As the court reporter reached for the document, Jackie couldn't help noticing the woman's arms were both covered in chill bumps. She was still having difficulty sitting through such a deposition."

The deposition went forward, and the attorney began to probe into the Tom's side of the case. "Mrs. Kennard, you previously stated Tom called you every day. What did he call you for? And what time of the day did he call you?"

"No particular time. I guess whenever the desire hit him. He would discuss day-to-day events at work and inquire about how things were going, or more specifically, had I been able to obtain my husband's fingerprints for him yet."

"Fingerprints? What do you mean?"

"Tom needed a set of fingerprints to turn in as his own. Each employee was required to provide those because of their licenses with the state and the amount of money and the sale of insurance we were involved in."

"I don't understand, Mrs. Kennard. Why did he want to use your husband's fingerprints?"

"Because he said he is not really Tom Kerakasco because he is in the witness protection program, and not everyone in the company was aware of his past. He went on to tell me he was in the witness protection program because he had killed someone."

"Mrs. Kennard, did he say who he killed?"

"No sir. I just know where it was supposed to have happened."

"And just where was that, Mrs. Kennard?"

"Pennsylvania."

"Do you have any proof, Mrs. Kennard?"

"Only that he told me," she replied.

"Do you have any proof that he told you this, any record of his phone conversation?"

"Well as a matter of fact I did buy a recorder and start recording his phone conversations after that."

Attorney Woodcock shouted. "EXCUSE ME! Did you say that you recorded his conversations? Serendipitously? Without him knowing?"

"Sometimes. But then there are several phone calls he left on my telephone recorder that he knew he was recording of his own free will."

"Mrs. Kennard, what exactly do you have on tape?"

"Well, I have him describing one of the general managers at another location masturbating on one of his female employees. I have him describing his sexual encounters with different women who work for the company, plus several other conversations. In some of the conversations, he described the managers' meetings, which were usually held at Richard's house and how the managers would brag about their sexual accomplishments with different salesladies while they passed the pipe."

"What do you mean, *passed the pipe?*"

"The crack pipe. Apparently they would partake in smoking crack or pot with one another while the meetings were going on."

"Mrs. Kennard, did he tell you who was present?"

"Sure," she replied. "But he told me to NEVER tell anyone."

"Well, I'm afraid that no longer applies. Can you share that information with the court?"

"He stated all the managers were there, plus the owner of the delivery company. Also a couple of corporate people from the corporate office in Houston. You see, it was a required monthly meeting."

Immediately, Attorney Woodcock turned to Ms. Bernard. "I want those tapes delivered to my office tomorrow by 9:00 a.m., along with the recorder used to record these conversations. Then I want the record to reflect that I have not been told of these tapes before."

Mrs. Bernard replied, "Well, I think we need to talk about that first. I'm not finished with the tapes just yet. My assistant is still working through them, dictating the conversations into a form we can all read while we listen to them at the same time."

Attorney Woodcock replied, "We'll have a discussion about this withholding of information with the judge later today. In the meantime, Mrs. Kennard, please tell me exactly what Tom told you about his past life."

"He said he'd spent most of his adult life behind bars in the penitentiary and he knows his way around a court room. Then he bragged that they'll never be able to pin anything on him, adding, 'I'm too smart.' Then he stated, the last job he did, he had over thirty-five people who witnessed against him."

Jackie had to pause for a drink of water before she could finish. The more she talked about it, the more she shook as she described to them what Tom had confessed to her. She was petrified with fear about the probable consequences from Tom, but still she described the details of how he bragged about the murder he committed. She'd kept this story to herself until she almost suffered a nervous breakdown before she confided it to the therapist. Still, this was something that would not go away—it had to be told so it could be checked out by the authorities. Jackie felt a deep sadness for the victim and his family. Even though she didn't know exactly who the person was, she still felt a profound obligation to him.

Jackie held her hand over her mouth for a moment, trying to stop her lip from trembling as tears began to run down her face. She talked in almost a whisper as she continued telling his story. "He said..." but before she could get the words out, she had to pause again. She struggled with her emotions for several more minutes before she finally gained enough control to tell them what he had confessed to her. With her voice cracking she continued. "He told me, 'the last motherfucker who was gonna rat on me wound up with his brains all over the walls before he made it to city hall.'"

Jackie then leaned forward, gasping for air as she clutched her chest while she cried uncontrollably. Everyone in the room watched and listened in complete shock and disbelief, none of them sure what to do as Jackie struggled to repeat Tom's story. "He said he had no other choice; the guy was an 'arch enemy' to him and his family. Then he told me how he waited just inside the guy's apartment for him to come back upstairs, and when the victim stepped off the elevator, Tom said it was like slow motion. 'I raised my gun and we stared at one another down the barrel. The look in his eyes whenever he saw me— he knew he was mine! I smiled, told him, Thank *your partner and kiss your ass good bye* right before I splattered his brains all over the wall.'"

Then Jackie broke down again before she could finish the story. Everyone looked around the room at one another in silence, waiting for someone to take control, but no one knew what to do or say. They could hardly comprehend what Jackie had just told them. Was she telling the truth or just making it up? No one was sure. The defense's legal team realized they needed to take a break and reorganize.

Attorney Woodcock said, "Off the record. Let's take a break. What say, thirty minutes?"

Mrs. Bernard nodded agreement as she stood over Jackie with a box of tissues, trying to help her regain control of her emotions. Jackie was sobbing so hard she had trouble catching her breath. Everyone who'd been in the room and heard her testimony was in a state of shock. Not one of them could comprehend it might possibly be true. And if Tom's story was true, who within the company knew about it and kept the secret hidden under the corporate ladder?

Attorney Woodcock immediately went outside and sat in his car while using his cell phone. He talked for several minutes before he emerged and reentered the law office.

"Ms. Bernard, I've decided to take a lunch break before we reconvene this thing, which will also allow Mrs. Kennard to take a breather. I'll return in an hour."

Ms. Bernard frowned at him. "Don't be late again, or I *will* go to the judge."

"I'll be on time," he snapped.

After the midday break, they regrouped in the conference room to continue where Jackie had left off.

"Mrs. Kennard, when we left you had described an incident to us. Is there anything you need to add to that?"

Jackie paused again before she raised her bowed head and looked directly at Attorney Woodcock. "Yes. My husband had dropped me off at Tom's house on his way out of town to do a job for Midway Housing. I was there because Tom previously called my husband and arranged for him to take me. Now, its obvious to me that Tom was lying to him when he said I had to attend a required meeting being held at his house. He wanted to make sure I was there so he could threaten me. In fact, he staged the whole business meeting to ensure I'd be dropped off there so he could have control of the situation and put the fear of God in me about involving him in the harassment case I had filed with EEOC. Then he sealed it with his confession of being in the witness protection program.

"He told me that if his wife hadn't talked him out of it several months earlier when I figured him out, he'd planned to knock me off, adding that he was not going to lose another family over my being pissed off about something Dexter and Hillary did to me. He meant that he would be in trouble with his parole officer for the charges being filed against him, not the company being upset with him. He later told me that Richard Spaniel knew about his past and had told him to 'just get somebody's fingerprints' to turn in, and he would personally take care of it for Tom. That's when Tom thought of using George's fingerprints."

Jackie took a sip of water and continued. "Then Tom drove me home and tried to come inside the house, stating he promised George he'd make sure that I got home safely. He told me I could not leave the company with this much information. If I did he would hunt me down and kill me."

"Mrs. Kennard, when did George drop you at Tom's house? Do you recall the date?"

""Yes, it was the same date that the other attorney questioned me."

"What other attorney?"

"Attorney Worthlittle," she replied.

"Attorney Woodcock's face turned red and he shouted, "Mrs. Kennard, are you referring to my assistant, Ms. Littleworth?"

"Yes sir."

"Then I demand that you show respect to her when you speak her name!"

"Sir, I'm just doing what you demanded earlier. Last name first!"

"Mrs. Kennard, did you ever get George's fingerprints for Tom?"

"No. I refused, and then I was terminated. He and Dexter made up the story that I threatened them with George when, in fact, Tom simply used that story to make it look like I threatened them with George over another issue. Tom told me that if I didn't furnish him with George's fingerprints, he'd already arranged with someone else to take over the business contract George had with the company."

"Did you explain this to George?"

"No."

"Why not?"

"Because he probably would have done physical harm to both Dexter and Tom. At all cost, I wanted to avoid any confrontations between them, so I chose to use the legal system to resolve my issues with Midway Housing."

"Mrs. Kennard, did Tom hunt you down?"

"Yes, he and Todd showed up at my new job one night right at closing time and they both had been drinking and appeared to be drugged. They were talking loud, and Tom took hold of my arm and led me down the hallway to my office where he closed the door. He asked me if I had been good, or if I'd talked to anyone. Then he took a pencil from my desk and held it in front of my face as he stated, 'Don't forget, IF you don't keep our little secret then I can have this done to you.' Then he snapped the pencil in half and threw it to the floor. He placed his foot on it and ground it into the carpet."

"Was there anyone who witnessed this, Mrs. Kennard?"

"Just myself," she replied.

"Attorney Bernard, since it's almost 6:00 p.m., I'd like to suggest we stop questioning today and resume at a later date agreeable to both us."

Jackie's attorney said, "Actually, I was hoping we could wrap this up today."

"Well, there are several issues that need to be addressed, so we need at least one more day with your client."

Attorney Bernard stated, "I have a trial starting tomorrow and, really, I don't have another day free until next week."

"Okay, then we'll just plan to finish up next week."

Attorney Bernard was not happy with the decision, but since the defense attorney was conducting the investigation, she really didn't have any say in the matter. And there were many more things he felt he needed to investigate, so they agreed to make the final arrangements via a telephone call early the next week.

# CHAPTER FORTY-TWO

Jackie was mentally exhausted after two days of testimony and more than ready to go home. She looked forward to getting some rest for the next couple of days before reporting back to her new job. She thought about so many different things on the drive home that time seemed to fly by. Before she knew it, she was pulling into the driveway.

She all but ran through the door, eager to see George, as she shouted, "Honey, I'm home," dropping her purse onto the kitchen counter.

George didn't respond. He just sat there with his arms resting across his chest, staring at the telephone answering machine until she found him sitting at the desk inside the office waiting for her.

"Are you all right?" she asked.

George pointed to the machine and said, "You need to listen to this then tell me just what the hell is going on." Then he pressed the play button. There was Tom's voice, and he was very drunk. "Geeeooorge, hey Geeeooorge. I just wanted to let you know that your ole lady really fucked up today. She broke omerta when she remembered and talked about something she was supposed to forget. You need to watch out for her. She might just step out in front of a car if she's not careful."

"Give me that tape!" Jackie shouted. "I'll take it to the lawyer's office on Monday. This idiot needs to be locked away."

"Locked away?" George said. "He needs his ass beat and that's what I'm about to do."

"No, please, George, listen to me. You can't just go over there and start beating on this idiot. That exactly what he wants you to do, so he can claim self-defense. Please let me handle this through the court!"

She spent the next few hours convincing George they needed to let the legal system to do its job and that he didn't need to defend her, because that's what Tom wanted him to do.

However, on Monday when Jackie arrived at her attorney's office, she was shocked and surprised to see two police cars out front. Her heart raced as she made her way toward the door, scared of what might be going on inside. She was met at the door by the legal assistant, who told her that their office had been broken into and ransacked.

"Let me guess," Jackie said. "My tapes were stolen."

"Well yes, but we think it was probably homeless people. They took a microwave oven too."

Jackie stared in disbelief as she asked, "Just where would a homeless person plug in a microwave?"

The legal assistant shrugged her shoulders as she walked away. Just then Attorney Bernard came out front and asked Jackie to step back into her office. She shut the door, motioned for Jackie to take a seat, and asked her, "What all was on those tapes?"

Jackie went into detail about many of the conversations she'd taped between herself and Tom.

Mrs. Bernard replied. "Well, we now have a problem, because whoever broke in here last night stole the tapes and the recorder. I don't know what we're going to do now, because I'm supposed to turn them over to the defense."

Jackie chuckled. "Don't you get it? Tom had someone break into your office and take the tapes. That way it truly is his word against mine."

Mrs. Bernard replied, "Well, as soon as they finish your deposition, then it's my turn. We'll get him pinned down, and he'll have to answer our questions. Then we'll get a handle on this crap."

"You're never gonna get a handle on this crap! Don't you understand? You're dealing with a hit-man mobster here!"

"Well, that's what he told you, but I have a different opinion of the guy. I think he's psycho." She sighed and looked out the window a moment. "By the way, Jackie, why did you stop by?"

Jackie described the message George had found on their answering machine, including the part about breaking omerta.

Attorney Bernard's jaw dropped. "What are you saying? Do you have the tape with you? I'm calling the judge right now on this one."

"Ms. Bernard, I just want to make sure you understand this maniac is very aware of what he's doing, and he IS playing with a full deck. His mind is just 100 percent criminal, and he is NOT afraid to carry out threats on anybody. He made it clear to me he will never go back to prison, no matter what he has to do to prevent it."

In spite of Jackie's words, Ms. Bernard held onto the belief that she could wear Tom down during the deposition and prove him a liar. She didn't want to believe the defendants had ransacked her office. Jackie still held onto her gut feeling. She felt Tom had either stolen the tapes himself or had it done. Why else would the intruder leave cash in the office safe, along with other valuables sitting around the office? She could not convince Attorney Bernard to put these suspicions on the police report. It was obvious Ms. Bernard felt uncomfortable accusing the defendants of such an act. Therefore, the report stated, "possibly a homeless person looking for food or something to sell for food."

# CHAPTER FORTY-THREE

*Tuesday, December 7, 9:30 a.m.*
*Deposition, Day Three*

Richard Spaniel attended this day of testimony, along with the defense's legal team. He always looked down, never at Jackie while she testified. He constantly scribbled in a notebook and appeared to be working on something far more important to him than her deposition. Jackie could tell it really pissed him off to have to sit there and be part of it.

Attorney Woodcock started the proceedings with, "Off the record. We are going to have another court reporter finish this deposition. The original court reporter asked to be removed from this case. Therefore, Mr. Joe Harris will be our court reporter through the remainder of the deposition.

"Mrs. Kennard, today we need to discuss something that will probably be very upsetting to you. You previously reported that one of your customers had physically assaulted you. We will have to have you go into some detail about that today."

Immediately Jackie felt sick to her stomach, but she tried to not let her feelings show as she quietly replied, "Yes sir."

And with that reply, she began another gut-wrenching day as the defense attorney made her recall the horrid assault and how she feared that the attacker was going to kill her if she didn't do what he told her. The attorney made her describe the entire assault in detail, right down to the blue flowers on the bedspread. Afterwards she sat in silence, stared at her hands, and no one made a sound. Jackie appeared to have sunk into some sort of a daze, her head bent downward, tears dripping from her eyes. It seemed as if she was unable to focus on anything outside her thoughts for several minutes. Finally, the defense attorney seemed moved by her detailed description when he asked, "Is that all you want to say about that incident Ms. Kennard?"

She whispered, "Yes," and quietly nodded, wiping tears from her cheeks. Then he scribbled onto one of his many legal pads for about five minutes, allowing her time to gather her thoughts before he moved forward with additional questions.

"Mrs. Kennard, did anyone from the company do anything about the assault?"

"Yes, I believe they did. Although I don't know how. Tom did tell me that he and Dexter had taken care of it and that nobody there was to ever bring it up to me or discuss it again or they would be terminated on the spot."

The remainder of the morning was taken up with what appeared to be followup questions about previous day's questioning, with no apparent rhyme, reason, or pattern.

Richard Spaniel reached for his cell phone, taking it from his belt loop before writing something on a piece of paper and passing it over to his attorney.

Attorney Woodcock then removed his cell phone from his belt loop, apparently to look at a message he'd just received, before requesting a break around 11:45 a.m. It appeared that something other than this deposition was heavy on both their minds.

As they always did during a break, Ms. Bernard and Jackie stepped out to allow the defense team time to discuss their next plan of attack in private. However, before they were out of hearing range Attorney Woodcock called out, "Ms. Bernard, can I see you for just a moment?"

Jackie continued toward the office as Ms. Bernard turned to hear what he had to say.

After a few minutes, Attorney Bernard came back to her office and instructed Jackie to go ahead to lunch with out her, but to be back in forty-five minutes.

"Is something wrong?" Jackie asked.

"I'm not certain yet," her attorney responded.

Jackie didn't go very far to find something to eat for lunch, the anticipation of the defendants' actions was all she could think about as she quickly ate a taco and rushed back to the law firm.

She was taken without hesitation back into the deposition conference room where Attorney Woodcock sat alone with his court reporter waiting for Jackie and Attorney Bernard to return.

As Attorney Bernard came in and sat down, Attorney Woodcock flipped open his appointment book and glanced through it before he declared, "Off the record. I think we will conclude for today and resume again tomorrow at 9:00 a.m."

Jackie sighed with relief. She was completely agreeable to that suggestion.

Ms. Bernard declared, "What!" "On the record! I think we need to talk about this before you make decisions prior to consulting with me. I don't appreciate the inconsiderate way in which you have wasted our time today, not to mention I may not be available tomorrow at 9:00 a.m."

"Well then, can you check you calendar and let me know?" he asked in his smart-ass, demanding way before adding. "I have an emergency that has come up that I need to attend to right away."

Ms. Bernard sighed, left the room and returned with her appointment book waving open in the air. "I'll have to move a couple of appointments around. How much time do you need to wrap this thing up?"

"As much time as it takes!" Woodcock shouted.

Jackie stared at the attorneys in amazement. That statement alone proved that he planned to wear both Jackie and her attorney down by dragging out the proceedings as long as he possibly could. And he knew that he was doing a good job of pissing Attorney Bernard off.

That was his strategy, piss her off and pull her off track as often as possible.

Ms. Bernard replied. "Tomorrow at 10:00 a.m. Then, we need to discuss anything past that time, but I hope you'll wrap your deposition up by the end of the day."

"Sure," he replied with a smirk on his face as he packed up his briefcase.

*Wednesday, December 8, 10:00 a.m.*
*Deposition, Day Four*

Attorney Woodcock announced, "The topic of discussion for today is going to be health issues." After that announcement, he spent the first three hours discussing every illness, childbirth, cold, flu, influenza, illness, or surgery Jackie had ever gone through. She even had to suffer through the embarrassment of discussing her personal female problems in the presence of Dexter and Richard.

"Mrs. Kennard, you previously consulted with a therapist before you filed your charges against my clients. I'll need to know exactly what you discussed with the doctor about Midway Housing and Tom each time you counseled with her."

"Objection!" Attorney Bernard shouted. "Doctor-patient privilege. You don't have to answer that, Mrs. Kennard. That is privileged information, just like attorney-client information."

Then Attorney Woodcock produced a list of medications, each prescribed to Jackie at one time or another in the past ten years. He'd obviously subpoenaed everything he could locate on Jackie that might damage her character. Then, he went through each medicine name-by-name, asking what each was for.

Jackie was uncertain about many of the drugs and couldn't remember either why or when they'd been prescribed.

The attorney said, "Mrs. Kennard, there was a drug listed in your file that's normally prescribed to chemo patients for upset stomachs. Why was this prescribed to you?"

"It was the only medication that would settle my upset stomach after I developed a bleeding ulcer."

"Mrs. Kennard, then there was headache, nausea, and stress medication that went along with that prescription also."

"Yes," she replied.

Just as quickly as that questioning began, Attorney Woodcock switched to a totally different line of questioning. "Okay, Mrs. Kennard, on another note, regarding the position you now hold with the Golden Gate Finance Company. Do you make credit decisions on loans?"

"Yes, of course," she replied.

"Do they finance manufactured homes?"

"Absolutely not," she replied. Just as the word "absolutely" rolled off her tongue, Attorney Bernard kicked her on the ankle. Jackie immediately leaned over and looked underneath the table to see if it could have possibly been an accident. Once she realized it was on purpose, maintaining herself proved to be the hardest thing Jackie had to accomplish that day. When they took a break, Jackie blasted Attorney Bernard.

"Why did you kick me?"

"Because you said 'absolutely not!'" the attorney replied.

"Are you crazy? Don't you EVER kick me! What the hell did you think you were doing? The answer was ABSOLUTELY Not. Maybe if you'd been paying attention to the question and not resting your head on the table, you would have understood the question." Jackie glared at her attorney, awaiting her response.

"I'm sorry," Ms. Bernard replied. "Just try to keep your cool when you go back in there, and we'll finish this thing up today."

"You kick me again, and you'll be finished right then! I don't need the aggravation from you on top of that asshole Woodcock hammering me!"

As they reconvened in the deposition room, the questioning returned to a subject they'd discussed earlier.

"Mrs. Kennard, you stated that you had worked for DeDe and Dawn Dryer at another location. Would you tell us about that?"

"Objection," Mrs. Bernard stated.

"You may answer the question," Attorney Woodcock stated.

"I thought I already did," Jackie replied.

"NON RESPONSIVE!" he shouted. "Answer my question!"

"Honestly, I thought I already did," she replied.

"AGAIN!" he shouted. "Answer my question."

This went on for a several minutes before Attorney Bernard interjected.

"She's already testified regarding her prior employment. Can we move on to another subject, or better yet drop the line of questioning and just move forward."

But time and time again Attorney Woodcock went down the same line of questioning he'd already covered days earlier, apparently trying to throw Jackie off balance so she'd answer something in a different way that he could use to impeach her in court.

Finally, Attorney Woodcock announced, "We're going to conclude our deposition for today and resume tomorrow again at 9:00 a.m. Off the record. Ms. Bernard, please have your client here tomorrow at 7:30 a.m."

"We need to discuss this, Mr. Woodcock. On the record." The two attorneys didn't discuss anything, they argued back and forth for thirty minutes, screaming like two children, both determined to win. Finally, Attorney Woodcock responded, "I'll go to the judge and tell him that you're blocking our right to depose this witness if you don't agree to let us complete what we feel is a necessary fact-finding deposition."

Attorney Bernard sighed, shook her head no, and replied. "Against my better judgment I will allow you to go forward one more day with deposition. But, I expect that you are not going to go down the same road as you have today, questioning my client on issues that have already been established."

There was no reply. Attorney Woodcock just continued gathering his belongings before leaving the room.

*December 9*
*Deposition, Day Five*

On this day, no one was present from Midway Housing, only the defense's legal team. "Mrs. Kennard, today, we are going to discuss your previous education and each job you have held in the past twenty-five years."

Jackie thought, *God this guy must be really desperate for a case if he has to spend this much time discussing every detail of my boring life.* Then she watched as he placed on the table for all to see her past school history, even as far back as high school more than twenty years earlier. Then he presented her college information and compared it to what she'd written onto her original job application with the Midway Housing Corporation. He was trying to find anything he could to prove Jackie a liar. He then proceeded to question her about issues so far back in her past that even she had forgotten them. He'd managed to discover the time she got into trouble for skipping school in her senior year.

Jackie was a little shocked at his comments and thought he must've talked with her ex husband for that information, because no one else knew.

"Mrs. Kennard, your ex husband tells us that you owe him money. Do you owe him money?"

"I don't know," she replied. This statement really hit a nerve in Jackie. The defense had stooped to a new all time low.

"Well, he said that you would know what he was talking about. As a matter of fact, he offered to testify if we needed a witness of character against you."

"That doesn't surprise me," Jackie replied. "How many ex spouses wouldn't take you up on the offer to get to say something dirty about their ex in public, plus get paid for saying it?"

"Does that bother you, Mrs. Kennard?"

"Why should it? We're divorced."

"Who filed for the divorce?"

"I did," she replied.

"Ms. Kennard, he stated that discussing your sexual preferences in court would be no problem for him."

"Good for him! Good for you. Good for your... clients. Maybe then you can get your..."

"Your what? Mrs. Kennard"

"Your answer!" Jackie replied, as she bit her lip to keep from saying what she was thinking.

"Why did you file for divorce, Mrs. Kennard?"

"I don't remember. Why don't you ask him?"

Then the line of questioning flipped again, this time focusing on George and his prior business, along with his past marriage and the whereabouts of his two children, Brandon and Jason.

"Mrs. Kennard, where are George's children?"

"With their mother."

"Where is that?"

"Somewhere in Florida," she replied.

"I thought they lived with the two of you."

"They do. She and George have joint custody, and the children split their time between the two households."

"I'll need their address."

"I don't know it," Jackie replied.

"Then you'll need to find it and get it to your attorney, who will forward it to me for the record."

It was obvious with that request that the legal defense team was grasping at straws to find something to use against Jackie. They were desperate to find anyone they could who had a dislike of Jackie, and they were running out of options.

"Off the record. Lets break for lunch and return at 2:00."

After lunch, they returned to the conference room. This time, Jackie noticed that both Richard and Dexter were present for the afternoon deposition. They all waited patiently as the defense attorney prepared himself and then he resumed the line of questioning about the thirty-four different sexual charges. Again and again, Attorney Woodcock questioned Jackie about the incidents, and each time she responded with much the same answers she'd given in previous days' testimony. The only difference was this time Dexter was sitting directly across the table from Jackie, alongside Richard.

During the description of the snake in the pants issue, Dexter got up and excused himself from the room. It appeared he couldn't take the embarrassment of hearing her describe him unzipping his pants and reaching inside to pull out a live snake! He turned blood red in the face and simply excused himself. Several minutes passed before Dexter returned, and by then Jackie was describing how he would fart at her, how he told people she was a swallower and not a spitter, how he put out a $50 bounty for one of Jackie's pubic hairs, and the time he grabbed a thread attached to her pants zipper and pulled it—completely revealing her crotch. Jackie told again how he often offered to allow her to suck on his dick as he unzipped his pants in front of her. This detailed testimony went on for hours while Dexter sat there completely expressionless, either with the color completely drained from his face or shining beet red, listening as Jackie never missed a quote or detail of his abuse and harassment.

"Mrs. Kennard, are there any witnesses to any of these accusations you bring forth?"

"Yes."

"I'd like a full report on my desk tomorrow, including the names along with the time and events that you are aware of witnesses to."

Jackie was about to reply when Attorney Bernard shouted, "I OBJECT! She cannot possibly complete that list on such short notice and get it to you by tomorrow morning."

"Then I'm going to the judge and request that the case be dropped, based on the fact that there are no witnesses to her charges. Our investigation concluded that Ms. Kennard is bringing false charges and these accusations are merely made-up lies because she was angry her husband lost the flooring contract with the company over his bad work performance. Again, we conclude she has no grounds to bring these charges forth and needs to drop her charges against my client."

"Not a chance," Attorney Bernard replied.

Jackie's knuckles turned white as she squeezed her hands together and glared at Dexter, who had a smug grin on his face.

Attorney Woodcock: "Then we will conclude today's testimony and resume tomorrow at 9:00 a.m."

Attorney Bernard: "I'm not going to stand for this! I'm going to call the judge today and have a ruling issued to put a stop to this deposition immediately! This should have been finished days ago. You are simply harassing and aggravating both myself and my client, and now you are starting to go over the same questions that were asked and answered days ago."

"Go ahead," Attorney Woodcock drawled. "Like I said, we'll adjourn today and return tomorrow. "

Attorney Bernard was outraged by Attorney Woodcock's lack of consideration. She immediately stomped out of the conference room and placed a call to the judge, asking him to have the deposition stopped. After talking with both attorneys, the judge gave the defense attorney only four additional hours to complete whatever he needed to ask Jackie. Then the judge assigned the time on the deposition for the next morning at 7:30 a.m. sharp, to conclude at 10:30, with any cleanup questions to take place between 10:30 and 11:30 a.m.

*December 10, 7:30 a.m.*
*Deposition, Day Six*

They assembled again in the conference room, and Attorney Woodcock quickly began his questioning. He was all over the place, sometimes even helping Jackie along with her questions so he could quickly move onto the next one. Jackie purposefully took her time answering some questions, which obviously upset Attorney Woodcock. Then as the 11:30 time limit came, Jackie stated, "I have to go now. I'm already late for work."

"Wait!" he shouted as he held up a book in his left hand while writing something down with his right hand. "I'm not finished yet. I still have several questions to ask."

"I'm sorry," she replied. "I really have to go to work now, or I'll be fired for missing too much work."

As soon as those words were spoken, Attorney Woodcock slammed a book onto the table directly in front of Jackie, causing her to jump. "Well, I'll be fired for not finishing my job if you don't answer all these questions."

Jackie shrugged, stood up, and walked away from the table.

Attorney Woodcock screamed her name. "JACKIE KENNARD, I'm talking to you! Sit down until I've released you to go!" He slammed another book onto the table.

She looked at her watch, then back at him as she reached for the doorknob and opened the door. By now both Attorney Bernard and Attorney Woodcock were shouting back and forth so quickly the court reporter couldn't keep up.

Then Mr. Harris shouted, "HEY, take a break! I can't keep up when you're both shouting at the same time."

Jackie had already gone down the hallway for help, because she wasn't about to put herself in between those two in what would apparently be a duel to the death. Then Attorney Bernard's partner instructed Jackie to go ahead and leave, and she would rescue Ms. Bernard.

After all was said and done, the six days of deposition plus the prior deposition taken by the defense's first attorney, Ms. Littleworth, totaled more than 3,800 pages, including exhibits and documents obtained from Jackie. There was absolutely nothing they did not ask about, from her height and weight to her sexual preference and religious beliefs. Jackie felt she'd relived her entire life, plus the last three years' aggravation, all over again.

With that ordeal finally behind her, it was their turn to ask questions. Jackie could hardly wait for the depositions to start against the defendants. She still desperately wanted to know Tom's true identity. And she held onto the promise that her attorney would somehow break Tom's cover during his deposition.

Once the judge ruled to have the deposition wrapped up, even the lawyers wanted to take some time off from the case. As Jackie's focus turned to getting ready for Christmas, she knew she still had research to do. Since it was her case, she wanted to know everything about it from the legal standpoint. Many times she was so busy the hours slipped away, and before she knew it, it was time to go to bed. One Sunday evening the phone rang just as she had retired for the evening. It was Brian.

"Hey Mom, what's going on?"

"Not much," she replied.

"Mom, I want you to know I'm behind you on this, and I think you should see it through, no matter what. I've thought about it a lot since you were here, and I want you to promise me that you will see this thing through to the end. I want you to get justice!"

"I intend to," Jackie added.

"Well, I believe in what you're doing and I want you to know you can count on me to help in any way." He paused and she heard him take a deep breath. "Mom, I have something I want to tell you."

There was a long silence on the phone before Jackie thought she'd lost the connection. "Brian, are you there?"

"Yeah. Mom, I need you to pick up something there in Dallas for me. Actually, it's two things. Two gold rings."

"For what?" she asked.

"Because I've met someone, and I'm going to ask her to marry me."

"Oh my God! Are you really! That's the best thing I've heard in a long time!" Jackie screamed with excitement. "When and where are you planning to marry?"

"Well, IF she accepts, I thought we might get married in Las Vegas."

"I can't believe it! My baby boy is getting married!"

"Mom, I'm not a baby. I'm a twenty-six year old Marine. I'd like for you to pick up the rings and then have them engraved on the inside with our names and the date before you send them out to me."

"I'd love to do that," she replied. "But, you haven't told me what name should be engraved inside hers."

There was another pause before Brian said, "Her name is Jackie. Jackie Claxton until we get married, then she'll become Jackie Weatherby."

"You're kidding! Is she anything like me?" Jackie asked.

"Absolutely... positively not!" Brian replied with a chuckle. "My Jackie is nice!"

The two of them laughed hysterically and continued talking for over an hour. Jackie was full of questions. "When do we get to meet her? And just when is this wedding going to take place?"

"Well," Brian hesitated. "I was thinking about New Year's Eve. That date was lucky for you and George. Then we can come home to Dallas and have a party when I get a leave in April."

"That will be perfect," Jackie said. "Your Aunt Gail and I will get everyone together and give you two a wedding party in the spring."

As Jackie finished her conversation with her son, Brian, she felt a warm glow of happiness. This event felt like a fresh breath in her life. She genuinely welcomed the change from her everyday struggles with the impending trial and depositions. The next day she went to the jewelry store and picked up the two simple gold bands. She called Brian an hour later to tell him she had the rings and was sending them to him right away.

What do they look like?" he asked.

"They look like two gold rings. Each one has the other's name engraved inside, along with the date of 12-31-97."

"Well, do ya think she'll like it?"

"I'm sure she will." Jackie kissed each ring before placing them inside the box and closing the lid with a snap. "I'll send them by overnight express at the earliest pickup time tomorrow."

"Mom, how are things really going with the lawsuit?"

"We're moving along. Don't worry yourself about it. Your wedding and Regina's graduation in May are far more important to me now than anything else."

# CHAPTER FORTY-FOUR

*April 1998*

For three months the defense legal team managed to stall any attempts on behalf of the plaintiff's attorney to begin taking their depositions. Every appointment was canceled, several at the last minute. Numerous times, the defense attorneys claimed they couldn't make the date because of personal reasons. Once they stated that Tom was out of the country on business and wouldn't be back for a while. Then there was a company trip to Hawaii that could not be avoided. The excuses went on and on until Attorney Bernard had to go before the judge again and obtain a ruling to make them comply.

Attorney Bernard wanted to depose Tom first, hoping she could quickly prove her point that he was in fact living a lie and was not part of the witness protection program. Finally, the judge set the date for April 17 and confirmed, via telephone conversations, that everyone could be present. Then he stated, for the record, that he was getting tired of having to rule on every issue to make things move forward with this case. He advised the defendants' counsel that if they continued dragging their feet he would either sanction them heavily or just take a ruling in the case without it having to go to the jury.

With the deposition date only days away, Jackie was still thinking of questions she wanted her attorney to ask. She knew she had one shot and one shot only to ask these questions—inquiries that could point her in the direction she needed to go in order to find Frankie Paige's real father and Tom's real identity. Keeping in mind what Tom had previously told her about being able to manipulate the system from his lengthy experience, she knew they must carefully word each question so he would have to answer truthfully. For example, instead of asking, "Do you know Frankie Paige's father," they would ask, "Do you know the name of Frankie Paige's father?"

Jackie had spent another long day working on this and before she realized it, Sunday night arrived. George came into her office and asked, "Hey, are you going to come to bed or work on your project all night?"

"I'm coming to bed right now." As they climbed into bed, she said, "I'm really tired. I've pushed myself to stay up too late this time." They talked together for a few minutes before saying good night and turning out the lights. Having spent the entire weekend doing research work on the witness protection program, Jackie had no trouble falling asleep. Then at exactly 4:30 a.m. she sat straight up in bed gasping for her breath and panting as though she'd run a marathon. She startled George awake.

"Honey, what's wrong with you?"

Jackie couldn't answer. She could hardly catch her breath. She shook her head back and forth, trying to shake herself into reality as she stumbled to the bathroom.

"Honey, what can I do?" George asked in a panicked voice. Jackie sank onto the bathroom floor, still gasping for breath. George's first thought was that she was having a heart attack. He quickly retrieved a wet washcloth and wiped her face, before she was finally able to start breathing.

"What just happened to me?" She asked George. "I thought I was dying. I was disoriented. I guess I had some kind of horrible nightmare, but all I can remember is Brian standing there in front of me in a fog, calling 'Mom! What's wrong with me? Where am I?' Then I woke up feeling incredibly hot and couldn't catch my breath."

George was visibly shaken by it all and wanted to take Jackie to the hospital right away, but she convinced him they should just go back to bed. Too scared to sleep, she lay staring at the clock until the alarm went off two hours later. Still feeling peculiar from the incident and unable to figure out what happened, she got up and dressed for work. Even after arriving at work, she couldn't shake the eerie feeling, and she tried to find ways to keep busy and occupy her mind. She felt a sort of emptiness but thought it was just fatigue from having worked all weekend.

Jackie finished work early and drove home, planning to crash into bed and catch up on all the sleep she'd lost the night before. Just as she stepped onto the porch, she heard the phone ringing. She fumbled with the keys and hurried to grab the receiver, but only heard a dial tone. Moments later, the doorbell rang. "Grand Central Station," she mumbled, hurrying to get the door. She snatched it open to find George standing there with several other people. Instantly she knew something wasn't right, George wasn't his usual jovial self.

"Why'd you ring the door bell?" she asked. "What's going on?" By then the other three people had stepped around George, and she realized they were all wearing military uniforms. Jackie smiled, thinking Brian must be with them. He was due to come home any day, on leave for his wedding party.

The men filed through the door as one of them spoke. "Mrs. Kennard. It is with deep regret and sorrow that The United States Marines has come to inform you that your son Lance Corporal Brian Weatherby was killed this morning at 4:30 a.m. on Highway 5 in San Juan Capistrano, California. His car was hit from behind by another car traveling at a high rate of speed. He was alone in his car. The car burst into flames." The chaplain paused as Jackie slumped against George. "I'm really sorry, Mrs. Kennard, but they were unable to get him out of the car before he perished."

Jackie could not believe it was true. She heard nothing past the word *killed*. She violently shook her head and screamed, "No! You're wrong! It can't be him! He just got married and he's coming home in a few days, bringing his new wife to meet us. You must be mistaken!"

"I wish we were wrong," the chaplain replied as he helped lower Jackie into a chair. "Mrs. Kennard, we have something to give you." He knelt in front of Jackie. "Brian's wife knew you'd never accept this news without proof, and she asked me to give this to you." He held out his hand, and Jackie waited to see his offering. He opened his hand to reveal a gold ring. It had been burned on either side. Jackie trembled as she took the ring and held it to the light to reveal the engraving, Jackie 12-31-97. She could no longer deny her greatest fear as she collapsed into George's arms and cried uncontrollably. "How could this happen?" she cried. "I don't understand! Why?"

Two days later, Jackie sat alone in the sanctuary, awaiting the arrival of her son's remains. She specifically asked to be alone because she wanted to talk to God, one-on-one, before she saw the casket. As she sat in silence, a lifetime of thoughts ran through her head. At that point, she had no physical feelings. Absolutely nothing mattered to her—she felt an indescribable emptiness inside. Then the door opened, and she watched as they rolled in a steel gray casket draped with an American flag. She bowed her head and pressed one hand over her eyes, desperately trying to hold her emotions at bay until they were alone. But she could no longer hold back the tears as one of Brian's fellow Marines approached and offered his condolences as he handed her an envelope. The envelope contained letters from several of Brian's friends at Camp Pendleton, each expressing their sympathy since they couldn't attend the funeral. She sobbed uncontrollably for a moment, and then asked everyone there if she could be alone with her son.

She wasn't allowed to view Brian's body, so she sat on the prayer bench and leaned onto the casket, resting her head against the cool metal as she cried and talked to her son, desperately trying to make sense of the tragic accident. Then, like any mother would, she told Brian how much he meant to her and how much she loved him. Jackie wasn't sure, how or if she could survive the loss, but she had to be strong to help Regina through it. So she asked Brian to help her find a way to cope with his death. As she closed her eyes and talked to him, she felt his presence all around her.

Perhaps it was a mother's instinct, or the bond shared between mother and child, but Jackie had obviously experienced something unusual the morning Brian was killed. She prayed for strength as she lay across Brian's casket. She was exhausted. She hadn't slept in days, and soon she fell asleep. Lying there, she dreamed his entire life, from the first time she saw him at birth until the last time she saw him boarding a plane as a Marine. She vividly recalled every event of his life—almost like a spectator. She watched as the two of them laughed before he handed her a red rose, and said. "Mom, I'm free. Please don't grieve for me. I'm following the path God has laid for me. I took his hand when I heard Him call; I turned my back and left it all. I couldn't stay another day to laugh to love to work or play. Tasks I've left undone will just have stay that way, for I found peace at the beginning of my day. If my parting you has left a void, fill it only with remembered joys. A friendship shared, a laugh, a kiss. Oh yes, these things I, too, will miss. Be not burdened with times of sorrow. I wish you the sunshine of many tomorrows. My life's been full I savored much. Good friends, good times, a loved one's touch. Perhaps my time seemed all to brief. Don't lengthen it now with undue grief. Lift up your heart, and peace to thee. God wanted me, Mom, He set me free."

Then Jackie felt someone pulling at her and she awakened. It was George. "How long was I out?" she asked.

"A couple of hours," he replied. "I thought I probably needed to get you up because people are starting to come in."

Jackie shook her head, rubbed her eyes, and ran her fingers through her hair, preparing herself to meet the people who were waiting to pay their condolences. Jackie was amazed at the number of people who stopped to offer their love and kindness during the next twenty-four hours. It gave her the strength she'd prayed for.

Then, on April 10, 1998, Lance Corporal Brian Weatherby was laid to rest.

# CHAPTER FORTY-FIVE

On April 17, 1998, just one week after Jackie had buried her son, she was back at the conference table. This time the meeting was held in their attorney's office. Jackie purposefully sat directly across the table from Tom, showing no emotion or expression, as she waited for his deposition to begin. No one from the defense knew about Brian's death because Jackie knew that they would somehow make an issue of it, and she preferred to keep that part of her life private.

Attorney Bernard swore Tom in then introduced herself and explained the proceedings. She asked Tom if he'd ever had a deposition taken before, and he answered, "Yea, once."

"And what kind of proceeding was that?"

"It was for an accident case."

"What state was that in?"

"Pennsylvania."

At that point, Jackie picked up a pen and began taking notes as the questions continued.

"What county was it in?"

"Allegheny."

"Do you recall what year?"

"Either 1973 or 1974."

"What was the outcome of that particular lawsuit?"

"They settled, and a cash award was given to me." Tom suddenly rose from his chair and began pacing around the room. All eyes watched in wonderment. No one was sure what he was going to do. Then Attorney Woodcock said, "Ms. Bernard, before you go on, let me explain that Mr. Kerakasco has a stomach problem. Rather, he has a nervous stomach and it gets upset easily, which causes discomfort. Therefore he feels better when he moves around. But please be aware that sometimes when his stomach does acts up he regurgitates. Therefore, he may burst from the room if he has to."

"Great," Ms. Bernard replied. "We'll deal with that problem when it comes up."

As she continued the questioning, Tom asked her to call him Tommy. She replied, "Thank you, but I'd rather call you Mr. Kerakasco, if it's all the same to you."

Tom shrugged "Okay, whatever."

"Have you ever testified in any other depositions?"

"No ma'am."

"Have you reviewed any documents for your deposition today?"

"Yes. I've read all the deposition given by Jackie, I mean Mrs. Kennard."

"And you do realize that the information that you have read was not supposed to be passed along to you?"

"Nope, I sure wasn't."

"You do realize that you are still under a restraining order not to have any contact with Mrs. Kennard or anyone in her family."

"Yeah, yeah, I know. They told me that already."

Attorney Woodcock interrupted: "For the record. We need to make it clear for all involved here that a gag order has been issued under federal rule, and there will be no discussion allowed outside this immediate legal arena about this case or anyone directly involved with it. Attorney Bernard, you can continue now."

"Thank you," she replied. "Mr. Kerakasco have you ever gone by any name other than Tom Kerakasco?"

Attorney Woodcock intervened, "I'm going to make an objection, and at this point I would like to state on the record, that prior to this deposition, there were discussions between the plaintiff's counsel and Attorney Marion Littleworth. The witness has been, or is currently in a witness protection program, and we have discussed with Attorney Bernard that because of that program, and the necessary secrecy related to that program, we would not allow or would advise Mr. Kerakasco to not go into matters related to the witness protection program."

Tom stared at the ceiling as his attorney continued. "However, Mr. Kerakasco may recount any conversations he has had with Ms. Kennard regarding the witness protection program. Also, he will provide testimony regarding prior convictions to the extent that the federal rules of evidence would permit the admissibility of such convictions in a court of law. Beyond that, as we discussed with Attorney Bernard, Mr. Kerakasco will not answer questions that go beyond those parameters."

He paused and then said to Tom, "And based on that, Mr. Kerakasco, I advise you not to respond to that question."

Attorney Bernard added, "And I just want to indicate for the record that I have spoken to Attorney Littleworth regarding this issue. My understanding of the agreement we reached was that I would ask questions I felt were pertinent, and if counsel and/or Mr. Kerakasco did not feel he should answer, a refusal would be recorded. Then I would seek a motion to compel that testimony. And so, my preference is that I'm going to go ahead and ask the questions. If you don't want him to answer these, then you can direct him not to answer."

Finally, after much discussion, Attorney Bernard said to Tom, "I believe—I've forgotten the question, but I think I asked if you've ever gone by any other names." She then addressed Attorney Woodcock. "I think that's the question you directed him not to answer."

"That's correct," said Attorney Woodcock.

"How many other legal names have you gone by?" she asked Tom.

"I advise you not to answer," said Attorney Woodcock. "I'm going to object on the grounds of relevance."

The sparring continued as Attorney Bernard asked about Tom's other names and the witness protection program. Attorney Woodcock advised Tom not to answer most of the questions. Tom looked at Jackie, smiled, shrugged, and jerked his head as though to say, "Yeah, I'm bad. I'm above all this!"

Attorney Bernard concluded, "Attorney Woodcock, I prefer that Mr. Kerakasco refuse to answer himself, rather than his attorney speak for him."

Attorney Bernard then asked Tom which branch of the government handled the witness protection program and to whom he reported. Tom replied that the federal marshals were in charge of the program, but he would not reveal to whom he reported or their location. She then asked Tom why he entered the program, and again his attorney advised him not to answer.

When Tom refused to answer further questions about his past names, Attorney Bernard asked about his current and past social security numbers. Again, he refused to answer. Tom did reveal that he was born in Pennsylvania on November 27, 1954. Attorney Bernard then searched through a stack of papers before she produced Tom's original job application, where he listed his birth date as August 24, 1954.

Attorney Bernard smiled as she handed him the job application and asked him to read it aloud.

Tom read the document and smiled back at her. "Damn! See how stupid I am?"

"Strike that!" Attorney Woodcock ordered. "We need a fifteen minute break."

The two attorneys argued over whether or not to take a break and finally agreed to fifteen minutes. Tom and Attorney Woodcock returned twenty minutes later, and Tom seemed more subdued as he returned to the table.

Attorney Woodcock spoke first. "On the record. Attorney Bernard, before we took a break we were discussing my client's job application. I want to state for the record that upon entering the witness protection program, he was advised to create a new background for his own protection. Therefore I advised him not to answer any further questions until I've had the opportunity to decide if each question should be answered or if he should plead the Fifth Amendment."

"Thank you, Mr. Woodcock. Again, it is my understanding that I will ask the questions, and if there's a disagreement, we allow the court to decide whether or not the answer is allowed into use or not. Now, having said that, Mr. Kerakasco, did you graduate from high school?"

"Yeah, from Hill South High School."

Attorney Woodcock immediately turned to Tom and said, "Did you answer that question?" Tom leaned over and they discussed something in private before Attorney Bernard interrupted.

"Is there anything you'd like to share after your private discussion with your counsel?"

"No," Tom said.

"Exactly where is Hill South High School located?"

"Nowhere. It was destroyed several years ago."

"Did you grow up in Pennsylvania?"

"Yeah."

"Whereabouts?"

"In Pittsburgh."

"Did you live in the actual city of Pittsburgh or in the suburbs?"

Attorney Woodcock shouted, "Objection! I don't think this is relevant to the claims, and I'll advise you not to answer."

Tom looked directly at Attorney Bernard, leaned toward her, and replied, "Okay, I ain't gonna answer your stupid question. On advice of counsel, of course."

Attorney Bernard responded, "That's not necessary, Mr. Kerakasco. You don't need to add any adjectives to your answers. Mr. Kerakasco, are you a barber?"

Immediately Tom leaned forward, and all the color drained from his face. With a most peculiar expression on his face, he shouted, "Excuse me? What did you say?"

"Mr. Kerakasco, you don't have to get upset. I just asked if you are a barber? By that I meant, did you regularly cut people's hair at the Midway Park office?"

"No," Tom snarled.

"Did you ever cut anyone's hair at the Midway Park office?"

"Yes, I did."

"How often did you cut Dexter's hair?"

"I don't know."

"Well, was it once a week or once a month?"

"Probably once a month," Tom said.

"Then I would call that regularly," Attorney Bernard said. "Mr. Kerakasco, did you ever tell my client that you learned to cut hair in the Big House?"

Tom bit his bottom lip and appeared to ponder how he should answer. "Maybe," he replied, glaring at Jackie.

"Did you go to school to learn to cut hair?"

"Maybe."

"Mr. Kerakasco, do you have a license to cut hair?"

"No," said Tom.

Attorney Bernard continued, asking a series of questions about Tom's educational background and pointing out discrepancies on his state license to sell manufactured homes. Then she focused on his job at Midway Housing, asking, "What is your title now with Midway Housing Corporation?"

"General manager," answered Tom.

"What was your position to Jackie when the two of you were employed together at Midway Park?"

"I was her supervisor."

"Can you explain to me when you got the title of general manager?"

"When I transferred from the Midway Park East location."

"Did you ask to be transferred?"

"No, I got a promotion."

"Did you get your transfer before or after Jackie filed a claim naming you as one of her offenders?"

"After," Tom said, leaning back in his chair interlacing his fingers.

"Mr. Kerakasco, isn't it true that all the male witnesses named by my client who are still employed at the Midway Park location were promoted to some sort of management position after she filed her claim?"

"That's just a coincidental thing. They were all up for a promotion."

"Mr. Kerakasco, how many times have you been married?"

"Twice," Tom said as he held up two fingers.

Attorney Bernard asked several questions about Tom's marriages, including the names of his first and second wives. Once again, Tom's attorney advised him not to answer. Tom also pled the fifth when asked about his children and his current address. He did reveal Lucrezia's name and stated they met in a bar. Attorney Bernard asked, "Do the two of you have any children?"

"Yeah two, a boy and a girl," Tom replied.

"Is the little girl your child?"

"No."

"Do you know her father?" Attorney Bernard questioned.

Tom turned and smiled directly at Jackie before he answered, "No, I don't."

Jackie knew he was lying, but there was nothing she could do about it. Her attorney had messed up on delivery of the question, and Tom was able to truthfully answer it with a lie. He knows who the father is, but he doesn't personally *know* the father. Jackie tried to not show her disgust but made a note to share it with her attorney later.

Attorney Bernard next asked Tom when he moved to the Dallas area and where he lived prior to that. She then inquired about his criminal background, asking how many felony convictions he had.

Attorney Woodcock interrupted, "Mr. Kerakasco, before you answer that question, let me advise you the parameters we have set for this deposition are that you may respond to any question regarding felony convictions to the same extent that the federal rules of evidence allow."

"Two," Tom answered again holding up two fingers.

"What two felonies have you been convicted of?"

"Conspiracy to distribute cocaine."

"When were you convicted of that offense?"

"1984. I think."

Further questions revealed that Tom was convicted in Allegheny County, Pennsylvania, and received a twenty-year sentence after pleading guilty. He served approximately four years in Terre Haute Penitentiary in Terre Haute, Indiana, a federal facility, from 1985 to 1989. After that, he was transferred to a federal facility in Kentucky and then to a county jail in West Virginia, where he was brought in to testify. Tom's attorney did not allow him to discuss the case in which he testified, but Tom did reveal that his testimony was the basis for being placed in the witness protection program.

"What did the trial involve, or who was the defendant in the trial?" Attorney Bernard asked.

"I don't remember any of their names. Just that there were thirty something codefendants on trial."

Tom would not reveal any names, but he did state the trial was drug related and the defendants were convicted. Attorney Bernard asked, "What happened to you in terms of where you were transferred after you testified in that trial?"

"I was transferred into a witness high-security unit."

"Where was that located?"

"New York," he replied as he glanced toward Jackie again.

Jackie glanced at Tom. She'd asked him when they first met if his accent was New York, and he had said no. *Wow, imagine that*, she thought. *He lied to me about that, too.*

Tom would not reveal the location in New York, stating he was led underground through heavy steel doors and was not allowed to know the exact location.

"How long did you stay there?"

"Two years."

After that, Tom said he transferred to another witness protection unit in Minnesota, but he didn't know why. He also stayed in that facility for two years prior to his release. That was when he came to the Dallas–Fort Worth area. Attorney Bernard then read aloud from an affidavit describing the second felony charge, which was also conspiracy to distribute cocaine.

"I refuse to answer," Tom blurted out.

"I didn't ask you anything yet, Mr. Kerakasco," Attorney Bernard stated.

"Okay," he replied. "I was just preparing myself for your next question."

"Well, I can probably make it easy on you. If you're going to take that attitude and be uncooperative, I can stop the deposition right now, go to the judge, and ask for a ruling."

Attorney Woodcock and Tom conversed in hushed voices for several minutes before Tom replied, "I'll wait for your next question. Then I'll refuse to answer."

Ms. Bernard proceeded to ask a series of questions regarding businesses Tom had owned and his previous income-tax payments and if the references he provided on his original job application were actual people or just names made up. Again, Tom took the Fifth Amendment on most of these questions and at one point stated they were an "invasion of his privacy."

Attorney Bernard burst out, "Mr. Kerakasco, you have violated my client on so many counts that I can't list them all on a single sheet of paper. You have now pled the Fifth Amendment 147 times. You obviously have a past life you want to avoid sharing with us. My client submitted to ten days of intense personal testimony that was often extremely embarrassing, harassing, and more than personal in its nature. My client has answered questions about her life, her jobs, her children, her marriage, her divorce, her surgeries, and her personal medical conditions. She has even replied to questions about her sexual preferences. And you refuse to answer a simple question about the reality of a reference you put on a job application because it interferes with your privacy?" She slammed down her pen in disgust.

Attorney Woodcock answered for his client. "Attorney Bernard. It is our position that the situations between Mrs. Kennard and Mr. Kerakasco are not comparable. We have no objection to counsel going into certain areas, but because of the nature of why Mr. Kerakasco was placed into the witness protection program... well, I'll have to continue advising my client to not answer certain questions."

"Would you please allow me a break?" Attorney Bernard answered. "I need to confer with my client here and make a decision."

Ms. Bernard paced the floor in her office, obviously upset by how the deposition was turning out. She had not expected Tom to exercise his Fifth Amendment right on every question. She and Jackie used this break to discuss the fact that they'd probably need to go before the judge again and ask for a ruling in order to piece together anything about Tom's past.

"I really don't think we've learned anything useful, much less what it is he's hiding. Without a name, we're lost." Attorney Bernard sighed. "What do you want to do, Jackie?"

Feeling frustrated, Jackie said, "I don't know yet, so let's just keep going. I'll think of something." She paused. "Why can't we go to the judge and ask him to make Tom testify?"

"I can do that, but there's no guarantee he'll make it happen. If this guy was some big turncoat in the Mafia, then they won't make him testify and disclose who he really is."

"Damn this bastard!" Jackie exclaimed. "How could a creep like this be given immunity? There must be something we can do to get information!"

Then Attorney Bernard confessed, "Jackie, up until a few days ago, I didn't believe Tom had ever been in a witness protection program. Now I'm thinking the story he told you is probably true. We'll just have to work through it all and go to the judge for a ruling. But, in the meanwhile, keep yourself out of the limelight. I don't feel comfortable about the restraining order being helpful if this idiot gets pissed off like you said he does. He appears to be either a sociopath or psychopath, or both. Let's just get through this questioning and see where we end up today. Then I'll go to the judge tomorrow morning for a ruling."

Jackie agreed to this, and her attorney resumed questioning Tom.

"Mr. Kerakasco, before we took a break we were discussing your personal life. You made it very clear that discussing that part of your past could bring you possible harm. Well, I'd like to avoid being a part of anything that would bring you harm, so we'll take a different road and go over your present life. You have worked for Midway Housing for approximately two years? Is that correct?"

"Yep!" Tom slouched in his chair, grinning at her.

"And during that time Mr. Kerakasco, have you ever had an affair with any of the female employees?"

There was a long pause before Tom answered. "Well, I wouldn't call it an affair."

"What would you call it, Mr. Kerakasco?"

"A blow job here and there. Once I went out to dinner with Linda Lambert, and she took off her panties while I was driving down I-75 and threw them out the window. Then she proceeded to finger-fuck herself right there in front of me. Then she unzipped my pants and while I was driving she went down on me and—well, I pulled over. I was afraid I might cause a wreck. When we got to the restaurant, we sat in the bar and jacked each other off under the table while we were waiting on our food to arrive. Then we finished eating and left, but before we got out of the parking lot, she gave me another blow job."

Silence hovered over the room like a heavy fog. No one knew what to say or do. Every head in the room was bowed downward because no one wanted to make eye contact.

After a long pause, Attorney Bernard asked, "Mr. Kerakasco, who did you say this person was?"

"Linda Lambert. Hey, can I please add something or tell you something else about that?"

"Why not?" Attorney Bernard replied.

"Well, the day after this happened, I went into Jackie's office and told her about it, and I thought she was going to come in her pants when she heard about it. She clapped her hands together, like this—pow, pow—and yelled, 'Tell me more! Tell me more!' Then she rubbed her hands together like this and laughed hysterically! She's a sick fuck, herself! Then she opened her desk drawer and took out a magnifying glass and told me to stand up. Then she placed the magnifying glass next to my crotch and said, 'Nah, you're not big enough for me!'"

The conference room again fell silent. Stone cold shock was etched on everyone's face. No one in that room thought Jackie was capable of such crass action. She hardly seemed like the type of person who'd say those words or examine Tom's crotch with a magnifying glass. Jackie felt waves of embarrassment radiating from her face. Attorney Woodcock snickered out loud as everyone sat in complete disbelief.

"Are you finished Mr. Kerakasco?" Ms. Bernard snarled.

"Yea, I am," he replied as he crossed his arms and leaned back in his chair.

"Thank you," Attorney Bernard replied.

Tom's attorney requested a fifteen-minute break at that point. When the men left the room and closed the door behind them, Ms. Bernard turned to Jackie and begged, "PLEASE tell me he's lying!"

Jackie stared at her in total disbelief. "What do you think? Do you really have to ask, after we've worked together all these months? He's trying to make me mad enough to come across the table for his throat, he's seen me get livid for less than that at work, and he's hoping I'll lash back at him." She smiled grimly, "What you've just witnessed from Tom is a sample of his everyday demeanor. I've told you, he says whatever comes to his mind whenever he thinks of it. That was a shock treatment for all of you. Don't worry. Nothing affects me after I buried my son last week."

"What? What are you saying?" Ms. Barnard asked.

"Just that," Jackie replied. "I don't want to talk about it."

"What happened, Jackie?"

"He was killed last week in a car wreck, and that's all I want to say about that right now. Please don't bring it up, because I'm okay with being here."

Attorney Bernard silently stared into Jackie's face, and Jackie added, "Really, I'm fine. Let's just keep this thing moving—and please don't let them know!"

Just then the door opened, and the defense team announced they were ready to resume the deposition. Attorney Bernard was obviously concerned about Jackie even being there, but she had no choice other than to go forward.

"Mr. Kerakasco, were you ever disciplined because of complaints made by other women from Midway Housing about your sexual profanity?"

"I don't understand the question—the question is very broad. I'm confused."

"Well, let me ask this way: Were you ever or have you ever been reprimanded by any one of your supervisors in regard to complaints by any female employees other than my client while you have been employed with Midway Housing?"

"Yeah, Dexter said something to me once about something I said in front of one of the ladies."

"And what was that, Mr. Kerakasco?"

"Suck a dick!"

"Was that a one-time thing, or did you say it on a regular basis?"

"Regular basis, four or five times a day. Whenever the thought crossed my mind," he replied as he shrugged his shoulders in disregard.

"Mr. Kerakasco, will you please tell us the names of the women working for the company that you have had an affair or sexual relations with?"

"No, I won't. That's personal information. I don't kiss and tell. I'll just say I'm refusing to answer, I'll plead the Fifth on this one."

Frustrated with his refusal again to answer the question, Attorney Bernard just shook her head. "Mr. Kerakasco, are you aware that my client was assaulted by a customer of Midway Housing while at work?"

"Yes, I'm aware."

"Would you please tell us exactly what you did about this incident?"

Tom looked directly at Jackie, shrugged his shoulders and replied. "Nothing. It wasn't my place to do anything. Her old man shoulda took care of it for her."

Jackie immediately wrote something down on paper and slid it over to her attorney. They exchanged looks before she continued. "Mr. Kerakasco, did you tell my client that you 'took care of it' in order to make her feel comfortable enough to return to work?"

"Yeah. I lied to her. I knew that was the only way she'd ever come back to work, and she had several deals hanging that she needed to close out for the month. Oh, by the way, closing out her deals made our location the number one location that month."

Jackie sat glaring at the worthless piece of slime. She could not believe he'd just bragged about lying to her in order to profit. Now she was really pissed!

"Mr. Kerakasco, did you discuss with Mrs. Kennard the fact that you were in the witness protection program?"

"Yeah, maybe."

"Why?"

"Because she figured me out and kept saying things in front of people, so I just called her aside one day and confessed to her. I told her it didn't need to be discussed with anyone outside the two or three of us—meaning myself and my wife."

"Did you go into detail about the reason you were placed in the witness protection program?"

"I think I told her I had to testify against several people, but that's all that I said about it."

"Did you tell Ms. Kennard you'd murdered someone? And in fact I quote, "blown his motherfucking brains all over the wall."

"I don't know what you're talking about," Tom snapped as he leaped from his chair and paced around the room.

"Is it your testimony today that that conversation never happened?"

Tom shrugged his shoulders and yawned.

"I'll need a verbal response. The court reporter can't record a shrug," Attorney Bernard stated.

"I don't know what she's talking about. I never told her anything about that. I mean, like that."

"Did you ever threaten Ms. Kennard's life if she told the story?"

"What story?" Tom grinned at her as he sat back down.

Gritting her teeth, Attorney Bernard continued. "Mr. Kerakasco, did you ask Mrs. Kennard to obtain her husband's fingerprints for you to use as your own for your license?"

"Maybe," Tom drawled.

"Why did you need George Kennard's fingerprints?"

"Because Richard Spaniel told me to just get some fingerprints for my license and he would take care of the rest."

Attorney Woodcock screamed out. "Objection! Attorney client conference."

A few minutes later, Ms. Bernard continued. "Then I take it that Mr. Spaniel knows about your past?"

"He knows I'm in the witness protection program."

As the deposition went on for the remainder of the day, Tom confirmed almost everything Jackie had stated in her complaint against Dexter and others. However, he refused to confirm many of the charges she brought against him, offering the impression that the two of them were as he put it, *very good friends*. He did confess that the two highest people in the company knew about his past and, because there was a need for only two people to be licensed at each location, Dexter could have been one and Jackie the other, but Tom would still be presented as the front person. It was now even more obvious to Attorney Bernard that Tom had a past, and it was probably on the dark side.

"Mr. Kerakasco," she asked, "When and how did your 'very good friendship' end with my client?"

At this point, Tom became a bit tongue-tied. "Whenever I told her about, I don't know. Probably—I can't remember. She changed her phone number and moved when she left the company."

"I take it, that's when you searched until you found her then paid her a visit her on her new job."

"Objection!" Attorney Woodcock shouted.

Attorney Bernard continued, "For the record: I would like to state that I intend to go before the judge for a ruling before I complete my deposition with Mr. Kerakasco. Therefore, I would like to end for the day and reconvene after the judge has made a ruling on discovery issues regarding Tom's past."

# CHAPTER FORTY-SIX

Late that afternoon, Attorney Bernard called the judge's chambers to arrange a hearing. Instead, she learned from the clerk that the defendants had just filed a motion to have the judge disqualified from the case, making it impossible to proceed until a ruling was reached on that filing, which could take weeks or even months. Attorney Bernard was furious! What a back-stabbing, unethical thing to do!" she screamed as she slammed her hand onto the desk. She dreaded calling Jackie with this bombshell.

Jackie cried when she heard the news. "I wish you would call with something positive just once. I don't know how much more I can take."

Hanging up the phone, Jackie decided she could no longer sit still and allow them to continue taking advantage. She called the Dallas federal marshal's office and asked to speak with anyone who could possibly give her information. Instead of receiving information, she was asked to *leave* information—her name, phone number, and the name of the person she was referencing. A secretary said someone might call her back at a later time.

"That's not good enough," Jackie snapped. "I really need to talk with someone—preferably right now."

The receptionist stated "That's not possible, ma'am. I'll try to have someone call you back."

Jackie hung up even more confused than when she called, but with the intent of going to the federal marshal's office right then and demand to meet with someone. Just as she was about to walk out the door, the phone rang, and a man identified himself as Frank Franklin, US federal marshal. "What can I do for you?" he asked.

Please, can you help me obtain some information? I'd like to know who takes responsibility for people in the witness protection program. Are you the person I talk to when someone in the program does something wrong?"

Mr. Franklin said, "Well, ma'am. I can't give you that information. I can't even tell you whether or not someone is in the witness protection program, but I'm willing to hear your complaint."

"I don't need you to reveal anything, because I already know that this asshole is in the program. What I want is to have the creep picked up and disposed of before he crashes any more lives." She then told Mr. Franklin about everything that had happened, not only to her, but also to the other people whose lives had been destroyed when Tom came into contact with them after being dumped into society in the Dallas area.

After a few moments of silence, Mr. Franklin replied, "Ma'am, I'm going to take some notes and check into your story, but in the meantime you should have your attorney contact the federal US Marshal's service in Arlington, Virginia." He then gave her a phone number and an address for Attorney Bernard to contact.

With that information, Jackie felt she'd reached a breakthrough. She immediately drove to her attorney's office to relay the information to her. Together they composed a letter outlining the case and requesting information on the person who identified himself as Tom Kerakasco. Though they now had a thread of hope to now work with, the case had reached a standstill until the higher court ruled on whether or not their judge would be disqualified from the case. This was another huge setback for Jackie. She had no choice but to accept the temporary shutdown and wait for a ruling.

It was now the end of May and time for Regina's graduation. As Jackie and George sat in the school auditorium waiting to see Regina cross the stage and begin another part of her life, Jackie listened intently as the guest speaker spoke of many things. He touched on many important issues, including how the graduates' past efforts had laid the groundwork for their futures, and what they should do to plan their futures. Then he uttered words that profoundly affected Jackie. She felt as though a light bulb had turned on inside her head when he said, "As I stand before you today, I ask that you take a moment to look around at your fellow classmates, because I can guarantee you that some of you will never cross paths with one another again, while some of you will see each other on a regular basis. The important thing for you to know is that you can determine or change your future. You have the ability to determine what happens to you and where you go from here. You have all worked very hard to get here today, and each of you earned your right to walk across this stage. To each of you, I say congratulations. This moment is yours and it will be recorded in history to forever remain the same."

That statement hit Jackie like nothing before! Recorded in history to remain forever the same! That was the missing key! Tom couldn't change history! She drew a deep gasping breath and George instantly turned toward her. She shook her head and patted his hand as she whispered, "I'm okay. I just thought of something." She now knew how to find out who Tom Kerakasco really was.

She could hardly sit through the ceremony as thoughts danced through her head about what the speaker had just said. *This is it*, she thought. This will break the case wide open. After the ceremony, Jackie and George went straight home and into her office where she immediately started looking back through the notes she'd taken during Tom's deposition. There it was! The name of the high school he'd attended.

George said, "I thought Tom said the school had been destroyed."

Jackie nodded as she picked up the phone and called information, requesting the number of the school. The operator did confirm the school was no longer in existence.

"Another dead end," George confirmed.

"Maybe not," Jackie whispered with her hand over the phone, before she asked the operator for the number to the Pennsylvania Historical Society. As she quickly jotted down the number, she felt confident that she'd found the key to something positive. She could hardly contain herself over the weekend waiting for Monday to arrive so she could make that phone call. Just as soon as she got into the office, her first phone call was to the Historical Society of Pennsylvania. They were very accommodating and confirmed that in fact Hill South High School had been destroyed several years previously. Then Jackie took a stab in the dark, confessed her absolute need of assistance, and asked if they'd been able to retain any information about the school.

"Yes, we still have records" the librarian replied.

Jackie asked the librarian if a copy of the names from Tom's graduating class could be faxed to her office for her to look over.

The librarian said, "Sure. It may take me a few minutes to locate, but I can do that for you."

Within fifteen minutes, Jackie stood at the fax machine, watching in total disbelief, as papers appeared bearing the names of the 300 plus members of Tom's graduating class. Jackie quickly looked through the sheets, but no particular name stood out. She called the Historical Society back and again spoke to the librarian, saying, "I'm sorry, but none of these names look familiar to me. Would it be possible for you to photocopy the graduating class pictures and send to me? I'll wire you the money today. Please, I really need your help on this. It's very important that I get this information as quickly as possible!"

Obviously, Jackie's desperation could be felt through the phone and the librarian agreed to help her out. "Yes, honey. I'll go ahead and send the information to you now, and you can just drop a money order in the mail for ten dollars."

"Ten dollars!" Jackie shouted.

"I'm sorry, but it's to cover the copies and labor," the librarian explained.

"Oh, no ma'am, I didn't mean it like that. It's just that I would be willing to pay much more than ten dollars for this information!"

Jackie's heart was pounding in her chest. Why hadn't she thought of this sooner? Immediately she gave the librarian her Fed Ex account number and then went to the bank for a money order. She got the money order for ten dollars, plus a thank you card addressed to the librarian. Jackie signed the card and placed a $100 bill inside.

Two days later, Federal Express delivered the package from the Historical Society. Jackie ripped open the box—she could hardly wait to see those pictures! Finally, the truth she struggled so hard for. She scanned over the pictures page by page, person by person, wondering if she'd even recognize Tom.

"Oh, my God!" she shouted. There, right before her eyes was Tom Kerakasco in his senior high school picture! He was wearing a pinstriped suit looking remarkably similar to himself still today, except for those dorky glasses. Jackie frantically searched the page for his name. "OH MY GOD! This is Tom—Oh my God, it's really him! But it's not Tom Kerakasco—it's Terry Barber!"

She immediately called her attorney, so excited she was hyperventilating on the phone and had to wait a few seconds before she could speak. "You won't believe what I just got in the mail. I'm coming to your office—I've got to show you!"

When she arrived, Jackie was immediately escorted to Attorney Bernard's office where she laid out the pictures and proof of Tom's true identity. Attorney Bernard laughed as she saw his true name. "Barber, that's why he turned white and acted so shocked when I asked him if he was a barber. He thought I was talking about his last name!"

Attorney Bernard's associates were all present to witness this, and they were amazed at how Jackie had managed to obtain the picture. Then Attorney Bernard said, "The problem is, I don't know if we can use this. It all depends on the new judge in the case. And from the looks of what's happened so far, the other side at this point pretty much controls things. The prior judge was favorable to our side, but now we have no judge until the higher court makes a ruling—and we really don't know who or what that decision might bring."

"Who appoints the judge?" Jackie inquired.

"Probably the President," Attorney Bernard replied.

"The President of what? Jackie asked, feeling confused.

Attorney Bernard looked at Jackie across the desk and leaned toward her has she replied, "The President of the United States of America."

"So what?" Jackie asked.

"Well," Attorney Bernard replied, "the President will appoint a Democrat to replace the Republican judge we had. Don't overlook the fact that Tom was released under the term of a Democratic President, and the decision to put him in the witness protection program was probably made by a Democratic Judge. Plus, Attorney Woodcock is close personal friends with a leading Democrat in California, and he just spent a lot if time there. I'll bet this case had something to do with his extended trip to California."

"Damn!" Jackie exclaimed. "Now it's political. How can I win with these odds stacked against me?"

Attorney Bernard added, "The new judge may rule to disallow any part of Tom's past, since Tom—or Terry—or whoever the son of a bitch is, is now basically the responsibility of the United States government. They made a pact to provide protection for him in return for whatever he did to put him in this protected witness program." She stared out the window and shrugged, "We'll just to have to wait out the ruling to see what happens."

Jackie sank in her chair. "You mean to tell me I've done all this work for nothing?"

"Maybe not. We just need the ruling from the judge to come down first. Then we'll see what we need to do next."

For the next six weeks, everything for the discovery process sat on hold, until finally, the President of the United States announced he was appointing Judge Lindsey Samuel, the first black judge in the Northern District of Texas. From that appointment, Judge Samuel inherited literally hundreds of cases, one of those being Jackie's.

"I'm really disappointed," Attorney Bernard confessed in her phone conversation to Jackie.

"I'm not," Jackie replied. "I'm glad the new judge is black, because now they have to testify before him about their prejudice and racism.

They can sweat over his ruling when he hears my complaints against the company about racial comments."

"That's not what I was referring to," Attorney Bernard stated. "His caseload will take a very long time for him to sift through. It could even take years."

Jackie and her attorney continued discussing their options. "I think you should petition the court to have the case moved," Jackie suggested.

"I can't do that, but I will ask that it be assigned to a magistrate judge—anything to move it from Judge Samuel's court," Ms. Bernard promised.

That was probably the best thing Attorney Bernard could have done. She literally sat in the judge's court all day waiting her turn to ask for the case to be moved into another court. Judge Samuel was more than obliging and readily signed the motion that would relieve him of some of his workload. Suddenly, the case was back on track and would move forward under a magistrate judge.

The defendants wasted no time appealing motions before Judge Samuel. As a common defense strategy, they requested and received a change in trial date, which again postponed the court date for several months. Second, the judge granted their request to have their own physician of choice examine Jackie. The defendants' lawyers immediately arranged to have two doctors examine her. One was looking for signs of a stomach ulcer. The other was a psychiatric evaluation, accompanied by a handwriting analysis.

The defense team contacted Attorney Bernard and told her to have Jackie at the hospital to submit to an endoscopic exam on the following Thursday. After that phone call it was hard to tell who was more upset—Attorney Bernard or Jackie.

"What the hell is this for?" Jackie demanded.

"I guess so they can be certain your doctor correctly diagnosed the stomach ulcer, and the psychiatrist is to see if you really suffer from post-traumatic stress syndrome, as our therapist stated," Attorney Bernard replied.

"Do I have to submit to the endoscope?" Jackie protested.

"I guess you do, because the judge ordered it."

"Does he know what that is? Do you know what that is?" Jackie's voice was trembling. "They run a tube with a camera attached to it down your throat while you're awake! I won't be able to stay awake while they're doing it. I won't be able to stand it. I gag whenever I brush my back teeth."

Attorney Bernard chuckled.

"It's not funny!" Jackie snapped. "You go have it done, then let's see how funny it is."

"Okay, I'll appeal to the judge and try to get it overturned. In the meantime, you will probably need to request time off from work, in case I can't get it stopped."

On Thursday at 7:00 a.m., Jackie arrived at the hospital, accompanied by George, determined to make the best of a bad situation. George tried several times to make her smile with his usual funny remarks, but nothing worked. He pulled her close as he asked, "Are you scared or just really pissed off?"

"I just want to get this thing over with so I can go home," she snapped as they entered the admissions office.

Half an hour later, Jackie changed into a hospital gown, sat on the side of a hospital bed and waited until an orderly took her down to the day surgery room. George leaned over to kiss her, and a tear rolled over her cheek as her bottom lip quivered.

"Let's go," she demanded, turning her face away. "I'm ready to get this over with!" Once inside the room, Jackie trembled as her fear escalated. She watched anxiously as the technician brought in the tube, laid it onto the table beside her bed, and prepared other equipment for the procedure. The nurse instructed her to open her mouth as wide as she could, hold back her head and close her eyes. Totally to her surprise, the nurse sprayed something directly into Jackie's throat that froze on contact and made her instantly unable to breathe. Panic set in as she started gasping for air and trying to swallow. She could see from the surprised expression on the nurse's face that something was wrong.

Unable to speak or breathe, Jackie began clawing at her throat. She fought and struggled until she passed out. When she regained consciousness, she was in a recovery room. The doctor told her that she had come very close to dying. They determined that the numbing spray contained something Jackie was allergic to. Looking up at the doctor, she tried to speak, but no sound came out as she mouthed, "No shit!"

The doctor then explained how they were able to finally get her stabilized enough to complete the endoscope, but her throat would be extremely sore for several days, and she would probably not be able to speak until her throat healed. Jackie thought, *How lucky am I? They saved my life so they could run a hose down my throat!*

The doctor warned her to avoid speaking for at least six to seven days. Jackie signed with her hands for a pen and paper, and then wrote, "Did you find an ulcer?"

The doctor replied, "We found where one had been."

Jackie nodded. There could be no denying it for the defendants now.

## CHAPTER FORTY-SEVEN

George took Jackie home from the hospital late that evening. As he tucked her into bed, he said. "Jackie, I've been thinking about something. Why don't you give this thing up?"

She shook her back and forth frantically, but he continued:

"Just hear me out and don't try to talk. I almost lost you today. For what reason? So they could have proof that *they* caused the ulcer that damaged your stomach."

Again, Jackie shook her head no.

"Is it really worth it?"

She grabbed a pencil and paper from the bedside table and scribbled, "It will be!"

"Why?" George asked.

"JUSTICE!" She wrote.

George shook his head and sighed. "I should've known better then to ask."

She smiled at him and nodded.

"Good night, sweetheart," he said, and then he turned out the light so Jackie could rest.

After this near fatal incident, Jackie's dreams became very detailed and vivid. Often she spent much of the day wondering what her dreams meant. Then she decided to keep track of these dreams in a journal.

Many of the dreams were violent and involved the people she'd worked with at Midway Housing. These dreams continued for weeks, and each one seemed to contain some sort of hidden message. Often she would wake up in the middle of the night startled and drenched in sweat because of what she'd just dreamed. One night as she was deep in sleep, bright lights encircled her. She counted them one, two, three, four, five, six, seven. Seven of the brightest lights she'd ever seen. What was this? Jackie wondered. What could it mean? She thought she was on an airport runway in her dream, because the lights came directly at her so fast that she couldn't get away from them. As they swooped down over her she saw nothing except bright light all around her. She awakened gasping for her breath as she leaped from her bed. This dream really concerned her, and she wondered if she was having some kind of delayed breakdown brought on by the death of her son, or perhaps it was just from the stress of it all.

Jackie didn't have much time to study the dream's meaning, so she tucked away her dream journal for another day and proceeded to prepare for Richard Spaniel's deposition later that day.

Depositions are designed to seek the truth. However, this deposition soon proved that Richard Spaniel wasn't ready for the truth to be discovered. He was extremely nervous, and Attorney Bernard asked the right questions to make him that way. But, like Tom, he too escaped several of those questions by pleading the Fifth. (Naturally, through the advice of his counsel.)

Jackie found it most interesting that Richard had attended the same university as the president of Midway Housing Corporation. Even more surprising was the fact that they'd been roommates in college. But his next response was an even more startling revelation: His prior job was as a police officer in one of the penitentiaries where Tom had served time. Plus, he and Tom hailed from the very same geographic area.

When questions came up about drugs, his personal drug use, and others within the company who used them, Richard either played dumb or conveniently pled the Fifth Amendment. By the end of his deposition, Richard used the Fifth Amendment 134 times. Although this didn't equal Tom's record of 200, it still hindered the plaintiff's search and fact-finding questions.

"Off the record. Attorney Bernard, can we take a forty-five-minute break? I really have to attend to something."

"Attorney Woodcock, if you continue to take forty-five-minute breaks and three-hour lunches, we are not going to finish this deposition until next century. I'd prefer to not take such long breaks, but if you have to take care of something important, then I guess we'll have to."

More than an hour later, they gathered back at the table of truth. The constant delays were a ploy by the defense attorney to distract Attorney Bernard's train of thought, but she still managed to question Richard about prior offenses filed against the company by other women. Richard cleared his throat and squirmed in his chair before he answered.

"Well, there was sorta—a few times. Um, I'm not certain of the times or the people."

"That's fine," Attorney Bernard replied. "Perhaps I can help you remember with this list." She passed Richard a sheet of paper.

Jackie didn't know anything about a list, but she was ready to hear about it. This meant strength for her case.

Watching Richard squirm was priceless, as he had to describe how a previous female employee brought charges against the company, accusing him, and five other male employees of sexual harassment, indecent exposure, sexual assault, and discrimination. Jackie was stunned as she stared at Richard's bright red face. She had no prior knowledge of this incident.

"Mr. Spaniel, please describe exactly what the charges were against you," Attorney Bernard said.

"Well, uh, she said that I, uh, fondled her breasts. She said I touched her inappropriately."

Attorney Bernard: "Did you?"

"No," said Richard. "Well, not exactly."

"Mr. Spaniel. Do you want to be specific or do you prefer I read from the charges for the record?"

"I'll explain. We'd all been out drinking, and things got a little out of hand. Someone pushed her into a pool and she got all wet." Richard stopped there.

"Mr. Spaniel, is that all?" Attorney Bernard nudged.

"Yeah, that's all."

Attorney Bernard then read the charges aloud, direct quotes from the woman's statement: "We were setting up a new location out of town. It was late, and we all went back to the hotel to eat. Everyone started drinking. We went out to the pool, and things got out of hand. Someone put some kind of a date drug in my drink. The next thing I knew I woke up soaking wet and naked in a room full of men with Richard on top of me jacking off with his dick between my breasts while the other men cheered him on."

Attorney Bernard continued, "As I understand this statement, Mr. Spaniel, as she lay unconscious, you were holding onto her breasts, with your penis resting somewhere in between them, and she was providing you with sexual pleasure and gratification as you preformed this act in front of a cheering group of guys. Is that what happened, Mr. Spaniel?"

Richard blushed. "Something like that."

"This is what you referred to previously as 'fondling her breasts?'"

"Yes," he answered.

"The second complaint filed by this young lady involved another manager, Brady Bragg. Seems he masturbated on her inside his truck while they were out of the office on company business appraising a mobile home. She then filed a second charge of indecent exposure." Attorney Bernard paused and set the papers on the table. "Were either of you ever disciplined at a corporate level about this?"

Richard shrugged, "No."

"And why not?" Attorney Bernard asked.

"Because she settled out of court."

"So in other words, you paid her a large sum of money, and she went away.

"Something like that," Richard agreed.

Attorney Woodcock immediately interrupted to ask for a lunch break. After much arguing, they finally agreed on taking a break for lunch. Over lunch, Attorney Bernard brought Jackie up to date on her findings about several charges faced down by the company in prior cases. Attorney Bernard continually glanced at her watch for the time because she was adamant about returning to the office before the defendants. As usual, Jackie and her attorney returned promptly, but the defendants were late again, this time by nearly an hour.

Attorney Bernard continued the same line of questioning for the rest of the day, revealing case after case filed within the Midwest Region managed by Richard Spaniel. A total of sixteen women in addition to Jackie had filed charges, and not one of them worked together or knew one another. Some of the cases were reported about the same male employees at the same location, which showed pattern and proved that the company had refused to resolve the problem of repeated inappropriate behavior.

The situation with Jackie was not an isolated incident as they had claimed. In fact the whole company was infested with indecency—nothing less than a den if iniquity, all the way to the top. The only difference in Jackie's situation compared to the others was the crazy twist of Tom's past and his identity, or lack of identity.

Attorney Bernard asked several questions, which revealed that Richard held the highest position in his division, and the only position higher than his was held by Richard's ex college roommate. Next, she asked about female employees, and Richard admitted that all the women employed in management positions were married to men who also held management positions within the company.

She then asked, "Why then was Jackie holding a management position without being married to anyone within the company?"

"I don't know," Richard answered.

"I do," Attorney Bernard replied. "So that her knowledge and ability and her husband's fingerprints could be used to cover Tom."

"Objection!" Attorney Woodcock bellowed. Attorney Bernard then questioned him about the corporation.

Q: Mr. Spaniel, your company has gone public, right? They are traded on the New York Stock Exchange?
A: Yes
Q: How many of your stockholders know about this case or the other sixteen women who have filed similar complaints against the company?
A: None.
Q: How many manufacturing facilities does your company own Mr. Spaniel?
A: Twenty manufacturing plants located in eight states.
Q: How many company-owned retail facilities?
A: Give or take, just a little over a hundred.
Q: But you have independent retail locations also?
A: Yes.
Q: How many do you think?
A: Give or take a few, I think on last court—I mean count—we had around four hundred retail locations throughout the United States.

At this point, Attorney Woodcock began whispering to Richard, and Attorney Bernard shouted, "Objection! I'm not going to stand for you coaching this witness like you did the last one. I'd like to state for the record that you conferred with the prior witness, Tom Kerakasco, twenty-four times during that deposition, and so far you've done the same thing sixteen times with this witness. That is not acceptable, and if it continues, I'll have to stop the depositions and have a phone conference right here with the magistrate." She glared at him. "I mean it. Do *not* instruct the witness again off the record! If something needs to be said, you say it on the record. That's what we're here for."

Attorney Bernard then returned her attention to Richard. "Now, Mr. Spaniel, I'd like to show you a list containing several names of women who have filed previous claims of discrimination, sexual harassment, indecent exposure, and various other charges against your company, all at different times. Mark this Exhibit No. 4."

Attorney Bernard handed the paper to Mr. Spaniel for him to look over before she continued. "These are seventeen cases involving seventeen different women at various locations within your jurisdiction. How many of these women still work for your company?"

"Richard Spaniel took a deep breath before he looked toward Attorney Bernard and answered, "None."

"Mr. Spaniel, of all the men who caused these charges to be brought forth, how many are still employed within your company?"

"Most all of them" Richard said.

"Were any of them disciplined?"

"Some were, yes."

Jackie slid a note to Attorney Bernard: *Ask him where the metal comes from to make the house frames.* Attorney Bernard raised her eyebrows, but Jackie just smiled at her, indicating to Ms. Bernard that she had a reason for asking such a question.

> Q: Mr. Spaniel, where do you get the material to build the frames for the mobile homes?
> A: Different places.
> Q: Like where?
> A: Mainly wherever we can get a supplier to provide us with it.
> Q: Would you please be more specific and just tell us a place that might provide you with a large amount of iron ore?
> A: Well, we get the majority of it from Colombia.
> Q: Is that Columbia, South Carolina, Mr. Spaniel?
> A: No, it's the country of Colombia. You know, in South America.

Again, Jackie slid a note to Attorney Bernard, and the questioning continued.

> Q: Mr. Spaniel, does Tom ever travel for the company?
> A: Sometimes
> Q: To Colombia?
> A: He has done so.

Again, Jackie slid a note to Ms. Bernard.

Q: Is the owner of the delivery trucking company your neighbor?
A: Yes.
Q: You two must be close?

"Objection! Don't answer that!" Attorney Woodcock interrupted.
"I'm refusing to answer that," Richard said.
Attorney Bernard continued:

Q: This delivery company does deliver all your mobile homes, right?
A: Yes.
Q: Is this the only delivery company that handles your deliveries?
A: Yes, the Midwest Corporation owns it.
Q: Oh, I see. The mobiles are built in your factory with steel frames obtained from Colombia, and then they're sold and delivered literally everywhere in the United States—by your delivery company. Now, who are these mobiles sold to?
A: Usually, they're sold to our four hundred lots all across the USA for individuals to purchase to live in.
Q: Who owns the delivery trucks?
A: We own several of them, and some are leased to us.
Jackie slid a fourth note to Ms. Bernard.
Q: Do you ever ship things inside these homes?
A: We do sometimes ship parts for other houses.

Ms. Bernard leaned over and whispered, "Anything else you want me to ask about that?" Jackie shook her head no. Now having covered that topic, Attorney Bernard changed her questioning back. "Mr. Spaniel, are you aware that a female employee in Oklahoma filed the second lawsuit against Brady Bragg, saying he unbuttoned his shirt and took off his pants in her office, and then told her, 'You know what you need to do if you want to climb the corporate ladder.'"

"I heard something about it," Richard said.

"And did you think it merited discipline, losing his job, or demanding that he attend counseling?"

"No," Richard replied, "because his old lady—his wife—is very religious."

"Because you chose to keep it hidden," Attorney Bernard said. "Mr. Spaniel, do you keep everything hidden under the corporate ladder?"

"Objection!" shouted Attorney Woodcock.

"Seventeen separate women, none of whom worked together or knew each other. Yet they all have similar complaints at different locations. Can you explain that?"

When Richard meekly answered, "No," Attorney Bernard began a new line of questions.

Q: Mr. Spaniel, how well did you know Alvin Waters?
A: He was an employee.
Q: Yes, I know. But do you know how he died?
A: I assumed a heart attack.
Q: Did you inquire?
A: (Clearing his throat) No.
Q: How, then, did you know he had a heart attack?
A: Some body told me.
Q: How long before he died had you last seen him?
A: (Reaching for a glass of water) I don't recall.
Q: Actually, he attended a managers' meeting in your home the night before he died, isn't that right Mr. Spaniel?
A: Thinking back on it, maybe, but I can't really say.
Q: Did you witness him using any drugs before he left your home that night?

Richard's head turned immediately toward his attorney as Woodcock shouted, "Objection! Don't answer that."

Q: Mr. Spaniel, who all attended that meeting the night before Alvin dropped dead from a drug overdose?

A: I—I don't recall (voice trembling).
Q: Mr. Spaniel, when you found out about Tom's past, what exactly did you do?
A: Nothing.
Q: You were told he was under a witness protective program, and you did nothing to investigate the situation?
A: No.
Q: Why not?
A: I trusted him. I believed he told me the truth.
Q: Did you ever notify the licensing board that Mr. Kerakasco had misrepresented his background?
A: No.
Q: Did you notify the State of Texas Licensing that Mr. Kerakasco had a criminal background he lied about on his application?
A: No.
Q: What title do you hold with either of these two organizations?
A: I hold a position on the board of directors for the insurance group, and I'm the Manufactured Housing president for the State of Texas.
Q: What exactly do you do for either of these two positions, Mr. Spaniel?
A: I attend a lot of meetings.
Q: How did you get these two prestigious titles?
A: I was appointed.
Q: By whom?
A: A lot of people.
Q: Obviously, but exactly who sat down and decided Richard Spaniel should have these two positions?
A: It was through closed vote.
Q: And the biggest organization with the most money gets the most votes, and it just so happened that your organization fit that position. So they appointed one of their own to these positions, and it turns out that was you. Correct?
A: Something like that, but our parent company owns the insurance company.

Q: Your organization has a lot of clout in the industry, right?
A: Yes.
Q: You weren't the least bit concerned that Tom might do something to harm the company or to corrupt the entire organization?
A: No, I trusted him.
Q: You trusted him only on his word because you liked him, yet you refused to even hold a conversation with my client and terminated her on the spot when she tried to report wrongdoing to you?

"Objection!" shouted Attorney Woodcock.

The proceedings were silenced as Attorney Bernard spent the next few minutes flipping back and forth through her notes before she stated, "It's now 6:30 p.m. I have no further questions of this witness today. I suggest we conclude questioning for the day. Immediately, Attorney Woodcock stood and escorted Richard out of the room. As they were leaving for the evening, Attorney Bernard, Jackie, and the court reporter all stepped onto the elevator at the same time. Jackie listened as her attorney spoke to the court reporter about how they felt the deposition had gone.

Jackie commented, "These depositions drain me. I'm exhausted from sitting and waiting on them."

"I know," Attorney Bernard agreed. "Today, alone, they took over three hours off between their breaks and the extended lunch, and because of that, I've decided to keep Richard Spaniel under the microscope and make his life miserable for several days just to show them how it feels! I'm going to ask him everything I can think of. I'll start with what kind of cereal did you eat this morning for breakfast, then I'll take a few breaks and have them sit for a while. Then I'll postpone them at the last minute and make them reschedule. I'm tired of this unprofessional inconsiderate attitude. I'll show them!"

Then she turned to Jackie and asked, "Is there anything in particular you'd like to know about Richard, like—boxers or briefs?"

They all laughed, and Jackie replied. "No thank you! I don't even want to imagine that."

Attorney Bernard asked, "How do you think that poor girl felt whenever she regained consciousness and found him on top of her performing a sexual act?"

"Oh my God!" Jackie wailed. "That made me sick! I can't imagine what I would have done."

As the elevator door opened, each of them looked at one another to see who was going to step out first, then Jackie made the comment, "Hey, you're supposed to protect me. You go first." They chuckled, but it was obvious they were all thinking the same thing as they stepped from the elevator into the lobby. Then Attorney Bernard told Jackie, "I'll call you Monday after we've scheduled the next session."

# CHAPTER FORTY-EIGHT

*June 20, 1999*

According to Attorney Woodcock, both Richard and Tom were out of the country on business and unavailable for further deposition. Therefore, Attorney Bernard decided to proceed with another defendant's deposition and return to theirs later. This time she chose Dexter Kuykendahl, and not a day too early, Jackie thought. It would be a pleasure watching Dexter squirm in the hot seat.

When Jackie entered the room accompanied by Attorney Bernard, she looked around to see who was there. Immediately, she and Dexter exchanged glances. He waved with one hand and smiled at her before she took her designated seat located directly across the table from him. Jackie ignored the wave and figured his smile was probably just a nervous reaction. Before they began recording the deposition, Attorney Bernard swore Dexter in and explained exactly what he could expect from his deposition.

Attorney Bernard asked a series of questions about Dexter's age, height, driver's license, to whom he was married, and his length of employment at Midway Housing. Dexter stated he'd worked for his brother's car dealership prior to that, delivering exotic cars.

As she paused in her questioning, the court reporter peeled some numbered sticky labels off a roll and applied them to the text of the material already run through the machine she was typing from. Almost as if on cue, she finished the numbering just before Attorney Bernard picked up the line of questioning again.

Q: Mr. Kuykendahl, have you been married before?
A: Yes ma'am. Um, no I've not. I take that back. No, I haven't.
Q: How long have your worked for Midway Housing?
A: About five years.
Q: How did you become employed with Midway Housing?
A: I was delivering a car to one of the company executives and asked him for a job.
Q: And just like that, he gave you a job?
A: Pretty much, because he already knew my brother-in-law.
Q: What exactly did you do for your brother-in-law?
A: I, uh, I basically just drove exotic cars around or delivered them to buyers or picked them up at the dock whenever they arrived at the Houston or Galveston ports.
Q: Did delivering cars pay that well, Mr. Kuykendahl?
A: At that time in my life, it did.
Q: Did you deliver anything besides cars?
A: Yea, I delivered papers, titles-different stuff that my brother-in-law needed delivered.

Attorney Barnard's questions then focused on his relationship with Jackie.

Q: Mr. Kuykendahl, when did you first meet my client, Jackie Kennard?
A: When she came to my office for an interview.
Q: And were you notified by Richard Spaniel that she was going to be coming in for an interview?
A: Yes ma'am

Q: What did you and Mrs. Kennard discuss during this initial interview?
A: Lots of things. Well, no not really. My wife interrupted us.
Q: Well, allow me to be more detail specific. Mr. Kuykendahl, did you tell my client that she reminded you of someone that you had wet dreams about?
A: Yea, but I meant it as a compliment.
Q: Are you in the habit of complimenting every woman you interview like that?
A: Well no, not unless they remind me of someone I have wet dreams about.
Q: Let's cut to the chase, Mr. Kuykendahl. My client has charged you specifically with more than thirty separate incidents of sexual harassment. I don't believe she took it as a compliment.
Q: Is it true, Mr. Kuykendahl, that your wife accused my client of having an affair with you?
A: Not exactly. Well, she actually referred to us, I mean Jackie and me, as "fuck buddies" because she, I mean my wife, was always jealous of Jackie.
Q: And did you ever discuss this with your wife?
A: (Chuckling) Every freaking day!
Q: What do you mean by that?
A: She, I mean my wife, did not like Jackie or want her having anything to do with me. She was very open about it and made both our lives miserable because of it.
Q: What do you mean miserable? Who are both?
A: Me and Jackie. I mean my wife was not nice to Jackie. Finally I had to make a choice, and it was Hillary who had to go. Since Richard needed a secretary, it seemed like the time to make the switch.
Q: How did you come by making the choice of which one to let go?
A: It wasn't hard. My wife's not going to hear this, is she?
Q: She isn't here, is she?

A: No ma'am, but I want to make sure you don't call her and tell her what I'm saying, or else she'll throw a hissy.
Q: Back to your answer, Mr. Kuykendahl.
A: Oh yea, well, Hillary wasn't able to close her deals and Jackie was steady, closing five to six, sometimes seven to eight deals a month without my help.
Q: Did that make things better?
A: It did for Jackie, but not for me. My wife wouldn't let it die.
Q: Mr. Kuykendahl, did you and my client ever have an affair?
A: Dexter lowered his head and mumbled.
Q: Excuse me, Mr. Kuykendahl, I wasn't able to understand your mumbling. Could you please restate your answer?
A: No, we did not.
Q: Mr. Kuykendahl, were you responsible for the hiring for your location?
A: Yes some of the time.
Q: Who else did hiring?
A: Richard and Tom also did hiring.
Q: Who hired you?
A: Richard.
Q: Who hired Tom?
A: Richard made the final decision on Tom.
Q: Are you aware that more than fifty-five employees have passed through your doors in less than eighteen months?
A: Not really.
Q: Why do you think that number is so high?
A: I don't know. I guess they couldn't take the long hours required by the job.
Q: Did any of these fifty-five previous employees ever complain about abusive language or treatment?
A: A couple of them did.
Q: What did you do about those complaints?
A: I dealt with them when the issues were brought up.
Q: Mr. Kuykendahl, did you ever have any complaints against my client by any of your employees?

A: Yes.

Q: Who would that be?

A: My service manager said Jackie scheduled something with a customer for a vendor without consulting her first.

Q: Isn't the service manager your sister-in-law?

A: Yes.

Q: Were there ever any other complaints against Jackie by any other employees?

A: Yes, my wife.

Q: Oh, I can't wait to hear this. And exactly what was that complaint, Mr. Kuykendahl?

A: My wife, Hillary, complained about Jackie's attire. Really, my wife complained about Jackie a lot!

Q: Were any of these complaints legitimate, Mr. Kuykendahl?

A: I guess they were to Hillary.

Q: Did you reprimand Jackie as the result of any of these complaints?

A: No.

Q: Mr. Kuykendahl, did your wife, Hillary, once threaten to slap my client?

A: Yes.

Q: Did your wife, Hillary, follow through on that threat?

A: No.

Q: Why not?

A: Because Tom and I both grabbed Hillary before she made that mistake.

Q: Mr. Kuykendahl, isn't it true that your wife constantly picked fights with my client on a daily basis?

A: Pretty much.

"Objection!" Attorney Woodcock said. "My client has already testified there was friction between Hillary and Jackie and that he moved Hillary to another location because of it." Ms. Bernard continued the questioning.

Q: Okay, Mr. Kuykendahl, why then did you allow it to happen?"
A: I had to live with Hillary. But after a while, I knew Jackie could handle Hillary on her own.
Q: Are you and Hillary still married?
A: Yes.
Q: Does she still work for the company?
A: No.
Q: Why not?
A: That was a decision made between her and Richard.
Q: Mr. Kuykendahl, did you once during an outburst of anger swing a door open so hard that the knob stuck into the wall next to Mrs. Kennard's head?
A: I was very upset, and I tried to apologize for it.
Q: Yes or no only, Mr. Kuykendahl.
A: Yes.
Q: Did you shout 'Fuck You' to Mrs. Kennard as you walked from the room during that incident?
A: Regrettably, yes, I did.
Q: Mr. Kuykendahl, did you threaten my client that if she didn't do what you told her, that you would quote 'sic your dick on her'?
A: That was only a joke.
Q: Mr. Kuykendahl, may I remind you once again, that my client's reason for being here is because she didn't take any of your snide comments, threats, or sexual remarks as a joke. Now, will you please just answer my question and also state for the record how you referred to your penis?
A: I forgot the question.
Q: Did you, or did you not, threaten my client that if she didn't do what you told her to, that you would 'sic your dick, Kujo,' on her?
A: Probably.
Q: Yes or no, Mr. Kuykendahl?
A: Yes, but I was only joking.

Q: Did you ever remove your trousers in front of Jackie in your office?
A: Well, I was running late to get to the golf course. I had to change, and I told her to close her eyes.
Q: Mr. Kuykendahl, did you once pull a live snake from your pants in front of Jackie?
A: (Sighing a deep breath) Yes.
Q: Mr. Kuykendahl, did you and Tom both laugh hysterically about how badly this scared Jackie?
A: We laughed. I wouldn't say at Jackie, but yes we laughed.
Q: Well then, Mr. Kuykendahl, was your laughter intended instead for the snake?
A: No ma'am.

Attorney Bernard stated, "Off the record. Let's take a fifteen- minute break." During the break, she confided to Jackie her disbelief at how Dexter was cooperating with his answers. "Could this really be happening? He's admitting to everything, and I can't figure out why."

Jackie chuckled. "I told you why. He's their front person. He'll do anything they tell him. That's why he's in management."

"But this is insane," Attorney Bernard said. "I can't help but wonder what their strategy is. Maybe they're just hanging him out to dry, and he's too stupid to know it? I'd at least expect him to deny something."

Jackie shrugged. "Maybe they plan to declare Dexter insane at the time of the incidents. Or else they promised him some huge payoff to take the fall."

"Oh my God!" Attorney Bernard hissed. "That sounds exactly like something these slimeballs would do. What they're up to, I'm sure we'll find out sooner or later."

Jackie said, "Ms. Bernard, there is one thing that he lied about that I am certain of. He said he hadn't been married before, but I've talked with his ex wife Cheryl on the phone, myself, and they even had a son together."

"Are you sure? He just swore he'd never been married before."

"I'm positive," Jackie told her.

"Is there any way you can prove it?"

"Probably" Jackie replied. "I can go to the courthouse and look that up. It should be a matter of public record."

"Why don't you do that and bring it to my office?" Attorney Bernard said. "I can't believe he'd actually lie about something so obvious." As they continued to discuss other things, they lost track of time until someone knocked on the door and stated, "Break's over." Jackie and Attorney Bernard then returned to the table of truth in the conference room.

For the remainder of the day, Attorney Bernard asked Dexter more than three hundred questions about different situations and charges Jackie had brought against him in her lawsuit. He barely denied any of them and even showed remorse a couple of times. After Attorney Bernard deliberated on what to try next, she decided to change her line of questioning away from Dexter and focus more on Tom's behavior. Dexter was quick to note that he had previously disciplined Tom on several occasions about crude sexual comments and discriminating behavior toward certain employees.

*Could this actually be happening?* Attorney Bernard wondered? First Tom and then Dexter were confirming the accusations Jackie brought against them. It had to be the easiest deposition she could recall in her twelve years of practicing law. But what was Attorney Woodcock up to? He never objected, he never interrupted, he never coached Dexter as he'd coached Tom and Richard Spaniel. He just sat there filing his nails watching as the whole thing unfolded before his eyes. Attorney Bernard had no idea what to make of it, but she decided to take advantage of Dexter's confessions and get everything she could on record.

Since the defendant was being so cooperative, the deposition finished much more quickly than Attorney Bernard had anticipated. However, before she wrapped things up with Dexter she said, "Mr. Kuykendahl, we've discussed many things here today and I would like to say thank you for being so cooperative."

Dexter smiled and tilted his head in acknowledgement.

"However, there is one thing that I would like to ask your opinion on." She kept him waiting for almost a full minute before she asked, "Mr. Kuykendahl, do you believe my client is a creditable person?"

"Oh, yes ma'am, I do."

Just them Attorney Woodcock reached over, took hold of Dexter's sleeve, and pulled him closer for a private attorney-client discussion.

Attorney Bernard called out, "Attorney Woodcock, we've discussed before your coaching the witness. Need I remind you, the judge has ruled it is not permissible? Therefore, I am again stating for the record that I ask you not continue to do that." She turned to Dexter, "Mr. Kuykendahl, is there anything you'd like to add after your private discussion with your attorney?"

"Yes ma'am. I'd like to change my last answer. When I stated I thought Ms. Kennard was credible, I meant that was only when we worked together. Not now." Dexter just shook his head no.

Attorney Bernard asked, "So now your testimony is that you thought she was credible when you worked together, but you no longer think she's credible. Is that what you're saying?"

"Yes ma'am." Dexter nodded vigorously.

"Well, Mr. Kuykendahl, please allow me then to ask you another question. Do you think Tom Kerakasco is credible?"

A: Yes ma'am.
Q: Even after you witnessed him in his deposition confessing to have lied time and time again, about things as minor as his birthday to things as important as his job application and state licenses?
A: Yes ma'am.
Q: Mr. Kuykendahl, just one last question. Who got Mrs. Kennard's customer files when she was terminated from the Midway Park location?
A: Reese Burton
Q: And will you clarify for the record who Reese Burton is?
A: He's the son of Emma Woods, the personnel HR Trainer.
Q: Thank you, Mr. Kuykendahl.

Attorney Bernard pushed back her chair. "I have no further questions of this witness today. However, I reserve my right to have the availability to recall this witness for additional questioning at a later time."

Immediately Attorney Woodcock spoke, "Attorney Bernard, I'd like to address an issue with you off the record. We previously asked that you produce some original tapes to us that the plaintiff had recorded of the defendant, Tom. Do you have those to give to us yet?"

"Don't you recall that my office was broken into and those tapes were taken during the break-in?" she replied.

"No, I don't recall that at all," Attorney Woodcock replied. "Do you have a copy of the tapes perhaps?"

"No I don't," Attorney Bernard said.

"Then I'll have to go to the judge about this! I'm letting you know now that I'm going to ask that the case be dropped and sanctions be brought against your client for tampering with evidence."

"Tampering with evidence?" Attorney Bernard asked. "What are you talking about?"

"You know damn well what I'm talking about," he replied. "You both faked those tapes being stolen just so you wouldn't have to turn them over to us for examination!"

That was the last straw. Attorney Bernard stood and shouted across the table, "You go straight to the judge! I reported the break-in on a police report. How dare you deny you weren't told about it when it happened? There's nothing my client or I can do about the tapes being stolen. This is again just a ploy on behalf of your defendants to stall the case and buy some time."

"No, actually I think it's your way of destroying evidence with a phony story," Attorney Woodcock drawled.

"Are you accusing me of evidence tampering?" Attorney Bernard asked.

Attorney Woodcock shrugged. "I'm just stating how things look to me and the defendants in this case. Why else wouldn't you turn over those tapes?"

"BECAUSE THEY WERE STOLEN!" Attorney Bernard yelled back at him.

"Well, regardless, I'm going to the judge on this and asking him to have the case thrown out," Attorney Woodcock replied.

"FINE!" she shouted. "Do whatever makes you feel good. And with that, Attorney Bernard, Jackie, and the court reporter left. As they walked down the hallway together, Attorney Bernard commented, "I knew that was too easy. He had this planned all along and let me go through the entire day, all the time knowing he planned on asking the Judge to rule a mistrial on grounds of evidence tampering! Damn! That really pisses me off!"

"You?" Jackie replied. "How do you think I feel? All my witnesses have either been promoted to management positions or bought off, and my only other real evidence is missing!"

As they paused outside the elevator, Jackie asked, "What can we do now?

Attorney Bernard sighed. "I'll have to call the judge, explain what happened, and ask him for a ruling. I'm sure it won't affect you as much as it's gonna affect me."

"I still think you should have put in the police report that we felt they were suspect or at least had motive to take those tapes."

Attorney Bernard shook her head no. She wouldn't even discuss it.

# CHAPTER FORTY-NINE

Attorney Bernard was up against a wall. She fully expected to be reprimanded by the court for the loss of those tapes, but before she took the verbal beating she expected from the judge, she asked everyone in her law firm to look once again for those tapes, hoping they were just misplaced somewhere within the office. Attorney Bernard then decided to make a phone call to Linda, one of the legal assistants who'd recently left their employment and moved away. Linda told Attorney Bernard she remembered taking the tapes home around the time the break-in occurred to do the dictation from tape to print. Linda thought the tapes were in the box of things she returned to the office before she moved. She said, "I really don't think I have them, but I'll look through the boxes I haven't unpacked yet."

Within an hour Linda called back with the news that she'd found the tapes, explaining that apparently the movers had packed them in the wrong box.

"Great!" Attorney Bernard shouted. "Fed Ex them to me right away! I'll call the defendants' legal team and let them know." Next, Attorney Bernard mapped out her strategy for filing a motion with the court to have both Richard and Tom complete their depositions and answer the three hundred plus questions on which they'd pled the Fifth Amendment. In her motion, she cited a ruling that stated the witness protection program did not allow a defendant to shield personal information in the context of a civil litigation. She added that Kerakasco's credibility was directly at issue, and evidence concerning his background, including prior criminal history, was extremely important to this litigation. She also mentioned a federal rule that stated, among other things, "evidence that any witness had been convicted of a crime shall be admitted if it involved dishonesty or false statement, regardless of punishment."

Moreover, Tom's pleading the Fifth Amendment more than three hundred times in his deposition directly blocked the plaintiff's efforts to carry forth the court's ruling to litigate the case prior to having a court hearing. "Therefore," Attorney Bernard continued, "the fact remains, being placed within the witness protection program does not shield the defendant from future charges. Therefore we ask that the court rule to allow the plaintiff to continue background search for evidence on Tom Kerakasco's prior charges in order to determine if there has been a pattern set with any prior cases involving the defendant."

With that out of the way, Attorney Bernard made the phone call to the defense lawyer, hoping to win a compromise by offering the tapes in return for Tom's agreement to answer questions about his past, plus Richard's agreement to finish the questions still outstanding on his deposition.

But the answer was negative. Attorney Woodcock told her he still planned to ask the judge to stop the case, and he would file charges against both Jackie and Attorney Bernard for evidence tampering. That telephone call resulted in the biggest explosion ever recorded between two law offices. The attorneys shouted back and forth for almost an hour. This created quite a disturbance among Attorney Bernard's associates. Each one popped in and out of her office to see what all the yelling was about. Finally realizing there could be no compromise with Woodcock, she slammed down the phone. After this incident, there was no longer even a semblance of professional courtesy between the two law firms. Whether the misplacement of the tapes was intentional or merely a mistake, the defense saw a weakness and they were going to take full advantage of it.

It was now August 1999, and once again the process was on hold until the new judge magistrate ruled on the issue of evidence tampering. Although the defendants were obviously grasping at straws to have this case thrown out, there was nothing Jackie's legal team could do except just wait it out. But Jackie wasn't comfortable waiting anything out. As she turned on the television one evening, the six o'clock news was just coming on, and the lead story captured her attention.

President Clinton is visiting Bogotá, Colombia, to emphasize US support for Colombian President Andres Pastrana. Clinton symbolically hands over a check for 1.3 billion for anti-drug aid. Jackie turned to George and asked, "Are you hearing this? He's the first US President to set foot on that soil and he personally delivers 1.3 billion for the drug cause. Do you believe that?" George watched from over top his newspaper.

Jackie shook her head and got up to leave the room, saying, "What exactly is his cause? Am I the only one confused here, or does it look's like he's purchasing drugs?"

Jackie snapped off the television. "I can't watch any more. Clinton makes me sick. I'm going to the library to do some research."

"Do you want me to come with you?" George asked.

"Not unless you want to be bored to death," Jackie replied. She was again on a mission for information that could help her case. It seemed that somewhere along the line the tables had turned, even though she'd proved Tom a lair and Dexter confirmed her accusations. She strongly felt something was lacking.

A few days later she received a phone call from Attorney Bernard. "Jackie, we received a reply from the Justice Department in Arlington, Virginia, today. The judge magistrate ruled they have to forward Tom's file to Dallas for him, and only him, to see."

"What does that mean?" Jackie asked.

"It means that the magistrate and the federal marshal responsible for Tom are the only ones who can look through Tom's FBI file. Apparently this stuff is so secret that another federal judge had to sign off on it, and he ruled that the file inspection could be done only under camera-tape surveillance."

"Why is that?" Jackie asked, winding the phone cord around her fingers.

"It's to make certain none of the information is removed, re-written, or passed to anyone else. Or that his true identity is not released. Apparently this guy was a pretty big operator somewhere else," Attorney Bernard replied.

"NOW DO YOU BELIEVE ME?" Jackie asked.

"Yes, I do believe you. I just don't know how the judge is going to rule after this. We'll have to let this thing play itself out."

"Do we get to know anything about what's contained in that file?" Jackie asked.

"I doubt it," Attorney Bernard answered.

"Then how does it help us?"

Attorney Bernard sighed. "I don't know yet. In twelve years of practicing law, I've never dealt with anything like this before."

It took the judge several days to look over the FBI file and brief himself on the entire prior case history of Tom Kerakasco. After researching it, the judge ruled on behalf of the plaintiff's request, allowing them additional time to research his background and further depose Tom Kerakasco regarding his prior federal charges. However, the judge had no choice but to set a ruling on behalf of the defendants' request regarding evidence tampering. He couldn't ignore their accusations, so he ruled to hold an evidentiary hearing on that matter to take place within sixty days. In the meantime, the tapes would be turned over to the defendants.

"Oh well," Attorney Bernard told Jackie, "You win some, you lose some. Either way, we need to get prepared for that evidentiary hearing."

Shortly thereafter, Attorney Bernard received a phone call from the defendants' legal team, this time from a new attorney who introduced himself as Red Freedman. "But please, call me Red," he told her. "I just wanted to call and offer a solution to make the judge's ruling a little simpler on all of us. If you agree, we'd like to avoid deposing Tom again. To save additional costs to you and your client, why not just have Tom sign an affidavit stating his criminal background? In return we'll share with you our audio report, once completed, on the tapes. Would that be acceptable?"

"It sure would!" She agreed. "Now, when can I expect that?"

"Oh, I figure I can probably get Tom's reply to you within the week. Well actually, I forgot he's out of the country right now—he and his family are attending some personal family business in South America. I'll get back with you on that." He paused and cleared his throat. "Now the audio portion will take a little longer. We're having them analyzed professionally."

"Okay," Attorney Bernard said. "Hey, Red, I really appreciate this."

"No problem," he replied. "By the way, Ms. Bernard, just between you and me, what do you think really happened to those tapes of Jackie's?"

"As I've already told everyone, my legal assistant mistakenly packed them in the wrong box, and when she moved back to Wisconsin the tapes went with her."

Red interrupted, "I was only asking your opinion. I wasn't aware the tapes were in your custody when they were misplaced. I thought they were always in the plaintiff's possession." After a short pause, he added, "Ms. Bernard, another reason I called you is because we need to schedule an appointment for Jackie to see a psychologist of our choice."

Attorney Bernard reminded Red of the guidelines set forth by the judge. "Don't forget, this psychologist has a time limit of three hours, and the line of questioning can't stray into her personal sex life, either past or present. He's examining her only to determine the severity of her post-traumatic stress syndrome."

"I'm aware of all that," Red answered.

After hanging up with Red, Attorney Bernard immediately phoned Jackie so she could make arrangements to take off work again for another meeting.

As Jackie discussed this with George, he made the decision that she would not see the doctor by herself, and he arranged to take time off from work and go with her. If nothing else, he could wait in the lobby and provide moral support. George didn't trust anyone around Jackie and wanted to make sure the appointment wasn't some stupid trick to have Tom show up and try something.

When Friday arrived and George was driving Jackie to her appointment, they got caught up in heavy traffic created by an accident. Jackie used her mobile phone to call Dr. Henry's office to let him know she was running late due to an accident on the highway. However, George was able to maneuver around the accident, and they arrived to the appointment only a few minutes late.

Once there, Jackie checked in with the office receptionist, like any typical doctor's office. They didn't ask her to fill out paperwork or answer any questions—they immediately opened the door and told her to come in. As George stepped through behind her, the doctor stepped between them and placed his hand against George's chest.

"You need to step back and wait in the lobby," he demanded.

George looked down at the doctor's hand resting against his chest then back into his face. He didn't like anyone laying hands on him, no matter who they were.

Immediately the doctor removed his hand and said, "We'll be taking a break periodically. In the meantime, there's a snack machine downstairs should you want something to eat."

George didn't acknowledge the doctor's words, but gently touched him on his chest with the back of his hand as he moved him from between himself and Jackie. He reached for Jackie, rested his hands on her shoulders, and said, "Honey, if you need me I'll be waiting in the lobby. You just call my name, and I'll come through the wall if I have to."

Jackie nodded her head yes as she turned and walked with the doctor down the hallway into his office. As they walked away, the man looked back over his shoulder time and time again at George, who stood in the doorway, waiting to see which office he took her into.

Jackie felt uncomfortable in the presence of a doctor she knew nothing about. For all she knew this guy was some schmuck hired by the defendants' legal team for who-knows-what. He didn't look like a doctor to George either because he wore baggy corduroy pants with the cuffs ragged from dragging on the ground.

However, Jackie thought it best to make the meeting as pleasant as possible, so she smiled and answered the first few questions. They sat facing one another with a small table to the side of them with a box of Kleenex on it. Then Doctor Henry told Jackie that since she'd arrived late he was going to tack thirty minutes onto the end of their meeting.

"I wasn't thirty minutes late," she responded. "I was barely five minutes late. Besides, I called you and explained that we were stuck in traffic."

"I realize that," he answered, "but we haven't yet started, and I'm just letting you know I have to make up the lost time somewhere"

"In that case," Jackie told him. "I'd like to call my attorney before we start, just so there isn't any misunderstanding about what time I actually arrived and what time you actually started. It's not quite 9:10. So may I please use your telephone?"

"Sure." He stood. "Would you like me to leave the room?"

"Yes, I would," Jackie replied as she dialed the office number for her attorney. Ms. Bernard was out, but Jackie waited patiently while the receptionist located one of her associates. When Mike came on the line, she said, "I just wanted to let someone from our side know that I was five minutes late getting here for my evaluation due to a traffic snarl. Now that I'm here, the doctor he tells me he's tacking thirty minutes onto the session because I was five minutes late. Sure, I'll get him right now."

Jackie laid down the phone receiver and stepped to the door to retrieve Dr. Henry. He talked with the attorney before he hung up and proceeded with his evaluation.

Uncertain exactly what was exchanged between those two, Jackie felt better just knowing she'd reported the problem to someone on her legal team.

Dr. Henry explained that like Attorney Woodcock, he was a graduate of SMU. However, he held a degree in sociology. Then Dr. Henry told her he frequently evaluated people for court appearances and in many cases had been able to stop the proceedings before the trial because he determined whether or not a person was telling the truth by his ability to read their thoughts. Dr. Henry continued outlining his accomplishments to Jackie, adding that he was considered brilliant among his peers because several high-profile cases had been won as a result of his evaluations.

Jackie decided right then and there that she would answer his questions using as few words as possible.

Finally, after several more minutes, Dr. Henry finished bragging about himself and turned his attention to Jackie and the reason they were there. He started off by asking, "Do you mind if I take notes?"

"No," she replied. "I certainly plan to take notes, myself."

Dr. Henry made a note of that remark, and then continued. "Jackie, how many sexual partners have you had?"

Jackie shook her head. She couldn't believe it—right off the bat he was asking questions the judge had ruled inadmissible. With that question, Jackie had to defend herself and let him know she understood what the parameters were for their meeting. She looked him directly in the eye and said, "Dr. Henry, I prefer that you address me as Mrs. Kennard, not Jackie. And I'm not going to answer your question because I'm sure you're aware the judge ruled you cannot ask questions about my personal life, my sexual partners, or my sexual preferences. So I'm simply going to say—None of your business!" She smiled and looked down her nose at him. That comment really set the Doc's pen in motion. He scribbled faster that Jackie could talk.

Then the doctor asked a bizarre question. "Mrs. Kennard, did you ever threaten one of the defendants with a gun?"

Jackie thought for a moment before she answered. "I wouldn't exactly say I threatened him, but I told Tom Kerakasco if he followed through with his threat against my family, especially my children, that I would kill him. And you can let him know, I still mean that, Dr. Henry."

"And why would he threaten you or your family?"

"Do I really need to answer that? In my prior testimony, I explained I'd uncovered the fact that he's in the witness protection program. He threatened my life if I involved him in my lawsuit or disclosed his dirty secrets—like the murder he committed back in Pennsylvania."

"Has he done any harm to you or your family, Mrs. Kennard?"

"Dr. Henry, I live in fear every day that he's going to strike."

"That's not what I asked you, Mrs. Kennard."

Jackie replied, "No, he hasn't, yet."

"Mrs. Kennard, did you and Tom once get into an argument in the office of Midway Housing and you screamed at him to shut up as you slapped him and dragged him outside?"

"Not exactly, sir. I yelled at him and threatened to slap him if he didn't shut up. I did lead him outside away from the office business because he was out of control, screaming obscenities about a child drowning."

"Mrs. Kennard, didn't you frequently have emotional outbursts during which you would leave the office and stay gone for extended periods of time?"

"I left the office on a few occasions, when I was humiliated or very emotional because of something that had happened to me. For example, the time I was assaulted."

Dr. Henry cut her off. "That's not what I asked you, Mrs. Kennard. I just want to confirm that you did have emotional outbursts in which you would leave the office."

"Not without reason," she replied.

"Mrs. Kennard, did you ever take a trip with Mr. Kerakasco?"

"I was on a plane going to a company function, traveling along with Tom, but not alone with Tom. I was not accompanying him on the trip."

"Mrs. Kennard, did you once go to Tom about a personal problem you were having with your ex husband and ask him if he knew someone who could remedy your problem?"

"No!" Jackie snapped. "He walked into my office during a private conversation and told me if I needed him to, he could have the bastard bludgeoned to death on his front porch with a hammer like that, as he snapped his fingers."

From the doctor's questions, Jackie could tell the interview was about as one-sided as it could get, and the questions had nothing to do with Jackie's stress. She realized they were questions devised by Attorney Woodcock, not by the doctor. After almost two hours of intense questioning, Dr. Henry said, "Mrs. Kennard, why don't we take a break and go to the restroom and get a drink, and be back here in fifteen minutes?"

Jackie shook her head yes as she leaned over to pick up her purse sitting on the floor beside the chair. As she bent over, she noticed an electric cord leading into the back of the table, probably indicating a recording device hidden inside the drawer. No wonder the doctor kept looking at his watch—he probably needed to flip the tape. Jackie wondered whether she should call his hand or just wait it out. After thinking about it, she decided against calling her attorney's office.

Jackie made her way to the main lobby where George sat patiently waiting. As she opened the door, George sprang to his feet. "Are we through?"

"I'm afraid not," she replied. "The doctor just needed a break."

Before the door closed behind her, the doctor appeared in the doorway and said, "Oh, by the way, Mrs. Kennard, everything we talk about is confidential."

George looked at him and replied, "Bite me, you bought-off think doctor!"

After the break, Jackie returned to the office and resumed her position in the hot seat as she waited to hear the next line of questioning. Much like the first round, Dr. Henry's questions favored Tom and Dexter.

"Mrs. Kennard, did you once have an argument with Mr. Kuykendahl's wife in which you told her you didn't fight fair and would run her down with a car if you had to?"

"Dr. Henry, I had many arguments with Hillary Kuykendahl. Which time are you referring to? Was it the time she accused me of "fucking" her husband or the time she felt compelled to strike fear and threaten me with her corporate connections?" Jackie paused. "Or perhaps you're referring to the day Dexter's son wrecked her car. She was late to work and so pissed off when she finally arrived that she tried to pick a physical fight with me. She threatened to slap me and even drew back her hand. That's when I warned her that I didn't fight fair and I would run her down with the car if she followed through with her threat."

Dr. Henry was now writing as fast as he could. Jackie couldn't help herself; this was so far out she had to made a snide comment. "Dr. Henry would you like for me to repeat that, or would you like for me to speak slower so you can get it all down?"

Dr. Henry looked over his glasses at Jackie, but he just kept on writing. Jackie could feel her patience and her temper wearing thinner by the moment. She could no longer take this mental beating and asked for a break.

"We just took a break," Dr. Henry replied.

"I need to go to the restroom," Jackie stated, and stood up to leave the room. Without another break, she'd never make it through without losing her patience. Again, Dr. Henry was writing everything down as she left the room. Jackie was outside the office and down the hallway when she realized she'd forgotten her purse. She returned to the office to get it, and as she walked up to the door she heard Dr Henry talking.

What she heard was shocking. She stood quietly, listening to the doctor as he discussed with Attorney Woodcock over the phone how the session was going. "Is there anything else you can think of that I need to ask her?" he asked. "Okay. Yeah I think I pretty much covered that. I can make it look like what you need it to. I mean she certainly appears to be capable of that. She's a very strong-willed person, and with the right amount of pressure she'll explode. For example, just now she had to stop the session and take a break because she was about to blow a gasket when I pursued questions about Hillary."

When Jackie heard that, it took everything she had to control herself. She had heard enough. When she returned to the room for the second time, Dr. Henry was sitting in the chair reading over his notes, obviously trying to appear as though he'd been sitting there all along. Jackie sat down without a saying anything and patiently awaited the next question. Dr. Henry appeared preoccupied, probably reviewing the additional questions he'd just received from Attorney Woodcock.

"Jackie, I know this meeting has not been easy on you, but I'd like to hear in your own words exactly how you feel about this."

"You'll need to be more specific," she replied.

"I want you to tell me exactly what you're thinking right now," he replied. "What do you think about this whole situation—the entire legal process, start to finish?"

"Well, Dr. Henry. This situation has completely devoured my life for over four years. There is not a day or an hour in the day that is not consumed by this situation. I have spent every day off, every vacation day, every sick day, and borrowed some I hadn't earned yet to resolve this situation. I've been cooperative, which is more than I can say for the defendants. I can tell you I've answered every question known to mankind with the exception of one, and frankly nobody cares which way I wipe my ass. So if there's anything you want to know specifically, you'll need to ask me outright because I don't follow where you're trying to lead. Is that what you or your client wants me to say?"

With that Dr. Henry replied, "Fair enough. I think we'll just take that as your answer."

Dr Henry seemed proud of himself when he stated with a chuckle in his voice, "Jackie, this pretty much concludes our session. I want to thank you for your cooperation. Is there is anything you'd like to ask me?"

That was an open door Jackie couldn't resist. She glanced out the window for a moment to regain her composure before she looked back at the doctor. "This is just between you and me, right? This isn't something you're asking for the record is it?"

"Oh no," he replied. "Strictly between us, of course."

"Can you read my thoughts right now?" she asked.

"Not exactly," he replied, "but why don't you tell me what it is you're curious about?"

"Well" she softly remarked. I was wondering why someone would go to school for twelve long years, struggle to become a doctor, and then live off the crumbs of his upper classman?" She waited for him to answer. There was no answer from the doctor, only silence as she continued her verbal war. "How challenging can it be for you as a doctor to evaluate each patient based on the defendants' specific needs?"

Dr. Henry's face reflected shock. Jackie couldn't stop herself. She just continued telling him exactly how she saw it. "I thought about it during your entire process, and finally I get it. Attorney Woodcock can't break down a witness, so you offer your professional opinion and sign some bogus statement that benefits whatever determination he needs. Of course, there is a pretty hefty price involved in all this for the right evaluation. Then, with your professional opinion and the swoop of your Bic, I'm made to look like an idiot or mental misfit, whichever your attorney friend needs. I'm curious, Dr Henry. What did this cost him?"

Doctor Henry sat stone-faced, refusing to acknowledge or answer her question. He just focused on the notepad in his lap. Jackie pleaded with him, "Please Dr. Henry, tell me. I'm curious to know just how desperate they are to make this go away by paying off a doctor for his professional opinion."

Still Dr Henry refused to answer, but Jackie could tell by his body language that she was making him very nervous. "It's sad to think someone who went to school for so long has to rely on handouts and falsified information to make a living."

She leaned toward the table and pulled open the drawer to reveal the tape recorder placed there, still recording their conversation without her consent. "Did you get that on tape too, Mr. Think Doctor? Nice try, but this is going with me." She flipped the tape from the recorder and took it with her as she hurried down the hallway and into the lobby. She dropped the tape into the pocket of George's shirt.

Flushed and angry, Dr. Henry pursued her and demanded she return the tape. Jackie smiled and replied, "I don't have your tape."

Just then George stood up, dwarfing the doctor with his six-foot-six-inch frame. George stood with arms crossed, waiting for the doctor to retrieve the tape from his pocket. Jackie said, "This concludes our meeting, and we're leaving now. You've already taken too much of our time."

Knowing he was defeated, the doctor retreated into the receptionist's office and slammed the door behind him.

# CHAPTER FIFTY

Jackie could hardly wait to call her attorney and report what Dr. Henry had done. She expected at least get a positive response from Attorney Bernard. However, Attorney Bernard screamed, "You did what? You took the tape from his recorder and refused to give it back? What were you thinking?"

"I was defending myself," Jackie replied. "He didn't have permission to record our conversation, at least not by me, and if he wasn't trying to hide something he would have put the recorder in plain sight instead of hiding it inside the drawer."

Ms. Bernard sighed. "Okay, Jackie, bring the tape to my office and I'll decide where it goes from there."

"You know what?" Jackie said. "Just once, I'd like to hear something positive from you. I'm starting to wonder about your integrity."

"What do you mean?"

"Just that," Jackie replied. "I'm not bringing the tape in now. I'll bring it later when I'm in the area. And while we're on the subject, what have you found out about my tapes or Tom's background?"

"We did a search and weren't able to come up with anything," she replied.

"A search on what?" Jackie asked?

"I'm talking about his background search," Attorney Bernard replied.

"Did you use his new name or his true name?" Jackie asked.

"I think they used his new name."

Jackie could not believe what she was hearing. "Why do you think they gave him a new name? So no one can find anything under his real name!" She was practically sputtering. "Never mind. I'll do it myself."

"Jackie, don't get yourself into any trouble. Before you do anything, you need to run it past me first."

"I don't have that much time," Jackie said. "I'm tired of waiting for someone from your office to do something. I need to know as much as I can about Tom's background before we go to trial! What about the tapes? Have you heard anything about that?"

Attorney Bernard replied, "I just told you, nothing yet, but I'll let you know."

Jackie was obviously upset by the lack of concern shown by her attorney. But more than anything, she was exhausted. As she and George left the parking garage, he suggested they have lunch together and take in a movie to relax.

"That sounds great," Jackie said, "and I'm hungry."

"I've got the perfect place," George said, grinning at her, "but it's a surprise. I want you to close your eyes until we get there."

She shook her head, and he added, "Well, at least lie back in your seat and rest."

Jackie agreed, thinking it was a good idea because she was exhausted from the mental beating she'd taken from the doctor. She'd just dropped off to sleep when she jumped and sat straight up, disoriented and gasping with a look of shock on her face.

George swerved the car and shouted, "Honey, what's wrong?"

Jackie was gasping for breath and couldn't answer. She pounded herself on the chest. "That dream again!" she gasped. "The one where bright lights surround me. They were swooping all around me so fast, and the lights came so close and were so bright that I got disoriented and I couldn't tell where I was." She raised her seat and cracked the window, gulping the fresh air. "But it wasn't like a dream. It felt as though I were somewhere else."

George took her hand and linked his fingers through hers. "I swear, you never left the car."

"I don't understand," she said. "It's the same dream I had before, and those lights surrounded me, covering me in the brightest light I have ever seen." She shook out her hair. "Maybe I'm just too stressed. I've need to take a break somewhere away from all this insanity."

"We're about to," George replied as he pulled into the parking lot of the very restaurant where he gave her the engagement ring.

"Oh, honey, this is great, we haven't been here—"

"In a long time," George added. "So, lets promise each other not to talk about this situation any more today."

Inside they were seated at exactly the same table they'd occupied before. Soon they lost track of the world around them as they spent nearly three hours eating, talking, and laughing, remembering various things that had happened over the years.

"I'd do it all over again," George told Jackie.

"So would I," she replied as she leaned toward George for a kiss.

"Do you still want to go to a movie," he asked?

"Yes, but first I noticed a little antique shop down the street that I'd like to browse through first."

As they entered the store and began looking around, George and Jackie ended up going separate directions. Neither was looking for anything specific, but different things captured their attention. After several minutes, Jackie made her way toward the back of the store, where she turned and glanced down the last aisle. Immediately she froze in her tracks and the hair stood up on her arms.

"George, come here!" She broke into a dead run down the aisle and snatched up a painting that sat on the floor, leaning against an old bucket. She held it up over her head as she turned full circle examining the painting.

"What is it?" George asked, coming up behind her.

"It's my dream!" she shouted. "This is the dream I had on the way here, the one I've been having over and over." She turned the painting toward George for him to examine. That's when she noticed the name Seven Sisters written on a label on the backside of the picture. The picture was actually of seven angels swooping down from heaven, forming a circle. Each of the angels carried at least one bright light.

"I have to have this painting," Jackie said. "I have to have it!" Her voice cracked and tears fan down her face.

This was like no behavior George had ever seen from Jackie before. He didn't question it; he knew she was serious about this. "Honey, you go to the car and wait for me. I'll pay for the picture."

"No," she said, "I can't let it out of my sight. The cashier will just have to see me crying." He offered a handkerchief, and she blotted her eyes. "I don't know why this has affected me, but I know I'm supposed to have this picture."

"It's okay," George said. "We're going to take it home with us."

As big tears dropped from her eyes, Jackie looked at George and asked, "You think I'm crazy, don't you?"

He put his arms around her. "I think you're really stressed and need some rest."

After they paid for the picture and left the store, George didn't even ask about a movie. He just drove Jackie and the picture straight home. There was hardly a word exchanged between them. George was deeply concerned and worried that the latest interrogation with the think doctor had been too much for Jackie to handle. After they got home, he suggested she take something so she could rest.

Jackie was still crying as she held the picture close to her while carrying it into her bedroom. She sat down on the side of the bed looking at the picture. She opened a drawer of the dresser sitting next to the bed, using it for a stand for the picture. George asked, "Honey, would you like me to hang that for you?"

"No!" she snapped. "It's fine right where it is."

"Okay," he replied. And that's where it stayed, no further than arm's reach away from Jackie as she slept and the first thing she saw every day when she awoke. George just accepted that the picture was somehow a comfort to Jackie and left it alone.

That night when Jackie slept, she had a new dream. This one made no sense to her at all. She felt as if she were walking inside a maze, but not an ordinary maze. This maze seemed to have no end, only back-and-forth pathways. It seemed to go on forever before she finally came to the end, which seemed more like a center than an end. Once inside, she found a message lying on the floor for her to read. Jackie bent over to pick it up, but she couldn't because the message was etched onto the floor. She didn't recall reading words from the etching, rather feeling the words in an unspoken language as if she were receiving instructions of some sort. She stood there for a moment focusing on the message, and then turned and retraced the back-and-forth pathways to return from within the maze. When she was outside the maze in her dream, she awoke to recall a very spiritual feeling around her. She wasn't frightened, but very curious what it was that she had just experienced. Not wanting to forget the dream, Jackie recorded it immediately in her dream journal for researching later, and then went back to bed hoping to get some restful sleep before she had to get up for work in a few hours.

However, as soon as she went back to sleep she started dreaming again. In the second dream, she was being held inside a cage with three white tigers sitting around her. She felt like a prisoner fearing that if she tried to escape the tigers would surely devour her. She could feel herself sitting flat on her bottom with her knees drawn against her and her face buried between her knees. In the dream she squinted her eyes open to look around, searching for a way to escape. Then she noticed standing outside the cage were all the defendants. They were laughing, making fun and pointing at her inside the cage. Jackie couldn't understand why until she looked down to discover she had no clothing on. She gasped with embarrassment and tried to cover herself, but it was too late—they were all staring and laughing at her every dimple, birthmark, and surgical scar! She was totally embarrassed and humiliated. Finally she awoke from the nightmare, still trembling from the fear of it all. Thank God that's over, she thought to herself. She lay there awake, refusing to go back to sleep for fear of another dream.

Jackie was so consumed by the court case that she didn't even get a break from it in her sleep. She decided she would have a talk with

Attorney Bernard and request some therapy or medical sedation or something so she could get some rest.

"You don't want to go into a hospital now," Attorney Bernard said. "If you do, they'd use it against you, or else they'll say you're just doing this to compound the situation and fake symptoms. There's a condition that can and has been used in court to say the plaintiff's mental damage occurred as a result of litigation and not the charge action.

"But, I really don't think I can take much more," Jackie said. "I really need a break."

Attorney Bernard's response to that was, "It's the weekend, take a couple of days off and relax."

"I can't," Jackie replied. "I'm working overtime to make up for all the days I was in deposition. Never mind, I'll work it out for myself." Although she felt doomed, Jackie desperately wanted to see this catastrophic situation to an end. That was when she came to the realization that what she needed was to attend church and ask for divine intervention. Otherwise, Jackie knew that she couldn't go on without help from somewhere. So at this point she asked God to help her or to send help so she could find peace and closure. Jackie knew she'd come a long way, but without proof of her allegations, she was pretty much done.

There were still a lot of missing pieces, and without any help from the defendants, Jackie was almost ready to have to accept the fact that she'd never be able to prove anything. It was a hopeless feeling, knowing she was on a cold trail with absolutely no assistance from anyone.

Just then George stepped into the room and handed Jackie a large brown envelope. "What's this?" she asked.

"I'm not sure," he said. "It came in the mail yesterday, and I forgot to give it to you."

Jackie chuckled. "I hope it isn't a bomb." As she took the envelope and peeled off the flap, she was stunned as multiple pictures of herself and George, Tom, Lucrezia, Frankie Paige, Dexter, Hillary, Todd Hunter, Stuart Carson, and even Alvin Waters fell out into her lap. "What the hell? Where did this come from?"

"I got it yesterday from the post office box," George explained. "It has no return address on it."

Jackie dug further into the envelope and noticed a folded letter inside. She opened the letter and read, "Keep these for yourself. Demand a list. You weren't the first and you aren't the last."

"What the hell does this mean? And these pictures were taken in and around the office and at different functions for the company, but I don't remember taking them."

George scratched his head and shrugged. "Don't ask me. I just picked them up. I don't have a clue. What are you going to do with them?"

"What the letter said to do—hang onto them until I can figure something out. Right now I want my attorney to get on the ball and get Richard back in there to finish his deposition." Jackie mumbled to herself, "A list? I wonder what that means?" By now she was again consumed with the latest twist and trying to figure it out. She already knew about the list of other women. Maybe this means there are still others who haven't come forth. Jackie made herself a note to discuss this with her attorney during Richards's next deposition.

## CHAPTER FIFTY-ONE

On Monday morning at 9:30 a.m., Jackie received a call from her attorney's office. "I need for you to come in as soon as possible," Attorney Bernard said. "We need to talk, and it isn't something I can discuss over the phone."

They made an appointment for 11:30 a.m., and Jackie found it difficult to concentrate for the next two hours. She kept focusing on the note of desperation she'd heard in Attorney Bernard's voice. Finally the morning meeting at work ended, and Jackie leaped from her chair, grabbed her purse, and headed straight to the lawyer's office.

"Jackie, we have a problem." Ms. Bernard frowned at her. "Red Freeman called me this morning with the results of the tape analysis. It seems there's a large problem. Someone had messed with the tape and done some addition and some deletion, making the conversation appear different."

"They can't get away with that!" Jackie exclaimed. "Those are my tapes, I made them, and they can't just do that to my tapes. That's my evidence against Tom!"

"Jackie, they're saying you altered the tapes—that you added and deleted parts to make it appear different from what Tom really said. You know, combining two different conversations into one."

"No, I don't know!" Jackie snapped. "I haven't done anything to those tapes but record pieces of several different conversations at different times in hopes of obtaining something concrete on the tape. Are they aware of that?"

"I believe they are," Attorney Bernard replied.

"Well, it sounds to me like you need to have the tapes examined by a different person."

"I don't think that's necessary," Attorney Bernard said. "I feel comfortable that Attorney Freeman is telling the truth, and he assured me these findings are legitimate." She sighed. "Besides, having those tapes reevaluated costs money, and unless you're willing to pay for it, I can't have it done. We've already spent far too much trying your case. We usually don't spend nearly this much money trying one of these cases."

Jackie could not believe her ears. She was absolutely shocked by Ms. Bernard's response. "Well, let me ask you this: Just how many cases have you run into like this one?"

"This one stands alone," Attorney Bernard replied.

"Don't we have a signed agreement that states you're working for contingency?"

Ms. Bernard nodded. "Yes, but there's only so much our firm can absorb."

"And just what is that number?" Jackie asked.

"We're there now."

"Okay, then, I suggest you get on the phone and call some of your attorney buddies and offer the case to them on a split basis or whatever it is you do, because I'm NOT going to allow them or you to screw me on this. I promise you, if you throw this case I'm going straight to the bar, and I'll take your license off that wall and use it as wall papering my bathroom." Then Jackie stood and leaned over Attorney Bernard's desk as she stared her directly in her face. "So you better make damn sure they make the payoff worth your while, because if you screw me, I'll make certain you NEVER practice law around here again!"

"Don't you threaten me!" Attorney Bernard shouted. "You're in a grave situation here."

"Oh, and you're just now figuring that out?" Jackie snapped. "I'm the one who initiated this lawsuit the one who's life was threatened if

I went forward with it, I'm the one who nearly died having a surgical procedure done at their request. I'm the one who did all the legwork to discover Tom's true identity and Dexter's divorce decree from having never been married before." She paused and took a deep breath. "I'm also the one who knows details about a murder that no one wants to check into, not to mention the other two deaths relating to Tom's behavior."

"You don't know that," Attorney Bernard replied.

"I DO KNOW THAT!" Jackie screamed as she slammed her hand down on top of Attorney Bernard's desk. "I know this slimy bastard was telling me the truth when he bragged about it and when he laughed about it and when he threatened my life if I ever told anyone about it. I've known I was in a grave situation from the very beginning. You just didn't believe me, and now that you see the truth you don't know how to handle it. You're overwhelmed, and you're looking for a way out!"

Attorney Bernard demanded, "Jackie, sit down. We need to discuss what we're going to tell the judge about this."

Jackie shrugged. "You have such a good relationship with the defense team, y'all need to get together and decide between yourselves what to tell the judge."

"I haven't had a good relationship with that firm in a long time."

"And why is that?" Jackie asked.

"You know why," she replied.

"I think I do," Jackie stated. "But I'd still like to hear it from you that they lied to you and didn't keep their end of the bargain AFTER we provided them with their requested information. They have lied to you so many times, just like I told you they would, and now you're asking me to trust the word of their paid expert because you trust this new attorney from their firm. Let me tell you about their paid doctor that I went to. He took breaks to call Attorney Woodcock so they could go over my answers to the questions. So you think they aren't lying now? Oh no, professional courtesy wouldn't allow that."

Jackie leaned forward in her chair. "So tell me, Attorney Bernard, what did you think about the tapes when you listened to them?"

"I haven't listened to them."

Jackie was stunned. "You what? You haven't even listened to the tapes, and your crucifying me? Who the hell are you representing here?"

"You don't know the law, Jackie. You just can't go around accusing people of murder."

"Accusing!" Jackie shouted. "I'm not accusing him. I'm confirming his confession." She stood up again. "You know what Attorney Bernard? I have major concerns about you right now. We both know you were responsible for those tapes, the tape player, the desk journal, and all that stuff called evidence that came from one attorney's office straight to yours. And now its not looking good for me because something happened to all that evidence while it was in your possession. Actually, we're no further along with their depositions than when we started. I think I'll go to the judge myself."

"You can't do that, Jackie. Get that idea out of your head," Attorney Bernard said. The judge will throw this case so far out the window, you'll never see it again."

"See it? I live it! And at least he'll know the truth—that this was not my mistake." Jackie replied. "It's not me who's afraid of the truth here. I'm already on the bottom with no place to go but up. I'm the one who lost everything I own to keep up with legal costs. Everything I've ever told you is true, and I've proved it time and time again. So no matter if you win or lose this case, I'm still going to get justice somewhere. With or without you, I don't care!"

Jackie bolted from Attorney Bernard's office feeling completely uncertain about the whole legal process and what she should do next. The only thing she was certain about was the fact that she had to do something for herself to bring the situation to some sort of closure.

## CHAPTER FIFTY-TWO

On the way back to work, Jackie stopped in a sandwich shop to get something to eat. She'd just stepped inside when she heard a radio advertisement announcing a psychic fair coming to Dallas that weekend. She didn't think anything about it at first, but the more she pondered over it, the more she thought—*Why not? It can't hurt.* So she called her best friend and talked her into going along, just to check it out.

When they'd arrived and paid their way in, they wandered around the hall set up for the presentation. They spent some time checking out the different things on display and items offered for sale before either of them decided on which psychic to get a reading from. As they walked around the market hall, Jackie came upon something called a labyrinth. It was actually a prayer circle in which one entered and walked through for nearly a mile before reaching the center.

"Looks like a maze," Linda remarked.

"Actually, this is exactly what I've dreamed about," Jackie whispered. As they continued strolling through the exhibits, they passed the booth of the psychic Glenn Hosting. It was then Jackie literally "felt" she wanted him to do her reading.

As she sat down, Glenn asked if she'd allow him to hold something of hers so he could meditate over it in order to do a better reading.

Jackie immediately took off her watch and handed it to him. Glenn closed his eyes and held the watch in both hands. Then Jackie watched as his facial expression changed from a smile to serious concern just before he opened his eyes and looked at her. "Wow, you really have a lot of things going on around you. May I confirm your name? Jackie?"

"Yes," she gasped. "My name is Jackie."

"Okay, Jackie. First of all, there are angels all around you, but I get the message that you already know that. I also see you have a son in spirit, and I'm hearing the name Brian. He wants me to let you know he is always with you. He also wants me to tell you that you're on the right track, but know what to call justice. I hear him saying the words semper fi. Do you know what he's talking about?"

By now Jackie was trembling and desperately trying to control herself. Completely shocked by what the psychic had said, her heart thumped as she reached into her purse for a tissue. It was all so unexpected that she couldn't hold back the tears. "How did you know that? How could you have known about my son! Do you communicate with the other side?"

Glenn nodded. "I have a gift that enables me to both see and hear from the other side."

Still trembling with emotion, Jackie wiped away her tears and listened as Glenn continued the reading. His voice was so soft that she had to really focus to hear his words above all the noise around them. "Jackie, you are in the midst of a sort of dispute. It appears to be something relating to your job. However, I see a man involved in this situation who is very bad. He is very dangerous. He's capable of—well let's just say anything at this time. Do you know who I mean?"

"Yes, I do," she replied.

Glenn shook his head and sighed with disbelief before he continued. "As a matter of fact, there's a murder directly relating to this man. Did you know that?"

"Yes, I think so," Jackie replied.

"However the problem is proving it. And eventually, you will prove it," Glenn stated. "But you'll need to be very careful and not create any noise when you're looking for the proof. This man has been able to keep this hidden by using a different name, and it appears to me he traded something to keep it hidden. Does that make sense to you Jackie?"

"Yes, I know what you mean," she acknowledged.

"Um, this man he killed, I believe he worked for the government, maybe as an informant or something like that. You're about to uncover this information if you haven't already. You'll need to make phone calls and buy some of the proof, but you already have enough knowledge to obtain whatever it is that you need, so stop relying on someone else to do the job for you. I see you making a few phone calls and having all the information to put the pieces together to solve this case. There is, however, one more thing that I need to make very clear to you."

"Okay," Jackie replied.

"Stay away from this man. I cannot stress enough how dangerous this man is. He is actually using this company, the company that you have a grievance with, as a distribution company or a front company, if you will, to deliver or transfer his product into and all over the United States. He has connections in Colombia from his prior life. Jackie, do you understand what it is that I'm telling you?"

"Yes, I think so," she replied, "but can I ask you something?"

The psychic acknowledged her question with a nod, and she continued. "Does anyone else within the company know about this?"

"Of course they do," he replied. "How do you think they're able to get away with it? They all keep it hidden under the corporate ladder. Haven't you heard that term used before?"

"Yes, I have."

"Didn't you previously testify yourself that everyone in management is related in some way or another?"

"Yes," she answered.

"With their hiring and promotion rules, they have to make sure you fit their profile before they bring you in to their 'family.' Otherwise, there's a lot at stake if they hire someone they can't manage. That's why you were released. They couldn't trust—or really they couldn't corrupt—you, and you got too close without them being assured you weren't going to bring them down. Therefore, they had to get rid of you. Really, they did you a favor." Glenn paused for a moment. "I see them thinking they got away with it only to lose it all because of a botched shipment into the US. When I say lose it all, I mean they are going to lose a shipload of Colombian goods so big that it causes them to have to file companywide bankruptcy to pay the debt to their Colombian connection."

"Oh my God," Jackie replied. "I really don't want to talk about this in detail here in a public place."

"I understand," Glenn replied. He then gave Jackie his personal card and told her if she ever needed him, he was just a phone call away.

"You don't know how much I appreciate this," she told him before they shook hands to end their session.

Jackie felt so much better after talking to this man; she didn't know why exactly, but she felt very peaceful just being around him. After that informative conversation, she decided to go forward as the psychic had advised. After contemplating things for a couple of days, she called directory information for the district clerk's office and the police department in Pittsburgh, Pennsylvania. She then placed her first call to the police department, where she talked to the desk officer about the situation. However, much to Jackie's surprise, he suggested that instead of the homicide officer, she should call a newspaper reporter in Pittsburgh. Jackie thought it was a little strange, but decided to go ahead and call the reporter. She was really surprised when the reporter answered on the first ring.

After she introduced herself and told him her story, she asked if he'd ever heard anything about this particular murder or if he knew of Terry Barber. "Terry Barber," he stated, "is currently in the Penitentiary serving oh, about a 150 years on racketeering, money laundering, drug trafficking, and God only knows what else. So, you must be mistaken, lady."

He sounded very sure of himself that Jackie had the wrong person. "I don't think so," she replied. "He's told me a lot of stories about his past, and I have a picture of him and a name identifying him as Terry Barber."

"Where and how did you come to know him?" The reporter asked.

"Well," she replied. "He was my boss."

The voice on the other end of the phone escalated. "Where? When?"

"Recently. At least until I filed charges in federal court against him and the company I worked for, and that was right here in Dallas, Texas, a couple of years ago. He told me he was released from jail in 1993 under a witness protection program."

"There's no way!" the reporter replied. "No way in hell that maniac is back on the streets."

"Obviously, you do know him," Jackie said, "because maniac is how I'd describe him on a good day." Then she added, "I guess I'm a little curious how he got out of murder charges and placed under witness protection."

"What murder charges?" the reporter asked. "He was never charged with that murder. As a matter of fact, I covered that homicide story myself, and the case remains unsolved to this day. Mrs. Kennard, I think you need to talk with the homicide detective who originally handled that case."

Jackie was by now so frightened that she was trying to convince herself this could not be true. Her fears were mounting as she asked him, "Are you sure it's the same case?"

He paused momentarily to think. "Tell me, Mrs. Kennard, do you know by chance when it happened?"

"I know when he told me it happened. He said it was on November 27, 1984, and he said he had to do it because the guy was about to "rat" on him about something."

"I'll be damned!" the reporter shouted. "You're not kidding!" Then he asked her, "Do you know where and how it happened?"

Jackie stated, "I believe so, yes. He told me the guy was just getting off an elevator and he shot him in the head several times and then shot both his eyes out."

"Hey lady! You really need to talk with a detective. You have me convinced. There's no way you'd know that unless the actual killer told you. There are other things around this that only the murderer would know, and I'm sure that the detectives will want to talk with you to determine if this guy was really the one who did the murder. I can't believe he's out, living the high life, and bragging about his crimes."

"It's true. Otherwise, how would I know him?"

"Mrs. Kennard, I'm going to send you some clippings from the newspaper about this guy, but you need to be aware he is BAD. I hope you don't have a relationship going with him or anything like that, but I'll tell you, you need to keep your distance. I cannot stress enough how BAD this guy is. If he would kill a federal informant and brag about it, he would kill anyone."

Jackie shouted, "A federal informant?"

"Yes, a federal informant working undercover," the reporter replied. "At one time this Barber guy was one of the biggest drug cartels in the United States with connections in three different countries. As a matter of fact, his whole family was involved in drug trafficking. Yeah, if memory serves me correctly, his father and uncle were very much mob related until one of them tried to step on the wrong people and got killed. Seems like his father was the "Don" of the family. If memory serves me correctly, someone attempted to blow him up in a car bomb. I don't remember all the details, but I'll pull those clippings and send them to you. What I do remember is they owned a bar as a front for the family drug business, and the uncle owned a concrete construction company. Terry ran a jewelry business—part of it, and his son, Levi, now runs a jewelry store here."

"Levi! Did you say Levi is his son?"

"I believe that was his name. Do you know him, too?" the reporter asked.

"I've talked to him several times on the phone," Jackie exclaimed! "I had a feeling Levi was his son. There's no doubt now that's who this guy really is, and if you could send me those clippings, I can sure use them."

"Sure thing," the reporter replied. "I just never thought this guy would make it out the other side. He was so dirty!"

Jackie couldn't believe it, and again she thanked him. "Adam, I really appreciate your information. This is a Godsend to me."

"My pleasure," Adam replied. "I'd do anything to help bring this creep down. Good luck!"

## CHAPTER FIFTY-THREE

Jackie hung up the phone in a euphoric state of shock. She'd never imagined she would hit such pay dirt with two phone calls. But now she worried how she'd ever convince her lame attorney of this. She finally then decided not to say anything until she had the newspaper articles in hand and could see exactly what they were all about. As she walked into the kitchen to get herself something to drink, the phone rang.

It was Attorney Bernard. "Hello Jackie, I just wanted to call and let you know I just received a signed sworn affidavit by Thomas Kerakasco that his only other charges were a DWI in 1978, for which he received probation, and carrying a concealed weapon in 1983, which was thrown out. So I wanted to tell you that it looks like your worries were for nothing. There are no other charges in his past."

Jackie could hardly believe Attorney Bernard was so completely trusting of this new-found information offered up by the defendants, but she simply replied, "Attorney Bernard I really appreciate you telling me this. I feel much better knowing that I was terrified for nothing. Thanks for calling."

Jackie realized she had to obtain undeniable information herself—otherwise there was no use discussing it further with her attorney.

"Oh, there is one other thing I called to tell you," Attorney Bernard added. "I'm going to be on vacation in Florida for the next three weeks.

Therefore, should you need anything before I get back, you can call Mike or Dorothy."

"I hope you have a good trip," Jackie said. After the call, she thought to herself how truly great this vacation timing was because she'd be able to obtain the information from Pittsburgh and then share it with Attorney Dodson, the owner of the law firm, while attorney Bernard was out of town. Jackie immediately placed a call to the district clerk's office, saying she was calling on behalf of her law firm, and asked if he would look up information relating to a Terry Barber. Jackie could hear the clerk typing something into the computer, and then he told her he needed to check on something and he'd call back. Jackie assured him that she really didn't mind waiting because she desperately needed the information for a pending trial.

"Well, in that case, I don't need to know any more," he said. "Where do you want the file sent?"

"Send it to my law office here in Dallas," Jackie stated.

"The whole thing," he asked?

"Well, just how much is there in the file?"

The clerk chuckled. "Probably a moving van full."

"What!" Jackie fumbled the telephone. "I don't want to see all that. Can you just send the charge sheet reflecting all the charges?"

She gave the clerk her home fax number and he agreed to send the pages right away. Jackie was absolutely astounded that she'd pulled this off so easily, while her attorney was completely crippled when it came to obtaining information. Just like the time before, within a few minutes her fax machine was churning out pages of information. Only this time, the pages showed that not only was Tom's sworn affidavit a lie, but the true charges filed against this man—whoever he was back then—were too many to list on a single sheet of paper.

Jackie shook her head in complete disbelief as she read the rap sheet. It looked more like a mobster's who's who list. There was extortion, drug running, possession, cocaine distribution, gun smuggling, organized crime, conspiracy, bribery, promoting mob violence, using a communications facility to distribute illegal drugs, and tax evasion. The district clerk's information also verified that both Terry Barber and his family owned and ran the drug corporation with the help of some 350 employees—thirty-five of whom carried titles like CEO, sales manager, or regional manager. It was much like any Fortune 500 company, with executives, salespeople, buyers, and movers, but in fact it was nothing but a criminal enterprise. The only difference was that his corporation dealt exclusively in illegal drugs.

If list of charges was incomprehensible, the trial outcome was even more shocking. He was found guilty in a jury trial and sentenced to 150 years in a federal penitentiary with no parole. The document further stated he was ordered shackled and placed in the Washington County Jail to stand by for transfer to the Terre Haute, Indiana, federal facility. But apparently this was just a dress rehearsal, because he had already arranged a plea and made a bargain with the feds to turn state's evidence against his own corporation, naming each of his employees as drug runners. This would result in sending them all to jail, but he was processed through the system, given a new identity, placed in the witness protection program, and moved to Dallas to start a new life. Where apparently the cycle started all over again.

"What a dirty bastard!" Jackie remarked. She had now lapsed into mental shock as she sat locked inside her closet in the bedroom. Devastated by this validation of her worst fears, she bowed her head, shaking it from side to side while sobbing uncontrollably. She rocked back and forth in an effort to comfort herself as she'd done so many times before. There was no denying it, she now had the proof and knew exactly what she was dealing with. From now on there could be no ignoring this or denying it by anyone. Tom was straight from hell, and from her point of view he looked like the devil himself. Still, she felt she needed to have the newspaper clippings in hand before she approached the owner of the law firm.

Several days later the newspaper articles arrived. When she opened the mailbox and saw the return address, Jackie knew immediately what it was. She could hardly wait to get inside the house, open it, and see first hand how the newspaper had reported the crimes when they first happened. There were so many articles she didn't want to read them word by word—she scanned each one and hit the highlights until something of importance popped out. She was surprised to find that each article contained something of importance, and each one outlined different areas of Tom's criminal lifestyle.

The most damning article of all was about slain drug informant John MacAlfie. It closely resembled the bone-chilling story previously told to her first hand by the murderer. She couldn't help but picture it now from the victim's side as she read the following article, which outlined the crime, leaving out the distinctive details Tom had described the night he drove her home. The article was dated March 1985.

Terry Barber, a Brockford man, was picked up this week by Custom Officials and Drug Enforcement Agents upon his return to the United States and charged with continuing criminal enterprise along with operating a large cocaine and heroin ring between three countries. During an interview, he told a federal informant that drug dealers had been trying to kill slain informant John MacAlfie for ages. In a taped conversation with another federal informant, Terry Barber described John MacAlfie as an "Arch Enemy." MacAlfie was shot last November 27th in his home in an unsolved contract killing while his girlfriend, Karen Gwen Smith, was at work. MacAlfie's death is under investigation by city and county officials along with the FBI. However, Barber is not considered a suspect in the killing at this time since he stated he had been out of the country on business right around that time. Barber is one of four men arrested Wednesday by the Drug Enforcement Administration and charged with distribution of heroin and cocaine as well as numerous other felony charges. DEA resident agent in charge, Adam Jamison said law enforcement officials believe Barber operated a sizeable drug organization, which spanned three countries and fifty states. This was the same organization that turned an 11-year veteran FBI agent, Doug Greenback into the first FBI agent ever to cross the line and join a Colombia-to-US drug-smuggling ring. Greenback was also the partner of slain informant John MacAlfie.

For the first time in more than four years, Jackie now knew the absolute truth. She had finally pieced it all together. Now everything made sense. He was never charged with the murder he'd bragged about committing because he immediately left the United States afterwards to lay low in another country. He then returned when he thought the coast was clear.

After reading this, it was hard for Jackie to sort out her feelings. She was both sickened and saddened by this information that confirmed what she'd believed for more than four years. After gathering this new information, she prepared for the trip to the law firm that represented her. She was confident Attorney Dawson would see things in a different light from Attorney Bernard, and this was the information she needed to turn the case around to her favor.

When Jackie laid it all out on the desk in front of Attorney Dawson, she could tell the woman had no words to describe what she was seeing. She was profoundly impressed by the tenacity and ability Jackie had displayed to obtain the information to prove her story was right. After several minutes of silence, still looking over all the newspaper articles and Tom's rap sheet, she shook her head and took several deep breaths.

"Jackie," she said. "I commend you on your ability to obtain this information. I don't believe I've ever seen anyone more involved in their own case than you are. That's not always a good thing, though. Let me tell you what you have here, and Ms. Bernard will confirm this with you. A discovery deadline is set in each case, usually by the judge presiding over the case. That means he allows so much time for each side to obtain and present whatever information they feel is pertinent to the outcome of the case. I think what you have here is very damning for the other side, but I'm wondering if it falls outside the discovery deadline set previously by the judge." She held up one hand before Jackie could interrupt. "Also, the judge may not allow this background to be brought into this case. And I'm sure the defendants' attorney will immediately file a motion to have this information quashed so the jury never gets the opportunity to hear or see any of it.

"I'm not sure about all this timing issue, and Ms. Bernard will have to research it when she gets back on Monday of next week. Until then, why don't you just leave all this information here and I'll see that Ms. Bernard gets it when she returns?"

At that moment, Jackie could visualize this evidence disappearing just as the tapes did. "If it's all the same to you, I'd rather keep up with it myself until Attorney Bernard gets back from vacation." She gathered up her articles and left the law firm. She was now more confused than ever, thinking that on a scale of one to ten her conversation rated about a negative three. Jackie thought the only thing left for her to do now was to take the investigation fully into her own hands and go forward any way she could.

On Monday morning at 10:00 a.m., Jackie received the phone call from Attorney Barnard saying she'd returned from vacation, but was swamped with filings on this case alone and it would take the entire day to just sort through it all. She added that she'd just received the official results of Dr. Henry's evaluation.

"Oh good!" Jackie responded. "I can't wait for this. I know it's gonna be a good one."

"Well, I've already read part of it and let's just say it's even less than I thought it would be. He referred to you as delusional and homicidal, among other things."

"But that's okay," Jackie said. "We're going to court next week, and the judge will sort it all out. By the way, Jackie replied. I need to talk with you about something. I've done some additional investigating myself, and I've come up with some very damning information."

"About what?" Attorney Bernard asked.

"Actually I brought it in for Attorney Dawson to take a look at last week while you were vacationing. I was able to obtain the information from a newspaper in Pittsburgh. I stumbled over it when I was searching for articles about Tom's criminal activity. Believe it or not, what I found is something much bigger than him!"

"What could possibly be bigger than him?" Attorney Bernard asked.

"The whole witness protection program," Jackie replied. "This article outlines the deceit placed on the American public by the US Justice Department and its witness protection program. I always thought the program did what its name implies, but apparently that isn't the case at all. According to these articles, the Justice Department uses this program to filter criminals of all kinds back into society where many of them start a new criminal life under their new identities—courtesy of the federal government." She stopped to take a breath. "Apparently, Tom isn't only the only one who's worked his way through the witness protection program."

"Jackie, I'll look at the articles but don't expect me to intertwine them into this case. They have nothing to do with this case, and I won't allow it."

"Actually, it already does intertwine with this case. It backs my story and verifies that their affidavit is a lie designed to keep us from knowing the truth."

"I'll look at it, but I won't promise anything. Now, what else did you have to discuss with me?"

Jackie said, "I have a friend in the private investigation who's offered to have my tapes analyzed in Quantico by the best hi-tech facility available in the United States."

"Are you talking about the facility in Virginia?" Attorney Bernard asked. "That's the FBI's test facility. How did you arrange that?"

"I told you, he's an old friend of my father's and wants to offer his assistance. Can you arrange for him to get the tapes sometime today?"

"Maybe. He'll have to follow an evidence chain with the tapes."

"He knows that, Ms. Bernard. He does this for a living. He wants to help me out, and he wants it to done properly so we'll have something to throw back at them when they make their one-sided presentation."

"I'll call him to make the arrangements," Attorney Bernard replied. "Give me his number." Then she added, "We do need to get together this week and prepare for the evidence tampering trial which is coming up next week, so leave your calendar open and your pager on. I'll be in touch later."

## CHAPTER FIFTY-FOUR

The evidence trial date finally arrived, and Jackie felt like she was about to give birth after a four-year pregnancy. They arrived early to the courthouse and parked underground as instructed, for security reasons. Then they were escorted to a courtroom on the sixteenth floor overlooking downtown Dallas. As she entered the room, Jackie was a little surprised to see the defendants' side was completely full of people, and several had spilled out into the other side of the courtroom, which was pretty much empty except for the legal team and Jackie. Not that it was required, but the defendants evidently viewed this like the seating arrangements for a wedding and placed themselves all together on the groom's side—an obvious attempt to make them seem more powerful.

The bailiff stood and announced, "All rise. The Honorable Judge Greg Garretson presiding." Everyone stood as the judge entered the courtroom and took his place on the bench. He glanced at the plaintiff first and then at the defendants before he looked around the entire room and announced, "You may all be seated." Then with a strike of his gavel he stated, "The court is now in session. You may proceed, counsel."

The first so-called professional expert witness took the stand. He appeared quite certain of his evaluation and proceeded to testify vehemently, displaying charts and graphs to further boost his expert opinion of Jackie's handwriting, her thought process, and even her malicious intentions in filing a bogus case. He mentioned her inability to cope in a corporate structure, and then added she probably needed serious psychiatric help. In conclusion, he offered up his own professional theory of Jackie's thought process, which he testified was made possible by listening to her voice in the taped conversations between herself and Tom.

The second professional witness, Dr. Theo Henry, testified that he had in fact interviewed Jackie for some three hours and found her to be polite and sincere, until she was asked about certain things. For example, her sexual preferences, which she refused to discuss. Then he said, "I asked her about a threat she made toward her boss, Mr. Tom Kerakasco, in which she had threatened to shoot him. Her reply was: 'It wasn't a threat, I meant it then and I still mean it today.' This convinces me she had strong homicidal intentions.

"As we proceeded with the interview, I asked her about her boss's wife. She became so upset that she had to take a break and leave the room to regain control of herself."

Jackie bowed her head and closed her eyes as she listened to them go on and on, portraying her as the aggressor in every situation. She couldn't help but feel concerned about what the judge must be thinking. She knew he probably had a low picture of her after hearing from those professional people. She even started to wonder about herself as she watched and listened through two days of damning testimony. Then came display after display of her handwriting and audio after audio of her voice as they played her over and over screaming at Tom in retaliation to a threat from one of his many phone conversations with Jackie. But, they never played any part of Tom's conversations or his threats for the judge to hear.

Some parts of it weren't even audible and they had filled in the blanks with whatever word they felt credited their needs. This presentation was one-sided; yet it was truly the most destructive thing in the entire trial against Jackie. It appeared her only hope was to take the stand in her own defense and then pray that her attorneys could destroy the destructive testimony by cross examining the expert witnesses.

On the second day, Jackie's team began their cross-examination. Attorney Bernard began with Dr. Henry, questioning him about the creditability of his practice before asking him to enlighten the court as to why he provided his services exclusively to the defendants' law firm, always provided an evaluation that showed positive results to them and grossly negative results toward anyone he evaluated, no matter the situation.

Dr. Henry coughed and reached for a pitcher of water to pour himself a drink. As he raised his glass and drank, he looked toward Attorney Woodcock with his hand noticeably trembling as he replied. "Actually, I do have a practice. However my services are better rendered through private necessity."

Then Attorney Bernard asked, "Dr. Henry, would you please tell the court just how long you evaluated Mrs. Kennard to arrive at your conclusion?"

"Approximately three hours," he replied.

"And would you please tell the court how much you were paid for this evaluation plus your two days of testimony."

"Actually, my expert witness fee is $15,000 per day. Whether I sit in the courtroom all day or I testify on the stand all day, it's the same amount."

Attorney Bernard replied. "Okay, Dr. Henry. Then let's assume you evaluated my client for three hours. What did that pay you?"

Dr. Henry shifted in his chair. "My office evaluation was approximately $25,000."

"Let's assume you received a check from the defendants in the total of $55,000.00 for two days of court testifying and the evaluation. What if you had told them my client was perfectly sane? Or that there was nothing wrong with Ms. Kennard? Or that her evaluations of Tom and charges were not at all made up, but in fact were all truths? Would you have received the same gross amount of money for you opinion, Dr. Henry?"

"I don't know," he replied.

"Did you ask about that, or did you just mold your expert opinion around their needs? Better yet, did you ever check into any of her allegations or charges before you provided this court with your expert $55,000 opinion?"

"No. I had a job to do, and that's what I did," he replied.

"Ah. And that job paid you very well, didn't it, Dr Henry? Well enough to make sure the defendants' were well served for your professional expert opinion." She turned to the judge. "Your Honor, I have no further questions of this witness at this time."

Jackie felt better, especially when she watched the judge making notes during the examination. The second expert witness she called to take the stand was the audio expert. He had never met or talked to Jackie prior to his testimony. During cross-examination, Attorney Bernard was able to ascertain that he, too, was paid handsomely for his testimony. Up to six figures for his valuable input because, as he implied, he could even tell the court just what it was Jackie was thinking when she spoke to Tom. At least he said he could after they paid him $90,000.

Attorney Bernard said, "That's a lot of money for just an opinion Dr. Audio. How often do you testify in cases such as this?"

"Well, not that often. Actually, I've been quite involved on the Branch Davidian's Mount Carmel tapes for several years, until recently when my friend—I mean Attorney Woodcock—called for my expert advise."

Then Attorney Bernard asked the audio expert where and how he obtained his license and what other cases he'd worked on.

At first the man seemed reluctant to answer. He hesitated and then replied, "Actually, this is my first case."

"And your license, Mr. Audio. Didn't you recently obtain it from the Internet?" Attorney Bernard displayed a copy for him to verify. "Isn't that correct?"

The judge intervened, bending forward in his chair. "Mr. Audio, is this true?"

The witness replied, "Yes sir."

Judge Garretson then stated, "Mr. Audio, I need to ask you one question before we proceed any further. Are you capable of determining what the true ratio or margin of error is in your evaluation of these tapes, along with the dates of the events actually recorded in the desk calendar?"

Mr. Audio appeared to be processing all the judge's questions through his mind. Then he stated, "After analyzing it from the audio side I'd say it's anyone's guess, because there are bits and pieces of different conversations on each tape. It could possibly be sixty to seventy conversations. Now on the calendar, there is probably a six-month overlap according to the ink analysis, either way."

The judge asked, "And what do you base that on, doctor?"

"Back in 1973, The United States government began placing small amounts of traceable lead material in ink. This traceable material enables us track and or date anything put in writing, with the exception of black ballpoint ink. For some reason the material does not cling to the paint cells in the black ink. Therefore, since most everything Mrs. Kennard wrote was with a black ballpoint ink pen, this created what we call a grace period in the material date writing."

The judge responded, "For clarification, you're telling me you have evaluated her desk calendar for proof that she maliciously planted false information about situations that actually didn't happen. Can you clear up for me how this is evidence tampering if the incident in question never happened in the first place?"

"Well, Your Honor, what we think happened—"

"Think happened?" The Judge asked.

"Yes sir," he replied. "We think the plaintiff, Mrs. Kennard, after she was terminated, went to her desk calendar and wrote this stuff, planning to use it to back her charges against the company."

"Okay," the Judge replied. "Let's say for the sake of argument that she did do this. Then, what is the result of the ink evaluation age process and the margin for error?"

The expert witness proudly announced without reservation, "Six months either way."

With that answer, the judge scribbled something down and appeared to be working a mathematical equation before he raised his head and looked directly at the witness. "Well, if that's true, then what she wrote five months ago would actually not even exist today, according to your evaluation. On the other hand, something she wrote twelve months ago could now appear to be only six months old."

"Yes sir," the audio witness replied with a nod of his head.

"I've heard enough," the judge said. "I think you need to have some concrete evidence to prove evidence tampering to this court, and not just a theory about what you think happened. Therefore, I'm stopping this trial and disqualifying both Doctor Henry and Doctor Audio. Dr. Henry, you may return to your office and resume your private practice or whatever it is you do between cases, because your services as an expert witness are no longer needed in this case." He turned to Mr. Audio. "As for you, your expert witness opinion with a margin of six months either way is too far reaching to play any significance in this trial, so you can go ahead and catch your plane back to wherever you came from because I've heard enough."

The judge paused and cleared his throat. "Attorney Woodcock, I'm completely disgusted and tired of this case dragging on and on through the legal system because of your shenanigans. Therefore, I order the trial to begin in one week. I am setting aside eight days on my calendar to hear the entire trial.

"Attorney Bernard, I order you to begin your jury selection immediately and be ready to proceed to trial exactly one week from Monday. NO MORE DELAYS. If either side tries anything, I'll enter judgment without any further assistance from either of you." He looked at both of them. "Do I make myself clear, attorneys?"

"Yes sir," they both replied in unison.

"You've wasted another two days of the plaintiff's time with this nonsense. Don't let it happen again!" Judge Garretson banged his gavel on the desk and announced, "court adjourned."

The bailiff called, "All rise," and the judge left the courtroom.

That was the closest thing to victory Jackie had ever seen in the last four years. She couldn't help smiling as she and three of her attorneys left the courtroom and stood in the hallway waiting for the elevator to open. The defendants were still huddled inside the courtroom, planning their strategy. Jackie and her attorney stepped inside the elevator, but before the door closed one of the expert witnesses caught it in an attempt to get on. Without thinking, Jackie threw her arm across the door, blocking him.

"You're getting on the wrong elevator," she said.

He replied. "I'm a doctor of theology and an audiologist. What I said was nothing personal against you, I was just doing my job."

"Really?" Jackie asked. "Well, I think it was personal. You don't know a Goddamn thing about me, but you were ready to offer up your expert 'bought and paid for' opinion to make me look bad. And you call yourself a doctor? You're nothing but a bad plan that failed, and I don't want to be closed in here with you." She lowered her voice. "So get off my elevator before you have to spend that ninety grand to have your family jewels reattached!"

He stepped back and they stared into each others eyes as the door closed between them. As the car moved to the ground floor, Attorney Bernard commented, "Well, I hope he didn't take that personally."

"He had it coming," Jackie said, and they all burst into laughter. They stepped from the elevator, and as they walked across the foyer an older gentleman approached and said, "Excuse me—are you Jackie Weatherby?"

Not certain what was about to happen next, Jackie stopped in front of him. "Yes I am. And who are you?"

He reached out, gently taking Jackie's hand, and he stared at her with a tear in his eye. He held a packet of folded papers in his hand. "Can I see you privately for just a moment?" As they stepped away from the group, he explained in a low solemn voice. "Your father, he was a very good friend to me. Please accept my apologies, but I never put it together until I saw you earlier in the courtroom. I thought you looked familiar, and then I asked my son your name."

Jackie wasn't sure what he was talking about. "Apology for what? Who are you?"

"It doesn't matter," he said. "Did you receive an envelope in the mail containing several pictures?"

Yes I did, Jackie nodded.

"Then take this and put it under your jacket. Don't let anyone know you have it. It will be self-explanatory."

Before she could respond, a man's deep voice could be heard echoing through the foyer, "Dad! What are you doing?"

Jackie could hear footsteps pounding against the marble floor rushing toward her. Quickly she spun around on her heel to see what was going on. She couldn't believe her eyes. Attorney Woodcock and his entire staff were in a foot race toward them; all the while Attorney Woodcock was calling the old gentleman "Dad." Jackie then wondered if his apologies were out of embarrassment, as she stood speechless, not knowing what to say.

Attorney Woodcock grabbed his father's arm. "You can't just go up and talk to her. She's the plaintiff here."

"I know that!" The man snapped back. "But her father and I used to be good friends, and I remember her as a child when you two played together. I just wanted to talk with her personally for a moment." Attorney Woodcock apologized to everyone, placed his arm around his father's shoulder, and led him away. Jackie stood there clutching the folded-up papers underneath her jacket as Attorneys Bernard and Michael approached her and asked, "What was that all about?"

Jackie explained about the relationship with her father and said goodbye to the attorneys. She immediately headed for the restroom, dying to see what the old man had slipped to her. Locked inside a stall in the ladies room she took the papers out from under her jacket. They were legal papers very similar to dozens she'd seen before, but as she read the documents she realized still another case was recently filed against the company though a Florida Court. The filing reflected charges almost identical to hers. However, the most shocking revelation was not the fact that Attorney Woodcock's law firm represented the defendants in that case also, but that Attorney Bernard and her law firm represented the plaintiff.

The date stamped on the case matched exactly the same days when Attorney Bernard was vacationing in Florida. Stuck between the last two pages was a picture of all the attorneys together at a bar, having drinks. Even though she was holding the picture in her hand, it was still hard to believe, but there it was Attorney Bernard, Woodcock, Littleworth and several she didn't recognize sitting around a table with the ocean in the background, toasting the occasion.

*Oh my God,* Jackie thought. This could not be a coincidence. She now knew who'd previously sent those pictures and what the note to make a list was about.

# CHAPTER FIFTY-FIVE

A couple of days later, Jackie received a phone call from Attorney Bernard, whose voice sounded agitated. "I just got off the phone with Attorney Woodcock," she stated. He wants us to get together one more time and try to settle this thing before we go to trial."

"No thanks," Jackie replied.

"Hear me out, Jackie! A trial of this size could be devastating to our firm, and we're up against a huge corporation with deep pockets. They can afford to keep this thing going on through eternity. We can't."

"Were we not in the same courtroom just yesterday when the judge said he was tired of their stunts and ordered this thing to trial without further delay?" asked Jackie.

"Yes, but they can keep this thing tied up in the appeals court forever if they don't get the results they want."

"So can I," Jackie replied. "Besides, let's don't lose focus of what I want from this. If you think back to when we first met, I told you, I didn't want this thing just settled and sealed. I really want justice. I mean that. I'm not willing to take a cash settlement with no justice."

"Well, why don't we give them one more try around the table to make this thing work before we go to court? After all, this is the first time they've initiated any kind of settlement."

"When do you plan to introduce that new information about Tom to them?"

"We can use that as a bargaining chip at the settlement table or hold onto it until trial, whichever works best for us."

"You know what," Jackie replied. "I think this is just another stall tactic, and I don't feel comfortable meeting with them. I prefer to just pass on this and go straight to trial next week."

"But there's an awful lot of work to do between now and then to get ready for trial. I don't know if I can have it all ready," Attorney Bernard said.

"You've had nearly three years to get ready for this trial," Jackie pointed out.

"I can be ready," she replied. "I just don't want to do all that work for nothing if we can possibly settle this out of court. I'll discuss it with my associates and get back with you later today."

Later that day, Attorney Bernard called Jackie back and told her they'd scheduled a third mediation to take place the very next evening. "I think the mediator who's handling this one will be able to control Richard because he used to be a cop."

"I hope so," Jackie said.

The next evening when Jackie and Attorney Bernard arrived at mediation, the opposing side had parked two pearl-white Mercedes and a Lexus end to end in front of the building, leaving no space for anyone else to park. Attorney Bernard pulled to the back of the building, which meant they had to walk a full block carrying heavy box-type briefcases.

As they entered the foyer, a large woman wearing a flowered dress greeted them. Jackie couldn't help but notice the lady's bright orange hair. Immediately the lady asked what they'd like to drink. In the next breath she asked, "Did you bring the check?"

"Yes," Attorney Bernard replied, handing over another thousand dollars for the mediator. They weren't there long before a middle-aged man entered the room, introduced himself as Craig, and instructed them that since this was a third attempt to square this thing up, he would skip the formalities and go forward. Then he stated, "I think they're ready to get this thing behind them. They brought in their big guns tonight—or should I say a room full of sharks. I believe they mean business."

"Good," Jackie replied.

Craig escorted them down a long hallway and up a flight of sixteen stairs into the room full of sharks. Jackie had great expectations before that door opened. However, she was less than impressed when she saw the same old people around the table—Richard, Dexter, and Attorneys Woodcock, Littleworth, and Freeman. Jackie could barely hide her disappointment. This was a setup to waste time, and she'd known it from the start.

Again, both attorneys presented their thoughts on the case to the mediator before Jackie and Attorney Bernard were escorted back downstairs to allow Craig distance between the two sides as he worked. Within a few minutes, Craig came downstairs with an offer.

"Five thousand dollars," he proudly announced as he slapped his tablet onto the table.

Jackie turned to Attorney Bernard and laughed out loud. Attorney Bernard became irate as she told Craig how they'd called her, practically begging to take this to mediation to avoid trial and they'd mentioned a six-figure sum as a starting point.

"I don't think so," Craig replied. "Richard said this is his final offer—take it or leave it."

Jackie stood up and started placing all the papers inside a briefcase as she told Attorney Bernard, "It's time we go. I told you this was a fix to buy some time. Now do you believe me?"

Attorney Bernard asked Craig to leave the room so they could talk privately. "We have to work this thing out," she said. "I cannot leave here without this case settling tonight."

"It isn't going to happen," Jackie said. "Give it up! They're professional hagglers. It's their job to wear their victims down until they give in or give up, and I'm NOT going to do either."

Attorney Bernard snapped, "I had things under control until you told him about those fucking tapes. Ever since then things have gone downhill."

"You know what?" Jackie replied. You need to think back. Those tapes are what are referred to as evidence. I'm not the one who misplaced them—you are. That resulted in him filing tampering charges. By the way, just when do you plan to enlighten them on the new evidence about Tom's past?"

"I haven't decided," she replied.

Just then Craig knocked, and he stepped inside, closing the door behind. "I have a message for you, Mrs. Kennard, from Mr. Spaniel. He said to let you know that he plans to bring charges against you for taping unauthorized conversations of his employees if you refuse to settle, and he wants me to remind you that he plans to fight this thing to the end, regardless of cost. He said to let you know they have deeper pockets than you and endless amounts of stockholder money."

Jackie held up her middle finger and she blew him a raspberry before she replied, "Craig, you can tell Mr. Richard Spaniel I don't give a big hairy crap about his stockholders' money because that's whose money he's spending. She paused to think about that for a second before stating, "Maybe it's time the stockholder's know just how their money is being spent. Then bring it to his attention that his lawyer is using him as a cash cow and milking him with all those unnecessary filings and endless days of depositions." She closed her attaché case with a snap. "And as far as filing charges against me, someone needs to wake him up and remind him the judge threw that out last week. Then tell him to think back four years ago when this all started, and all I asked for was my job back and an apology."

She started for the door and Craig backed out of her way. "Now if money is his issue, then we need to go home now and just let the jury decide next week how much it will cost him to break his company's bad behavior habit against women because I just want justice. Not just for me, but for all the other women who never made it this far, not to mention that family who lost their son."

"Jackie!" Attorney Bernard stepped in front of her. "I think he gets the picture." Jackie shrugged and stated, "I'm prepared to go all the way to the Supreme Court. I'll even knock on the door at the White House. Also, would you please ask him how many of his stockholders know what he's using their money for?"

Craig laughed at that reply. "I'll tell him right now. I can hardly wait to see the look on his face when I tell him that. He may fire his legal team on the spot."

As he left, Attorney Bernard became even more agitated. Her hands trembled as she shoved papers into her briefcase.

"Something's bothering you," Jackie said. "You seem really upset."

Attorney Bernard didn't answer. Jackie returned to the table, and they sat in silence for several minutes before Jackie asked, "Is this mediator from Pittsburgh, too?"

"I don't know," Attorney Bernard replied. "All I know is he used to be a lawyer."

"Really? When did he become a lawyer?"

"I don't know," Attorney Bernard snapped, "Why do you ask?"

"Because you told me yesterday he was previously a cop."

Just the Craig popped the door open and announced, "He's up to $25,000."

Jackie stood and began putting on her jacket, but Attorney Bernard shouted, "Jackie, sit down! We really need to finish this up here tonight."

"No! I'm not sitting here another minute. You can stay and play their games all night if you want to, but I'm going home, and you do NOT have my authority to settle this after I leave."

Then Attorney Bernard slammed her hand down on the desk. "I'm your attorney. I have over $200,000 in legal fees invested in this thing. I have the right to go into settlement if I think it's best."

Jackie stopped and stared directly into Attorney Bernard's face. "BEST FOR WHO? YOU OR ME! You seem to forget. Like the guy he murdered, he took away my life, too, only in a different way. I just exist now. So I'm not going away without justice, and justice to me is not $25,000. So, if you'll excuse me, my husband is waiting for me outside."

"She's right," Craig replied. "You can't settle on an amount unless you have her signature and approval. So I guess we're done."

Attorney Bernard's shoulders slumped. "We're done. I guess we're going to trial."

# CHAPTER FIFTY-SIX

Around eight the next morning, Attorney Bernard phoned Jackie at home to tell her she'd be out of touch for the next couple of days, in a secluded place preparing for the trial, and could be reached only through her secretary or by voicemail. But first she desperately needed Jackie to stop by the office right away and sign off on required court papers before she could proceed and begin the voir dire jury selection.

When Jackie stopped by to sign the documents, the legal assistant explained that Attorney Bernard had mistakenly taken them with her. "She just called and asked if you can drive down to her friend's ranch in East Texas and sign the papers."

"Is it really that important?" Jackie asked. "I have other plans for the day."

The assistant bobbed her head up and down. "I think so. Ms. Bernard said these papers are vital to the case."

So Jackie agreed to drive to a ranch on the outskirts of Tyler to meet Attorney Bernard. After driving for nearly three hours and trying to follow the directions she had scribbled on a torn piece of paper, Jackie began to think she'd reached the end of civilization. Just as she'd convinced herself to turn around, she saw the sign directing her to the main entrance of the ranch. At the end of a long driveway, sat the main house, looking like something from the English countryside. Actually, it looked like something from a Hollywood movie, as Jackie remarked out loud, "Damn! That's the biggest house I've ever seen. It must be ten thousand square feet."

What made the home even more outstanding was the twelve-foot high black iron fence that surrounded the perimeter. She pulled up to a security gate constructed of pointed iron rods and sat for a moment, staring into the world on the other side of the fence. Then she pressed the button on the security box. Immediately Attorney Bernard's voice came over a speaker. "Jackie, is that you?"

"Yes," she replied. The heavy gate rolled open and Jackie coasted her car through, still pondering how her attorney could afford such an impressive layout. She watched in her rear-view mirror as the iron gates rolled shut behind her car. Jackie felt a wave of insecurity, but she had no choice but to keep going. Attorney Bernard stood on the porch outside the main house to greet her. The house resembled an old English castle. The exterior was made from beautiful natural stone. There was an outside balcony between two upstairs rooms from which flowers and vines hung nearly down to the ground below.

Inside, Attorney Bernard showed her to a study at the back of the house, where she motioned for Jackie to take a seat at her desk. Every wall in the study contained a floor-to-ceiling bookshelf. Each one filled with books pertaining to legal issues. "I'd like for us to be comfortable when we talk. I know how much you like tea, and I thought you'd probably be thirsty, so I took the liberty of making some." A pitcher of iced tea and two glasses sat on the desk.

"As a matter of fact, I am." Jackie replied as she poured herself a glass. They chatted for several minutes before a man wearing a dark suit and sunglasses strolled through the office door. At first, he frightened Jackie, but she assumed he was probably Attorney Bernard's husband.

Without speaking, the man approached her. holding out a billfold containing an ID badge. He then introduced himself as Special Agent Doug Greenback with the FBI. Jackie glanced at the badge for a second and quickly turned to Attorney Bernard. Time seemed to stand still, and fear coursed through her veins.

"First of all," Agent Greenback stated, "please accept my apologies for having to meet with you under these conditions. However, it is necessary that I talk with you and let you know that when this case is finalized, I will be assigned to you should you ever need further assistance with this situation." He sat in the chair beside Jackie. "On behalf of the United States government and the FBI, we want to offer you our apologies for all the hardship and disaster this situation has brought at the hands of a participant within the witness protection program."

Jackie folded her hands in her lap and nodded but didn't answer.

The agent continued. "Now, in order to complete our investigation and properly bring to justice all the parties involved, I need you to turn over all the tapes you still have containing Tom Kerakasco's voice, whether these messages were friendly or threatening, so we can have them analyzed."

Jackie again looked at Attorney Bernard before she responded, "I've already given all the tapes to Attorney Bernard."

"Are you certain?" Agent Greenback asked.

"I'm positive," Jackie said.

He took a deep breath. "That's fine, then. I just wanted to personally hear it from you before we send them all off to be analyzed at our Quantico facility."

Having heard that, Jackie began to relax and breathe easier.

Then he said, "Ms. Kennard, you'll probably never see me or know I'm around, but I'll always know your whereabouts."

Jackie didn't quite know what to think of that remark or how she should answer, so again she said nothing. There was a brief silence before Agent Greenback added, "So, if you'll excuse me, it's a pleasure to have met you." Then he left the room.

Jackie frowned, trying to process what she'd just experienced while contemplating where she had heard the name Doug Greenback before. The agent's sudden appearance was like an actor on stage, playing a part. But so many strange things had happened that she decided it was best not to ask questions, but to be patient and allow the meeting to play itself out. That thought had barely left her mind when she began to feel disoriented and groggy.

"Something's happening to me," she told Attorney Bernard. "I don't feel well, and I'm really dizzy." Jokingly, she asked, "What did you add to the tea?"

"Just a little something to make you relax and help you through this," Attorney Bernard replied. "You'll be all right, but first we have to talk to you."

Jackie could hear Attorney Bernard talking and her own voice responding, but it felt as though she were watching everything from outside her body.

Attorney Bernard opened a desk drawer, pulled out a check, and slid it toward Jackie. "Take this. It's part of your settlement."

"What do you mean *settlement*?" Jackie asked. "I'm going to trial in a few days."

Attorney Bernard shook her head no. "Yes I am!" Jackie shouted in a loud, but slurred voice."

Attorney Bernard leaned toward her and shouted back, "No, you're not! That's why I had you to come all the way out here."

"Damn you! What do you mean? I can't believe I fell for this!" Jackie's tongue was so thick that her words were hard to understand, as she struggled to talk. "What are you planning to do to me?"

"Nothing, if you cooperate," Agent Greenback replied. Jackie jumped and gasped. She hadn't seen him reenter the office, but he now stood directly behind her chair. He leaned over until he was looking directly into her face. "Jackie, you have to understand. We cannot let you to go public with this thing. It's too big. You yourself don't even want to know how big this operation is. There are a couple of pretty well-known guys who have some big money invested in this. I'm not naming names, but you probably have a pretty good idea who they are."

Jackie was now struggling just to sit up in her chair. She could hear what they were saying, but she just couldn't get a grip on herself.

She was completely at their mercy. She feared this was going to be the end of her life.

Attorney Bernard then laid out on the desk a stack of papers and placed a pen next to it for Jackie to sign with. "What we have agreed upon is that you'll sign off on any and all charges against the company or any of its officers, shareholders, employees, or vendors. In exchange, they will watch and monitor you for signs of any attempt to go public about this or disavow the operation. They've agreed to set aside a very generous amount of money in a bank in the name of my law firm to avoid it channeling directly to you—in exchange for your life of course. Provided that you do not go public or disclose them in any way. There's enough in the account for you to live on comfortably for quite a long time."

She glanced at the agent. "Look, Jackie, this is what's best for all of us. Please, don't fight them anymore. We can't take this thing into a courtroom. The public could not—would not possibly believe your accusations that the witness protection program, as a branch of the Justice Department, recycled this drug lord back into society. Ever since the President Clinton situation, well juries feel they're just too overexposed. And believe me, they're tired of the whole sexual harassment thing."

Jackie began shaking her head no as she held up one hand and in a slurred voice shouted over Attorney Bernard "That's NOT what this is about!"

Attorney Bernard shouted, "REALLY? Well, that's what it would boil down to. Look, Jackie, I'm not going to debate this with you anymore. Do we have an agreement, or don't we?"

"Do I have a choice?" Jackie asked.

"You've always had a choice," Attorney Bernard replied. "You've just pushed us until we had to make this one for you. And trust me, if someone big at the top of this organization's corporate ladder didn't really like you, they wouldn't be extending you this offer. You could just as easily have wound up dead."

That statement brought a long deafening silence between them. Jackie struggled to hold herself together as she stared across the desk into Attorney Bernard's face as a grandfather clock ticked away time in the background.

After several silent minutes of staring at one another, Attorney Bernard broke the silence. "Really, Jackie, I mean that."

At which Jackie smugly replied, "I'm honored."

Attorney Bernard demanded, "No more smart-ass remarks, okay? Just sign it."

Jackie briskly rubbed her face with her hands trying to shake off the effects of her tea before she picked the pen up and began signing her name. Jackie now knew that signing her name to these documents was probably the only way she would walk out of there alive. "Do I get a copy of this?' she asked.

"No!" Attorney Bernard shouted. "You'll never see any of this again if you keep your end of the bargain." She slid a bankcard across the desktop. "Here's your credit card, and the account is fully operational at this time. By using this everywhere you go, the FBI will have constant knowledge of your whereabouts. That's one of their stipulations for this agreement. The good side to this is you can use as much as you need or want as often as you like. Pretty good, huh?"

Jackie nodded her head yes, but she refused to look Attorney Bernard in the eye. "Can I go now?"

Attorney Bernard gathered the papers and stood up. "My end of the bargain is that I keep you here until after the papers are filed with the district clerk. I'm about to fax these to my office right now for someone to take there immediately, and then you're free to go."

Jackie could no longer hold it together as she slumped further into the chair and her head rolled back. Special Agent Greenback then picked up one of her arms and felt for a pulse. Immediately she felt the stick of a needle. She moaned with pain and tried to pull away, but she couldn't move—she'd been injected with some sort of paralyzing drug. Even though she couldn't move or talk, she could still hear and see through her half-closed eyes.

As Special Agent Greenback laid her out onto the floor, someone knocked softly on the door. He turned and said, "You can come in now. She's sedated."

Jackie heard several people enter the room as she lay there feeling completely vulnerable, like a specimen in a jar, not knowing what to expect. She heard several familiar voices. Once of them she recognized as Tom, and the second voice was Attorney Max Mulligan straight out of Washington. A couple of other people she didn't know, but she assumed one of them was a doctor, since they addressed him as Doc. As they stared down at her, Doc said, "Oh, I remember this one, I did an endoscope on her for you guys last year."

Then Tom asked, "Hey Doug, did she fall for the Special Agent story?"

"I believe so," Greenback replied. "I never got close enough for her to get a good look at my 'past life' credentials."

Tom laughed. "We all know once an FBI agent, always an FBI agent, no matter what side of the law you're operating on—right?"

Then Max stated, "Gentlemen, if you'll be patient, I first need to make a phone call." Dialing on his mobile phone, he stepped beyond the doorway and waited for an answer. Jackie couldn't hear what was being said, but the conversation was short and to the point. As Max finished the conversation, he stepped back inside just in time for everyone to hear him say, "Goodbye, Mr. President."

Then he turned to Doc. "The Prez wants both trackers inside Jackie to be activated."

Special Agent Greenback looked up at Max and stated, "We only insert two trackers in the event of a terrorist threat or someone who could create a national disaster."

Max held up both hands and shrugged as he replied, "I'm just telling you what the Prez said." He glanced down toward Jackie. "Are you sure she's sedated? We don't want to take a chance that she comes to and notices us all standing here in the room with her. Could you imagine what that would do on top of everything else?"

Special Agent Greenback answered, "Yes sir, I understand your feelings about this."

"I hope so," Max said. "That's something I just can't take a chance with."

"Yes sir," Greenback replied.

The man they called Doc lifted Jackie's right arm, felt around on her upper abdomen, and placed a small hand-held computer wand against her. Next she heard a high-pitched noise while the device rested against her side.

"Cool!" Tom exclaimed. "What's that red light beam from?"

The Doc explained, "That's what activates the trackers."

"What trackers?" Tom asked.

"The trackers we put in her when we had the endoscope done."

"No Shit!" Tom exclaimed, "No one told me you were doing that."

Quickly Max questioned, "You got a problem with it?"

"No," Tom said. "I just had no idea they were gonna fit her with trackers."

Jackie then heard Max explain, "Like I said, we don't want to take a chance of her getting out of our sight. If one tracker gets damaged or goes down, we need a backup in her."

Agent Greenback replied, "Here, sir." He handed over a second computerized device taken from another silver briefcase, and again the doctor held it against Jackie's body and shot her with another red beam, somehow activating whatever they'd previously placed inside her. Jackie could not believe this was happening, and she prayed to die as she lay there paralyzed and helpless on the floor.

Then almost as if he knew she was able to hear him, Special Agent Greenback leaned over Jackie and whispered, "I'm really sorry that I have to do this to you but, after the ecstasy wears off, you won't remember a thing. When you wake up you'll think it was all a dream."

As she lay there helplessly fading in and out of consciousness, Jackie watched as the bright lights circled around her once again, and time seemed to stand still as she left the pain of her situation for a few minutes.

Then Jackie heard a phone ring before Max answered. "This is Max. I can't hear you very well, let me call you from a land line." He picked up the desk phone and dialed a number before he replied, "This is Max. Sure, as a matter of fact he's standing right here."

He passed the phone to Tom, who listened intently for several minutes before he responded. "Great! Thanks for letting me know. I'll tell everyone here." Then he hung up the phone and looked at Max.

"Is something wrong?" Max asked.

"Absolutely not," Tom replied with a big smile. "That was my Colombian ship captain calling to let me know our 1.3 billion dollar presidential investment is on its way, and they're just two hours from docking." He snickered his usual trademark tee-hee-hee laugh before he shook his head in disbelief and stated, "We can thank the Prez for making that happen. I still can't believe he delivered the check right in public view."

Max looked a little disgusted with Tom as he asked, "How would you prefer he do it Tom?"

Tom quickly replied, "Oh, I'm not complaining. That was perfect. I just can't believe the President actually delivered the cash right under the nose of the American public, that's all." Tom stood silent in his thoughts momentarily before he breathed a heavy sigh, raised his clenched fists in the air, and screamed, "GOD DAMN! IT'S GREAT TO BE THE KING AGAIN! I guess I should let the corporate big dicks know that we're actually ahead of schedule on this trip, and it looks like we're gonna turn the stuff pretty quick and get the company's investment money back to them sooner than we thought." Jackie watched his shoes move past her head as he paced the floor. "That should make them very happy, not to mention secure us more investment cash for the next time."

Max nodded affirmation. "That sounds like a good idea, Tom. Why don't you make those calls? And while you're at it, make sure your man's on duty with the Coast Guard tonight. I don't want to take a chance on something going wrong and having to abort this mission."

Tom laughed. "You're too paranoid, Max. That's never gonna happen. Listen to me. I've given specific orders that the ONLY way that shipment will be aborted is if my wife calls them and says 'MacAlfie is in town.'"

Before Tom could finish convincing Max he had everything under control, Max shouted, "Hey! Get someone over here and check her out. Her eyes are open. That's all I need is for her to see me standing here."

Immediately the doctor rushed to Jackie and leaned over her, flashing a light in each of her eyes before he replied. "Trust me, she isn't seeing anything, and she won't be for a while yet."

"See," Tom jeered. "Chill out man, you're making me paranoid."

None of the men had any idea that Jackie was only physically paralyzed as she watched them through the haze in her eyes and listened to their every word.

Then Max commented, "I can't take her staring at me like that, let's get the hell out of here before she sits up and wants an explanation."

Everyone in the room laughed, and Max instructed Agent Greenback to stay with Jackie until she regained consciousness and then head back to Dallas and start the satellite track on her. He added, "I want a weekly report unless something comes up or if she tries to contact anyone she shouldn't. If that happens, I want to be notified right away. Do you understand?"

"Yes sir," Special Agent Greenback replied.

Their voices faded out of hearing distance, and Jackie lay on the floor in silence. The next thing she heard was Attorney Bernard, who came into the room and asked Agent Greenback, "Is she okay? Can she drive yet?"

At which he replied, "She'll be okay after I give her a shot to offset the other sedative." Agent Greenback picked Jackie up off the floor, placing her back in the chair before he injected her again, this time with something to offset the paralyzing medication.

As she came to, he asked. "How do you feel?"

She cleared her throat first and replied in a scratchy voice, "My throat's sore! I must be coming down with something. Can I have a drink of water?"

"Sure," Agent Greenback replied. "I'll get it for you."

As he left the room, Attorney Bernard told Jackie, "You can go now. The jury was released, and the papers have been filed with the district clerk dismissing the case."

Jackie sleepily batted her eyes as she looked around the room and whispered, "What time is it?"

"Oh, it's about 6:30."

"That late? What have I been doing all this time?"

"Well, I think you took a nap."

"A nap!" Jackie exclaimed. "I must have passed out with my mouth open."

Just then Agent Doug Greenback reentered the room and smiled as he shook his head yes and handed Jackie her water. Agent Greenback then shook Jackie's hand and told her goodbye before assuring her that she'd made the right decision by settling the case.

"I think so, too," she whispered.

"Well then, if you'll excuse me," Agent Greenback said, "I really do need to get back on the road. I've still got another eight hours' work to do before I can call it a day."

"Have a safe trip," Jackie whispered as she rubbed her throat from the strain of talking. Then she smiled and waved as he left the office, leaving her alone with Attorney Bernard.

Struggling to talk above a whisper, Jackie asked, "Would you mind if I called George to let him know that I'm on the way. We were supposed to go out this evening with an old friend who came into town today, but I don't think I'll make it home in time."

"Not at all" Attorney Bernard replied. "Here, you can use this phone."

Jackie just smiled as she picked up the phone. She turned it around and pushed the redial button, calling back the number Max had previously dialed before he handed the phone to Tom to verify the shipment. Immediately a man's voice said. "Is something wrong?"

Jackie strained to say something, but she couldn't get the words to come out so she cupped her hand over the phone and whispered in a scratchy voice. "Attorney Bernard, would you please do this for me?

He can't hear me. Would you just say, 'MacAlfie is coming into town tonight?' He'll know what you're talking about."

"Sure," Attorney Bernard replied as she took the phone from Jackie and said, "Can you hear me now?" She paused momentarily, "Okay, I've been instructed to tell you, MacAlfie is coming into town tonight." She shrugged her shoulders before she said, "He hung up. Guess I lost him too."

Attorney Bernard stared at Jackie for a moment before she asked, "Do you know what you just did?"

Jackie was petrified with fear, awaiting her next words.

Attorney Bernard continued, "You'll probably never know, but settling this case today is the best way to handle it, and I am really glad this will soon be over with. It really has been a huge strain on me the past several years."

Jackie shook her head as she whispered, "I know what you mean. It was a strain on me, too."

Then Attorney Bernard completed her thoughts, "I do wish you good luck, and I do hope you'll be able to put your life back together."

"Thanks," Jackie said. "I'm sure things will get better day by day."

As they walked together to the door, Attorney Bernard continued the small talk and then shook Jackie's hand before she left. Jackie's heart was pounding so hard she was afraid that Attorney Bernard would hear it. She held her breath until she was on the other side of the gate and driving toward Dallas. As she drove along, she was deep in thought about what she should do next. Desperately wanting to get her mind on something else, she turned on her car radio, but it wasn't music she heard. Instead, it was a special news report.

"This breaking story just now coming off the AP wire out of Houston, Texas. A cargo ship has been seized with what is expected to yield the largest shipment of cocaine and ecstasy ever in an American port. Second only to a 1984 Florida shipment, this estimated five-plus tons of cocaine was camouflaged by iron ore originating out of Bogotá, Colombia. Authorities say its crew abandoned the ship before it docked just inside Houston. However, it was reported by Coast

Guard officials, the captain was last seen diving overboard into the water, but rescue efforts have failed to recover him. Authorities have not been able to trace the owner or the destination of the iron ore, but estimate the shipment to have a street value of $186 million, maybe even as much as a billion dollars. US Transportation and DEA officers estimate this amount of cocaine would measure out to at least one fix for every school child in America from preschool to high school. US Customs officials say it is the biggest cocaine bust ever by the agency in Texas."

"Imagine that," Jackie whispered. "A botched shipment! Exactly what the physic told me would happen."

Four months later:

Jackie opened her mailbox to find an envelope addressed to her from the Dallas Bar Association. "I'd forgotten all about this," she mumbled, quickly ripping it open. To her surprise, the letter came directly from the president of the Bar Association.

Dear Mrs. Kennard;

Please accept our apologies for the delay in getting back in touch with you. Your original letter dated November 1997 was somehow delayed in California and remained unnoticed until it was recently discovered and brought to our attention. Moreover, we are pleased to inform you, as the result of your grievance filed through this letter with the Dallas Bar Association against Attorney Bernard and the law firm of Bernard and Dawson, we have conducted a through investigation and have reached a unanimous decision to disbar Attorney Bernard for her unprofessional and unethical handling of your case. We have also discovered in our investigation that she unlawfully obtained and failed to disclose an amount of money paid to her by the defendants, which we have also determined should be paid to you instead.

The defendants' company CFO along with their attorneys, Ralph Woodcock and Max Mulligan, have not yet responded to our inquiries. They are apparently locked into a federal government receivership due to an unexpected bankruptcy as the result of bad overseas investments. However, when our investigation is completed, there may possibly be additional disbarments.

Mrs. Kennard, somehow the system failed you, and for that we hope you will accept our apologies, along with the enclosed check made payable to you. We here at the Dallas Bar Association all thank you for your persistence, your patience, and for having the confidence in us to assist you regarding this issue. We know that your ultimate goal was to achieve justice, and we hope that our decision has played some small part in achieving that for you today, but we also want to remind you that justice can be measured in many different ways. Therefore, we sincerely hope our decision, along with this check, will enable you to find some closure and move forward with your life.

Respectfully,<br>
Dale Greenberg, President<br>
*Dallas Bar Association*

Jackie bowed her head, and a tear dropped from her eye as she whispered, "Semper fi, my son. This is justice!"

## About the Author

J.K. LaMay grew up in Dallas, Texas.

Having worked in corporate America for many years and experienced corporate scandal first hand more than once, the author decided to leave the corporate structure for a quieter life in rural America to write about her experiences.

CPSIA information can be obtained
at www.ICGtesting.com
Printed in the USA
FFOW03n1051200417
34758FF